RED BULL MUSIC ACADEMY

FOR THE REC ORD

**CONVERSATIONS WITH PEOPLE WHO HAVE
SHAPED THE WAY WE LISTEN TO MUSIC**

RED BULL MUSIC ACADEMY

FOR THE REC ORD

CONVERSATIONS WITH PEOPLE WHO HAVE
SHAPED THE WAY WE LISTEN TO MUSIC

EDITORS: MANY AMERI · TORSTEN SCHMIDT

WE LOVE TO WITNESS WHEN THINGS HAPPEN

With us, it always starts on a couch. Usually there's two, sometimes three or more folks on there, talking. Talking and talking. Forget about the modern microscopical soundbite sprints, marathon to us reads only like the Uncle L dictum of "just getting warm." Back in 1998, the Red Bull Music Academy set out to provide music's true masterminds a space for

conversation, argument, pontification, titillation, outlook.

Whatever these illuminaries' agenda, we like to get it straight from the horse's mouth. Real Talk.

When we open a so-called term of this Academy in front of an intimate room full of up-and-coming producers, DJs, vocalists and musicians that made it through a grueling written application, my partner Many Ameri and myself tend to tell tales from the Dark Ages. The times (think around 1998 AD) when in the whole of Friedrichshain, Berlin, we couldn't find a fax machine to send a simple record review to an editor. When one used pencils to manually copy long lists in Japanese magazines as a guideline for your next record hunting spree. When only a handful of people in the room knew what an 808 was, let alone what it looked like or even, Lord Almighty forbid, how to program this devilish box of bass delight.

Boring technicalities aside, once we sat down with Mr. Jeff Mills on that couch, that empty Eureka-barrel hit us with all its might. Not that we hadn't done extensive interviews before.

But there was something slightly different in the air,

once the artist came down from the pedestal and the audience was sitting on eye-level, eager to learn. It took us a second until we figured out how well our bet paid off. But it probably couldn't have been more graphic then when this widely idolized world-travelling DJ's DJ talked about his notion of home: the pillow, where he lays his head at night. And the not so fancy sink in an often fancy hotel, in which he washes his underwear for another gig, on another continent for another night – by hand.

Over those two hours, Mr. Mills wasn't only obsessed with his life-style and current vision of the future. He also talked a lot about a certain Electrifyin' Mojo. A face that few know, but a voice everyone with their heart in music will be energized by immediately once the infamous intro to his Midnight Funk Association is booming through the speakers. So here's one of the most conceptual electronic artists of the late second millennium – whose own reputation as a rapid-rhythm-raising radio jock had earned him the honorary title of

"The Wizard" – singing the praises of this other rather unsung hero, the man who gave him a break.

Obviously this not only struck a chord with the young hopefuls in the crowd, but with everyone obsessed with history and the quest for all the influential elements that eventually result in greatness. And seeing that there was so little useful authentic information around,

we decided to document it all, properly. For the 15 years to come, we were fortunate enough to find couches in cities around the world.

And what began in the backyard of an unassuming Berlin ware-house would result in a yearly venture that has hosted workshops on every continent. Puts on some 500 nighttime events a year, many of which challenge and inspire. Curates stages at the most significant of festivals (including Sónar, Montreux, Movement). Hosts an online magazine, a 24/7 online radio station and a megaverse of couch conversations, all in its entirety watchable from your mobile device. We witnessed some of our participants going to the top of various charts, others turning doctor or graphic designer, but even more creating heartfelt, meaningful cutting-edge music.

For the volume in hand, we intended to change the proposition of the couch conversations. While we have been truly blessed with the plethora of talent we coaxed into joining us on said couch over the years, here and there it became apparent that – no matter how many people they entertain on stage – some folks just aren't cut out to be facing a room full of faces that hang on their every word. So what if we went to a private room and put some of the ones that made a difference in the way we listen to music with some of their fellow game-changing geniuses to see what they might have to say to each other? When turning the page, not every single entry on that list of conversation partners will immediately resonate with you.

But don't worry, and be assured: One thing we have learned in programming these Academies for one-and-a-half decades now is that it's usually the dark horses that take you to new territory. The combinations here are rooted in a multitude of considerations.

Different generations, diverse backgrounds, be it musically, politically, sociologically.

Every single time, we were curious what would happen if we sat these particular recording artists down together. What they would actually have to talk about, when often times facing each other for the first time ever.

How the ghosts of recordings they contributed to and the artists they worked with and learned from might find their way into the conversation.

No matter what part of the recording process these dialogues cover, seeing that it's all folks whose work in the words of Motown maestro Berry Gordy "left world-class impressions on people," we invite you to enjoy them.

You'll see how different generations and origins deal with cultural imperialism and hear from folks who started revolutions via open hi-hats while they were trying to capture the energy of the passing trains of their childhood. Learn about the importance of ear candy (are you really the only one who never adds the "uh" after karaoking "Like a Virgin" in the shower?) and how the curse of gold in the mercenary age they call the '80s is still subordinate to music.

You'll enter a world where milliseconds matter more than how many millions you sold (even to those who actually managed such feats),

where cheeky subwoofer tricks validate quality junkies more than an entire month of Oprah. Learn about the roles and road maps of mystical figures like producers, engineers, arrangers. Their side

jobs as psychologists, and why you can get easily away with telling President Carter some things, but less so with Marshall Mathers. About stage fright, diverse Daft Punk opinions and Japanese gardens, how the body reacts to bass and what emotions can be conveyed through rhythm.

You'll start to think about how to make sure that technology is serving you and not the other way around. How to listen to those little in-between notes, no matter whether you categorize them as blue or ghost, and deal with the moments when something isn't quite right. You'll find out how to get over them – and cherish the ones that just make you say: "Yeah!"

To round it all off, there's a selection of essays by some of our favorite music writers, providing context, biographical data and insights on how music is created.

We sincerely hope that some of the not-so-obvious but well-grounded characters portrayed here will be a little closer to your heart when you eventually put this book down.
To us, they are heroes.

After 15 years of creating a safe space where such distinguished characters let down their guard to be asked anything by the heroes of coming generations, we figured it was about time to provide them with the chance to ask those that inspired them. To which degree that would work, we didn't know. As Paul Riser, one of the greatest ever to arrange a piece of music puts it a few pages later, "I didn't expect to have a 52-year career out of it – but things happen."

We love to witness when things happen.

So please, read on, as you sit down. We hope there is a couch nearby – it has your name on it.

Torsten Schmidt, Red Bull Music Academy Co-Founder

Table of Contents

Essays

IT IS OFTEN SAID THAT THE AFRICAN CONTINENT IS THE ROOT OF ALL THINGS.

WHEN PEOPLE IN ALL CORNERS OF THE GLOBE TODAY CONSIDER AFRICA THE CRADLE OF CIVILIZATION, IT IS WITH THANKS TO AMBASSADORS LIKE MULATU ASTATKE, WHO HAS SPENT A GREAT PORTION OF HIS CAREER HIGHLIGHTING SAID ROLE – WHETHER IT BE THROUGH HIS MUSIC OR IN HIS LECTURES AND TALKS. AS PART OF LISBON'S BURAKA SOM SISTEMA, JOÃO BARBOSA AND KALAF ÂNGELO HAVE SIMILAR AIMS. THEIR MERGING OF ANGOLAN KUDURO WITH MODERN ELECTRONIC MUSIC PRODUCTION HAS THE SAME GLOBAL OUTLOOK AS ASTATKE. ON JULY 4TH, WE BROUGHT TOGETHER ÂNGELO, ASTATKE AND BARBOSA IN AMSTERDAM. ÂNGELO, A POET AND SOMETIME JOURNALIST, QUICKLY TOOK THE REINS OF THE CONVERSATION, ASKING QUESTIONS OF BOTH ASTATKE AND HIS BAND MATE BARBOSA.

Children of the post-colonial world and musicians of the global village, Buraka Som Sistema found their voice in Lisbon by taking the Angolan music hybrid kuduro out of its colonial bonds and fusing it with electronic genres. Composed of former Red Bull Music Academy alum **João Barbosa** (Branko) and Andro Carvalho (Conductor), poet **Kalaf Ângelo**, Rui Pité (DJ Riot) and dancer/MC Blaya, they have conquered the world with their unique synthesis of old and new, local and global. Since 2006 they've released three albums, signed to Sony BMG, set up their own Enchufada label and found fans and collaborators in the likes of M.I.A, Diplo and Santigold.

Kalaf Ângelo, João Barbosa and Mulatu Astatke

Informed by the five-note harmonies of his homeland and formal training that took place in the West, Ethiopian musician, arranger, and composer **Mulatu Astatke** birthed an entire genre almost by himself. Marked by undulating melody over a simmering groove, Ethio-jazz is the aural result of Astatke's curiosity in crossing the cultural expanse separating one continent from another. Despite a storied career and adoration by beat diggers the world over, it was a contribution to Jim Jarmusch's *Broken Flowers* in 2005 that re-introduced audiences to his unique fusion. Ever since, he's endeavored – both in words and music – to educate the world about the artistic contributions that come from his country and continent.

Moderator:
Torsten Schmidt

Photographers:
Till Janz and Hendrik Schneider

João Barbosa: Yeah, not everyone has that perspective. A lot of people look at it more as stealing. But the way you're saying it, it makes total sense because it makes all different generations connect the dots and whoever is interested is going to go and research and find what they need to know about it.

MA: That's what I believe. It's so great, because something might come from the mixing as well, you never know: something big, which can develop music in the world, sending it in different directions.

Kalaf Ângelo: With this meeting the first thing that came to my mind was that your music has been heavily sampled, and we come from that background...

Mulatu Astatke: The sampling.

KA: The sampling and the electronic approach. I would like to know how you feel about it, and how you see today's music from that perspective.

MA: Well, Ethio-jazz music is music with a lot of different materials. In Ethio-jazz you can almost feel South American music, you can hear jazz, you can hear beautiful voicings from America. So it's a beautiful combination of music. Berklee is where I put the things together. These lecturers at Berklee were always saying, "Be yourself." That's what always got into my mind: try to be myself all the time. At school we used to analyze Coltrane, used to analyze Miles. So I was saying, "OK, how can these people be themselves?" "How can I let myself become myself?" That's how the whole thing started off.

The fusion I made was five against 12, which means, like, five-tone scales against 12-tone scales. You really have to be careful of how you do it, because you can lose the feel, the beauty of the five-tones. It took me a really long time to fuse these two and come out without losing the character of Ethiopian scales. But I think it's great for the music. I love it. It's no problem. I keep only doing my jazz and somebody's doing something else with it, so it's cool.

Five-tone scales against 12-tone scales

KA: I don't know if you had a chance to listen to the music João's making now, but he is going to different parts of the world and digging, researching and then incorporating that into his own productions. João, when you look to Africa's music, do you feel like it's because it's hidden, because it's unknown or because it gives you that flavour that is necessary to the music today?

JB: I think it's a mix of both. It's trying to get something different and make it valid in an everyday music context. With Buraka the biggest thing we used out of Angola was the rhythmical pattern. We then put it into context with all these different other scenes from the world, and it ended up making sense and globalizing something. With Angola being an ex-colony of Portugal, there's a lot of Angolans in Portugal. And when we started this group, Buraka, it was kind of fun because we incorporated a lot of the stuff that we listened to while we were growing up. I think a lot of people in our generation were listening to the same things. But I don't think that there was a conscious understanding of that music. They didn't actually know that they had that in them, and when we picked up that rhythmical pattern and all these little different things – like using the voice as a percussion instrument – people really connected with it on a different level. It's almost like if you go into the subconscious and you bring out all these things that you grew up listening to… You don't even recognize that you know. It just creates a special connection with an audience. It's also a little bit of the Indiana Jones explorer factor of going out and discovering something new, which is always super exciting.

MA: I think Africans don't do enough research into their own work. There are people who do it, but most people are just looking for the money. It actually hurts you so much because when you really know about African musical instruments – and if you really go around to different places in Africa – they have so many interesting things that you should know about. I want to see most of the African peoples study classical music, study jazz, study everything, you know? I want them to know the culture, the musical instruments and the songs. Then, after that, they can do whatever they want to do. The problem now is that the bottom side of the culture is empty. They start from the middle and they go up. A man who doesn't know the bottom doesn't last long.

KA: I still have some problems with government involvement in producing culture or supporting culture. Education should be sponsored by government, and then education could help to build that ground, that first level of knowledge about the culture. But I always feel like, especially going to Angola, that people don't really want to look into their history because it's very dark. So people prefer to build from that point on. If you start building from the bottom, you definitely need to dig up issues that will not be pleasant. Do you think societies are ready to go that deep?

**A
scientist
mixes
chemicals
and,
when
we
are
writing
music,
we
mix
sounds
the
same
way.**

**OK,
how
can
these
people
be
themselves?**

**How
can
I
let
myself
become
myself?**

MA: I think culture and music and politics should have their own places. One bigger problem in Africa would be the educational system. If you go to more developed countries, usually music, art and dance are compulsory in schools. I believe music is no different from science, maths or chemistry. A scientist mixes chemicals and, when we are writing music, we mix sounds the same way. That's the way they should look at it. Without music, art and theater you can't be a complete person. You can't be complete, because these three subjects are so beautiful. How many great talents do we lose in Africa because of this? You finish the 12th grade and they say you should become a doctor or an architect, and you're sent to a university even though maybe you don't have it inside of you at all. Then you can become a regular doctor or you can become a regular architect. But you will never become outstanding, because it's not inside you. If it's compulsory in high schools someone will teach you how to develop it, how to love it. You don't have to get into other stuff. With more people educated in music, art and theater in Africa, we won't lose our culture, our resonance, our contribution to the world.

KA: These days I'm really enjoying Paul Simon's *Graceland* album a lot. And I'd like to ask your opinion. Do you guys feel an album like that could exist today on that level?

MA: Yeah, why not? There are so many interesting people coming to Africa and doing works. I always feel that there should be more of that. More people should do an African exploration. But I also would love to see an African doing the same, you know?

JB: If you watch the documentary about how the album was produced everybody was saying that he was crazy. The label was like, "We're not going to pay for this, we don't get this idea, we don't want this. Please don't go there. Just do something else." I'm OK to be crazy like that because no one is paying me $200,000 to make a record. But if you think about it in terms of a pop star, like he was at the time, now it would be Rihanna or someone like that. Everybody talks about a 30 year music circle, and I think those 30 years are getting smaller because people are consuming so much music. I think the 30 years are becoming maybe 15 years. Everything is just rotating super fast. And I think we're getting to that point again where pop is going to need adventures like that and is going to need to be different. Maybe somebody is going to do it. I don't know. But I don't think there is commercial drive to do something like that right now. So, unless an artist is really strong willed and wants to do it, it's not going to happen.

KA: How is the audience when you perform in your home country and abroad?

It's also a little bit of the Indiana Jones explorer factor of going out and discovering something new,

which is always super exciting.

There is one that has two types of scales used for jazz, for improvising.

The scales have been used by Debussy and Charlie Parker, the creator of modern jazz. This is the kind of thing I'm talking about. Their contribution:

MA: Well, at the beginning, when I went back from New York to Ethiopia with the concept of Ethio-jazz, it was about 40-something years ago. There was this instrument I was thinking about, the begena – a ten-string instrument used in Ethiopian church music. I wrote a score for a play and I used the begena, piano, drums and bass. All fusions. I remember people telling me halfway through to get off the stage. "How dare you use the begena on stage with pianos?" This kind of thing. After a few months I did the same thing using other Ethiopian instruments with trumpets and saxophones, and it was on television. So, after a while, I have no problems. The acceptance of the audience in Ethiopia now is much better than 30 years ago. Also, I had a beautiful radio program for about seven years, and that changed people's minds about world music a lot. At a school I can only reach maybe 100 people, but on the radio I can reach five million people a day. There are so many interesting tribes in Ethiopia. There is one that has two types of scales used for jazz, for improvising. The scales have been used by Debussy and Charlie Parker, the creator of modern jazz. This is the kind of thing I'm talking about. Their contribution: African contributions, you know? It's not only that. It's also the dancers. There is a tribe which has a dance that Beyoncé used. Exactly the same movement she uses. Nobody knows where this comes from, but it's from Ethiopia. I show them Beyoncé and those tribes together, fusing. We used to conduct music with a stick in the sixth century. Always you think Africa is only drums. It's not only drums.

RBMA: For you, Mulatu, it might be a little different because you were bringing something that you heard abroad back to Ethiopia. And that helped people connect with something they already had.

MA: Yeah. It was a new combination. Not exactly what I heard over there. Because, as I told you before, they were telling me to be myself. So I became myself.

JB: I think with Buraka so many people have such a strong opinion on what we do as a group and who we are. Even if they've never heard more than ten seconds of any of our songs, they've already decided that they hate it or that they like it or... And I don't really know how that works – having an opinion based on a preconceived idea of something. I think people come to the shows and they dance and they have the same sort of fun, but for one person it's just dance music with strange influences from around the world. If you're in Portugal or Lisbon, it's something a bit more complex and it's something that they put into a different context.

There are so many interesting tribes in Ethiopia.

African contributions

We should have a Noah's Ark for African instruments.

Just stack two of everything in one big warehouse with instructions.

Those people, before they die, are supposed to teach the kids. So much in Africa dies with the people.

So much beautiful stuff is just buried. We have to be careful, we have to teach the youngsters. So that it can be alive forever.

Exactly, exactly. I´ll be the guy.

How did your musician colleagues in Ethiopia feel that all of a sudden the neighborhood wannabe detective is like the biggest spokesperson for Ethiopian jazz? The character that Jeffrey Wright plays.

MA: Well, Jim [Jarmusch] told me he just fell in love with my music. Now, after that, he said he had to find an Ethiopian character. If you have the music, you have to find somebody for what you talk about. So that's how this guy went into the film. Then he was representing Ethiopia. The coffee drinking and that kind of thing. So, that's how it happened. But it worked. People loved it.

KA: Do you still buy records?

MA: No, it's a good question, really. I don't listen to anybody because at the beginning, at Berklee, they would make us listen to all types of music. Now I listen to cultural music, purely culture from the bushes. I don't listen to modern music because the more you listen, the more influenced you become and the more you start losing your ground. So I stopped a long time ago. I don't really sit down and listen to music. I go to the bushes and listen to different types of musical instruments.

KA: You record it?

MA: Yeah. I listen to how they interpret music. I listen to the different tones of the singers we have in Ethiopia. I listen to these beautiful voices. I listened to Coltrane and I listened to Miles. I've seen Bill Evans. I've seen my favorite guys. I used to listen a lot. I used to analyze everything, you know?

To which degree do you find that knowing what you're listening to is important?

JB: I don't think it's very important.

I think that the Jarmusch example is quite interesting in that sense, because before Broken Flowers your music was known really only to diehard music collectors. And when you went to the movie you're like, "How did Mulatu end up on that soundtrack here?" And you're in the cinema and it sounds like Mulatu, but it can't be. That doesn't make sense. How does that end up in a Hollywood movie? And then you look around and you see the people really getting into it, and they might not have any idea what they're listening to.

MA: Well, you see, there are two types of listeners. You have people who really listen to music, to how it's put together, what the elements are. And there are people who just listen for enjoyment. Just listen. They will love it or not.

I don't really sit down and listen to music.

JB: I want to go back a little bit to stereotypes. I think Americans do a really good job at painting stereotypes and using them to grab people's attentions to something. Like what you were just explaining about the movie and the Ethiopian drinking coffee. There are thousands of examples of that in Hollywood, in music, in everything. If you look at Conan O'Brien or something, every time he speaks something about someone in French he's going to use all these little stereotypes that he knows are going to make people react. I think it's really stuck in their culture – the fact that they always interpret other cultures through stereotypes. So that's why I think if you're making a movie in Hollywood you need this person who is introducing something to be a stereotype of that. And, in a way, that's helpful because it just puts things on the table and it's like, "OK, here is the Ethiopian guy. What do they usually do? OK, he needs to do that. And then we got the Brazilian guy. They're always, like, dancing samba." It gets to a point where they're only valid because they're stereotypes. It gets to a point where it's like, "Oh, I'm going to this African painter's exhibition." It's not just a painting exhibition. It's an African painter exhibition or it's an Indonesian painter exhibition. In the beginning we discussed this a lot, and it was like, "Whatever we do and whatever fusion we end up creating, it's always going to be about making good music that entertains people and that's broad enough to reach people without needing the whole…"

KA: Sub-label.

Using the Portuguese language on top of reggae instrumentals... That's good enough to grab my attention.

Better than trying to fake a Jamaican patois and completely incorporating someone else's culture and having dreadlocks.

JB: Yeah. We can have a cultural angle without having a super obvious cultural angle and that's doable. I remember there was a French guy who was trying to do this same thing around the same time and his promo picture was him holding an Angolan flag. It didn't make any sense because...

Yeah, but maybe that's like how beat bands tried to get British haircuts...

JB: Exactly. But I'm not saying that's right as well. I would never do that. That's why I never understood three guys who live in Lisbon that create a reggae band and speak in Jamaican patois. That doesn't make sense. As something to grab my attention, it doesn't really work. If there are thousands of musicians who are doing better than that in Jamaica, why am I even looking at you? It doesn't really make sense unless they're using whatever is in Jamaica and using whatever is in their own background. Making something that makes sense out of the way they grew up. Using the Portuguese language on top of reggae instrumentals... That's good enough to grab my attention. Better than trying to fake a Jamaican patois and completely incorporating someone else's culture and having dreadlocks. This is something that we really agreed on.

MA: I think it's great, these kinds of conversations, because you can always learn from each other. It's what really makes things very interesting.

I go to the bushes and listen to different types of musical instruments.

Graceland **was mentioned earlier. How do you walk the line between authenticity on the one hand and exploitation on the other hand?**

JB: With this sort of exploring, I think the difference is if you use it to create something new or if you use it to try and do more of whatever is already being created. It's like chemistry. It's like everything that Mulatu is saying. If I grab this chemical and mix it together with this chemical – and I'm going to make a new experiment – then I don't see anything wrong with that. For me, that's not exploitation.

But, when the borrowed musical influences are not explored carefully or treated with respect, you might argue that appropriation of musical forms can be a type of globalization in a negative sense. We can contrast that with your work – and even though there are decades between you – your musical outputs might serve a similar function in that there's something that is attributed to a different place and it's not coming from Berlin, London or New York.

KA: It's not your fault that the person who is listening will not do more research to discover what is behind a certain sound. When you give a formula to someone – if he is a trained listener – he always will separate the elements to understand it better, you know? To perceive what we do, someone should understand a little bit of modern Angolan music and also know a little bit more about Lisbon. The cultural context plays a huge role. Just like Paris or London in terms of music from that part of the globe.

JB: In a way, I think I would feel pretty stupid about having a band like Buraka without Kalaf and Andro in it. It probably wouldn't exist in the same way. I think the fact that some of the band grew up in London makes it different as well.

Even
if
you
don't
believe
you're
thinking
about
it,
it
will
be
in
the
back
of
your
mind.

Were you ever afraid of the whole colonialism issue?

KA: You cannot undo the slave trade. Same as Mulatu was saying. You cannot change the fact that you heard Miles and Coltrane. Even if you don't believe you're thinking about it, it will be in the back of your mind. It's the same with colonialism or anything like that. Am I abusing other people's culture? It will always be at the back of your mind. But the truth is that we cannot go back. We cannot redo history. I think the only thing we can do is understand it and try to evolve.

JB: And move on.

KA: Exactly. For me, when you see groups from Paul Simon to Buraka, it's impossible. We're all part of one. We all communicate. There's only a certain number of notes. Unless someone comes and brings some alien sound that no one has heard, those eight notes define every type of music. As Mulatu has said, he can write anything and go to a Chinese person and they will understand, even though he never met Mulatu, or never listened to Ethio-jazz.

You cannot change the fact that you heard Miles and Coltrane.

KA: We should have a Noah's Ark for African instruments.

JB: Just stack two of everything in one big warehouse with instructions.

MA: Exactly, exactly. I'll be the guy.

JB: It is kind of scary when you think that all these things are going to get destroyed.

KA: It's funny because I was in Berlin yesterday. I went to the Fashion Week, and there were some African designers. I remember the one from Ghana only wanted Rihanna and Chris Brown music for her show because she said, "I'm already African. I don't need African music." I think it's important to preserve identity and preserve culture.

MA: It's very important.

KA: At the same time I understand that Africans should be using computers, you know? But that's only to contribute your own story, to tell your own narrative.

That's what I love when you watch those You-Tube sessions. Obviously these African kids are using the same software as other people – and there's a whole lot of auto-tune – but they use it in a very different way. That's when it gets interesting.

JB: That's how all these local scenes blew up. I don't think the guy that invented Kuduro or Afro-house sat down and said, "I'm going to invent Afro-house." He sat down and said, "I'm going to make house music." And then suddenly all of this pre-stored information in his subconscious took him somewhere else. I think he actually thought he was making normal house music, but then when you play it sounds different. When you leave that space for a subconscious to work, it's going to make really amazing things for you.

MA: Chinese, Japanese, Ethiopians: we almost have the same scales and notes. You know? What is interesting is how they approach these notes their way, and how I approach these notes with Ethio-jazz. They love it because the scales are the same. Only the words are different. Ethiopian culture is so rich. In the north we have these kinds of scales. You go down to the south, and it's a different kind of music. West is different. Middle is different. We have so many interesting musical instruments. So many different types of dances. Globalization, though. This is a problem. Economically, globalization is something good and I accept it.

But culturally, it's a problem because the money changes the culture. Beautiful dances, beautiful voices, beautiful musical instruments suddenly start to fade out. That's why I'm talking about education. Those people, before they die, are supposed to teach the kids. So much in Africa dies with the people. So much beautiful stuff is just buried. We have to be careful, we have to teach the youngsters. So that it can be alive forever.

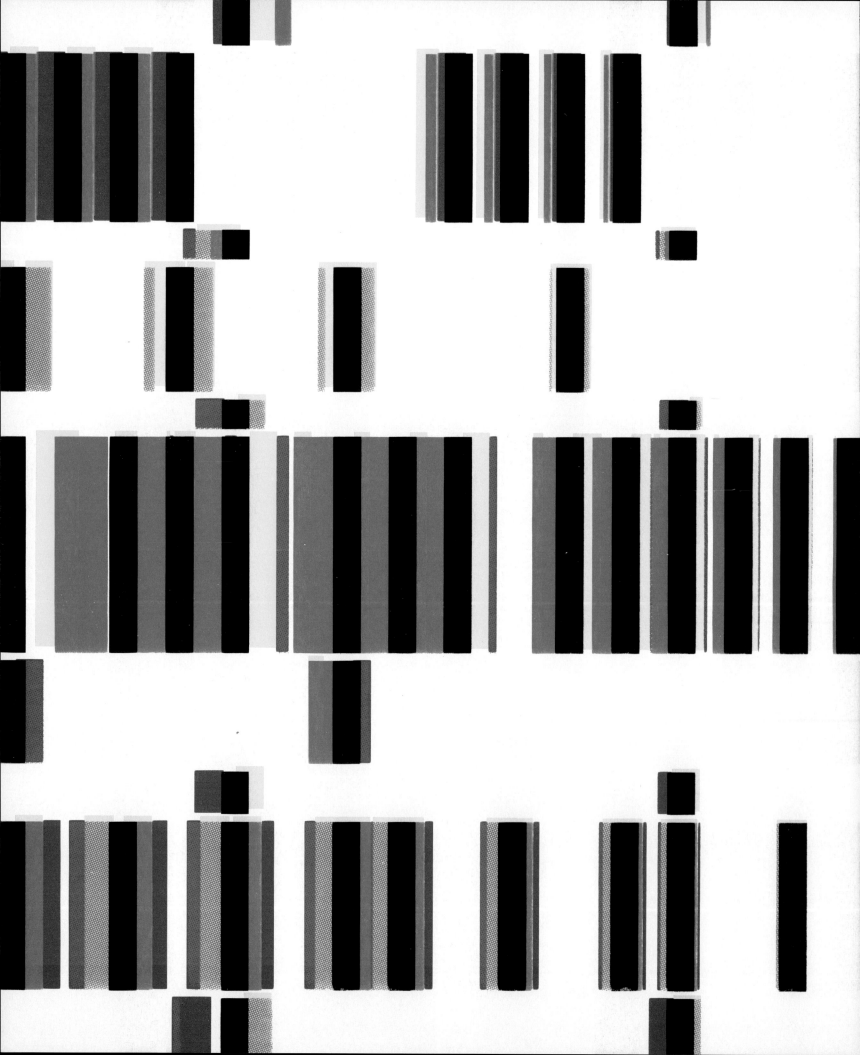

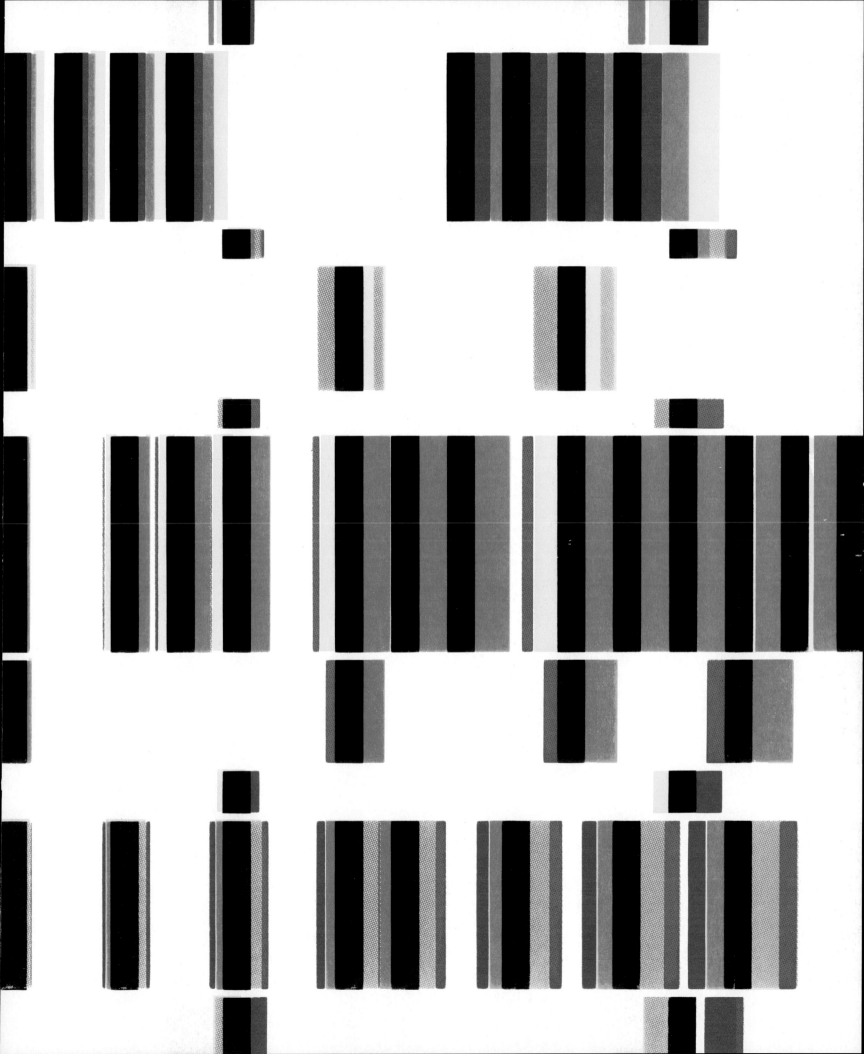

JAKI

Jaki Liebezeit's revolution was to not sound revolutionary at all. The drummer for Can played as if time was standing still. Oftentimes, he made it sound like it was. It took Liebezeit many years to come to his mature style, but once he did he mined it for all it was worth. His is an exploration of minimalism from all angles. Liebezeit's interest in alternative approaches to rhythm likely stemmed from a stint as a jazz drummer in Barcelona in the early '60s where he heard radio transmissions from North Africa. For him, the realization that Western music wasn't the center of the universe was an enormous one. Western music has never been the same since.

Bernard Purdie is a drummer's drummer, the consummate session player. The guy who keeps time when the regular drummer can't quite get it together. Over the years, his name has found its way onto plenty of big-name records, and – perhaps just as often – gone uncredited. Purdie moved to New York in 1961 before the Musician's Union would technically allow him to play in a group, but his chops and charm convinced the powers-that-be to sneak him in. He's proven them right ever since, anchoring rhythm sections for Aretha Franklin, B.B. King and Gil Scott-Heron along the way. Today, his legacy continues to grow, whether it be via his shows with Bernard Purdie & Friends or the legions of producers that have sampled his drumming for their own tracks.

Moderator: Hanna Bächer
Photographer: Peter Langer

LIEBEZEIT

AND BERNARD

PURDIE

The world's most sampled drummer and the world's most repetitive drummer. Two statements that may not be technically true, but you'd be forgiven for thinking so. Bernard Purdie's been a go-to session man for nearly 50 years, working for the likes of James Brown, Dizzy Gillespie, Cat Stevens, Hall & Oates, Steely Dan and – if you love a good rumor – The Beatles themselves. He not only keeps time, he invents new ways of doing it. (Just listen to "The Purdie Shuffle" for proof.) Jaki Liebezeit, meanwhile, is patience personified. He was the man behind the skins for krautrock giants Can, building his legend on playing the same thing for longer than you can imagine – and then for about 15 minutes more.

Purdie visited Cologne in May 2013, and the two met in Liebezeit's rehearsal space on the fourth floor of a former chocolate factory. It's where Liebezeit practices with his band Drums Off Chaos – a local quartet composed solely of drummers. When words failed the two septuagenarians, they simply played rhythms on their knees to illustrate what they meant.

Few drummers have played so little for so long. Fewer have sounded better doing it.

Bernard Purdie: Well, I have to say this: this is a treat and an honor for me because I've known about you, Jaki, all my life, you know? It's nice to be able to have this interview with you.

Jaki Liebezeit: You know me already?

BP: Oh, I know your work. I've known about you for a lot of years.

JL: No...

BP: Yes, sir. The thing is that I am a historian so when I want to know something about somebody, when people talk about someone, then I go to find out what they've done. And what you've been doing has really worked. For a lot of years. I have that kind of respect for you.

JL: I didn't know. I thought maybe you didn't know me at all because... I mean... I'm not as famous as you are.

BP: I don't think I'm that famous.

JL: Yeah, but I've known about you for ages.

RBMA: You're about the same age, though, right?

JL: To tell you the truth, I'm even older than you.

BP: Yes, you are.

JL: Yeah, one year older. But we are the same star sign. Gemini.

BP: Right on.

You moved to New York at a very early age, Bernard.

BP: I was almost 20. And in New York City at that time I was not allowed to work, because you had to have a cabaret license. Well, when I went to the union, the vice president of the union took a liking to me. I sat down and said, "I want to join the union." And he looked at me and he said, "Well, you're not quite old enough yet." I said, "But I'm a musician. I'm good! And I'm this, that and the other..." He said, "OK, alright. But in order for this to happen I got to take you downtown to the bureau to get a license for you." So we go down to get the license and when we walk in the lady asks me my name and he says, "This is Bernard Purdie." And the next thing she asks me is, "Well, when were you born?" "He was born in 1939."

But you were born in 1941.

BP: Yeah, I didn't say anything whatsoever. The vice president and the lady, they just filled out the papers. I walked out of there with a cabaret card two years earlier than I was supposed to. I'd only been in New York a month, so I had no idea what it meant to have a cabaret card. That's when I found out that Ray Charles couldn't have a cabaret card – and a few others too. They got caught up with drugs, so they couldn't have a cabaret card. That's why he wasn't able to work in New York all that time. But I could. Yes!

THAT'S WHEN I FOUND OUT THAT RAY CHARLES COULDN'T HAVE A CABARET CARD – AND A FEW OTHERS TOO.

Jaki, when did you first leave Germany to play elsewhere?

JL: Beginning of the '60s. I went to Spain. I had an engagement in a club in Barcelona to accompany musicians who came to the club. The most famous artist I played with was Ted Baker. There were some other people like Tete Montoliu, the famous Spanish piano player. He always accompanied the stars who came there too. The first time I was there I played, I think, seven months in a row with no days off. Every day. Seven months.

BP: I had one incident like that. I was in the Bahamas for six months. Seven days a week for six months. But I loved it. I absolutely loved it. I did not want to leave the Bahamas.

JL: It's the same feeling with Barcelona. It's like my second home. Sometimes I feel homesick.

You mostly played jazz, right?

JL: Yeah. I was a jazz musician at that time. Until about 1968 I was a jazz musician. At the end, I was a free jazz musician. But I was not satisfied with that. I need rhythm. With free jazz the band always stopped me when I started rhythm. "Stop that. Stop that." Although they were my friends, I quit. So I started with Can. That was the end of 1968 and finally I could play rhythm. I was happy to make a steady groove, which was forbidden before. That's why jazz was so popular in Germany after the war. It was forbidden at the time of the Nazis. They would put you away if you played jazz. So then jazz in Germany was so big. Music of freedom.

BP: I also went through the same thing. When I was ten years old I would take my teacher's place every weekend in a big band. It was a 14-piece orchestra. He would get drunk every Friday and Saturday night about midnight. I would actually finish the job. What I always wanted to do was play different rhythms because they'd play the same thing for so long. I would get to the point where I'd say, "OK, alright." And then they'd say, "C'mon!" When they would stop me I would actually continue and change the rhythm. And you don't do that when somebody's soloing. They'd turn around, "What!?" I'd go back and play the right rhythm, and the minute that they'd go too long again I'd turn around and play a different rhythm altogether. That was the only way to stop them from playing too long in one particular kind of music. So the rhythm: I *love* the rhythms. That's what I wanted to do all the time, but it's a big band so you have to play what they tell you to play.

How hard was it for you to get jobs at that time in Cologne, Jaki?

JL: I had friends in Cologne, and we had a band together. I didn't do so many gigs with other musicians. Occasionally I had gigs just to make money, but then I worked about ten years with Can. That was the first time in my life I got enough money to live without problems.

Bernard, I know you did jobs that were purely about the money. Like fixing other people's records, sometimes.

BP: I was doing that. I started that in the '60s. I was playing for Les Paul at his studio in Jersey. Most people don't know Les Paul invented multi-tracking. So he showed me how to play and fix drums. I would play over the top of other drummers because he could do it by shifting tracks back and forth. And he did a fantastic job, but it had to be precise. For me, that's fine. I didn't have a problem with it. What I didn't know is that it was not normal.

Why wasn't it?

BP: Most people couldn't overdub. They said 90 to 95% of the people could not overdub drums. You could overdub guitar, bass even some keyboards or regular piano, but nobody knew how to overdub drums. "Oh, you got leakage, and you got this and you got that." It was no problem for me.

JL: Yes, occasionally it happens. It was, for me, no problem [either]. I like to play with machines. That's what I have done for a long time. In the beginning of Can there was a recording with a primitive drum machine plus drums together. So that was one of the first recordings I think [where that happened]. Except for Sly and the Family Stone. They did that too. They sounded terrible, I think. This cheap [thing], used by organ players. You know them?

BP: That was me!

Bernard produced a record by them.

BP: And the thing was that he was a DJ. He was not a musician. Sly knew nothing about being a musician. He was a DJ that knew sounds. He loved sounds. And the idea that we were working on, we were doing it late at night. We had the same manager, who was the Vice President at Columbia, so they let us work at night. I'd go in there anywhere from 11:00 PM at night until 5:00 AM. And we'd cut the records. Whatever we had. The drums stunk. They were raggedy. They were the raggediest drums I had ever played on. But they were mine. It was a Scottish plaid bass drum and a floor tom. The smaller tom was blue and the snare drum was silver. That was my drum set and it was real, it was single-tension. Back then, if you had a crack in your cymbal you would cut it, so it would come out even, as much as you could.

That's the sound I had when I was doing all those different dates

SO THE RHYTHM: I LOVE THE RHYTHMS. THAT'S WHAT I WANTED TO DO ALL THE TIME, BUT IT'S A BIG BAND SO YOU HAVE TO PLAY WHAT THEY TELL YOU TO PLAY.

in the beginning, because I could not afford another cymbal. It was a trash sound, but it worked.

Is it true that the first instrument you learned was the horn?

BP: It was the autoharp. After that it was the trumpet. My teacher would not let me play drums in the band. He told me, if I'm going to be in the band I need to play another instrument. And the first instrument that he said was trumpet.

What about you, Jaki?

JL: I played trumpet too. They had an

orchestra for marching band in my school.

BP: The problem for me is that I was no good.

JL: Neither was I.

Anybody in that band, everyone in the band has to count. Most of them don't want to, so they want the drummer to do the counting for them. But they have to count or they're not going to know when to come in. So they do know how to count. They lied telling people, "Oh well, we don't count." That's a lie. Everybody, every musician

he knows the melody. But it's the rhythm that keeps him flowing. Always. We don't count out loud because we don't have to. But we have to count because we got to know where, when and how we come in and go out.

JL: Of course. If you play that kind of music. If you play free jazz, no counting at all.

THAT'S THE WORD: MELODY. RHYTHMS AND MELODY, AND YOU CAN DO ANYTHING.

BP: A year-and-a-half later I told him, "I can't play." He said, "You're right, you can't play the trumpet." So then he put me on flute. I had to learn how to play the flute. What he did for me, he forced me to learn music. That's what it was. I didn't know that then. You know, being 12, 13, 14, I didn't know that's what he was doing.

JL: Yeah, yeah. I think it's good to learn something about melody.

BP: Yeah, that's it. That's the word: melody. Rhythms and melody, and you can do anything. You can play with anybody simply because you can read it or understand it, write it: whatever it took.

I think you once said, "If you want to keep the peace in a band, you need to count." And another time I interviewed Jaki he said he never counted.

JL: No, it's too fast to count.

BP: You don't count out loud. But you have to count. In order to be a good drummer or anything else.

has to count. Now, the point is you don't do it obviously. You don't speak it, but it's inside you. It's in everything Jaki does.

JL: I can feel when it's four or eight or 16 bars. It feels like the division of cells.

BP: Division of cells, you're right.

JL: First you have one, then you have two, then you have four, then you have eight, then if you want, sixteen. But just by feeling you know how many bars, except if you have something which is maybe seven bars or eleven bars. Then you have to count. I could not do that without counting.

BP: You count. You have to count too because you can't do bar ten, bar 11, when you've got to be back here at bar one.

JL: But I'm never playing written music.

BP: Well, that's something different. The writing is something that you're forced to do when you have to learn another instrument. But the time… the time that you do things… we do it at all times inside of us. So we still got to know where one is. And that means that you are counting as long as you know where one is. Knowing time is where to count. That is the count. So he knows time like nothing else, OK. He knows it. He knows the rhythm and

BP: No, you might not seem like you're counting but when you and the bass player are not together somebody is going to be wrong, even with free jazz. You do a solo, it's the same thing. You want people to be able to follow you when you do your solo. So when you come out of your solo, and you go back to time for the rest of the band, you want the people to like what you do. That's what the Average Joe – anybody that comes to listen to the music – is going to appreciate. The rhythm is what's going to get to people.

I recently heard someone say in an interview that the biggest challenge for a musician would be to change the perception of time for the listener. So, when listening to a piece of music, you couldn't tell in the end if three minutes had passed – or 15. I think what you do often changes the perception of time that people have.

JL: No, no. I always keep the basic rhythm. It's possible to change some things within the rhythm, but the basic rhythm has to stay. It's like you play in a certain key. You have to keep that key. You cannot go to another key suddenly for no reason. It's the same thing with rhythm. If it's a certain rhythm, then you have to keep this rhythm. Some parameters can change, like loudness and the kind of sound, but the rhythm itself is fixed like a scale. If you play in C major then you have to stay in that scale. Same thing with rhythm.

DIVISION OF CELLS, YOU'RE RIGHT.

What I mean is different. Let's say someone listens to a piece of music that you have done and it's eight minutes with Bernd Friedman. At a certain point people lose that perception. They don't know anymore how long something has actually been going on.

BP: You're right in what you're saying. But I think what he's trying to convey to you is that you can go out of time and out of sequence. You can do that. But I guarantee you, when he's doing a solo, he still has to come back to some point to where "Bam, here is one." So you try to take the audience with you. There are times when I'm no different than anybody else. When I make a mistake, my mistake is so obvious. My mouth opens and I holler because I did something wrong. That bothers me more than anything. Because then I end up losing the audience. That's how I feel. But when I'm on,

Back in the '60s some of the members of Can were students of people like Stockhausen. Were you aware of electro-acoustic music in the '60s, Bernard?

BP: Sure.

JL: He was very popular but I, to be honest, was not so interested in Stockhausen because I was missing the most important thing, which is rhythm.

JL: I think it's a natural thing. No one can deny it. I mean, some people do. But I think it's like the division of cells. This system, you cannot deny it. Out of one cell you get two, out of two: four, and so on. It was forbidden in free jazz, to repeat something. I never understood this.

JL: It was free jazz.

BP: It was free jazz, but they're counting. I still had to think in terms of what their counting was. What he was good at is taking things and keeping some kind of time. Because they always had to count. All of his dancers. I did dance music all the time. See, I had one of the greatest teachers in the world, because my teacher played for the burlesque. And in order to play for them, you

BUT WHEN I'M ON, I'M ON. AND EVERYBODY IS WITH YOU. THAT'S WHY YOU SEE PEOPLE DANCE. AND FOR ME, THAT'S WHAT I NEED. I NEED FOLKS TO DANCE. WHEN YOU DANCE, YOU GOT 'EM. YOU GOT 'EM LOCK, STOCK AND BARREL. THEN WE CAN DO ANYTHING WE WANT.

I'm on. And everybody is with you. That's why you see people dance. And for me, that's what I need. I need folks to dance. When you dance, you got 'em. You got 'em lock, stock and barrel. Then we can do anything we want. That's what it comes down to. That's where the feel comes in. But, overall picture, the count is definitely in there. They have to know when they're going to come in, the rest of the band. If the rest of the band is struggling, trying to come back, what's the sense in having the solo?

BP: Rhythm and the feel.

JL: It's fantastic what he made… and new. But I think he was an enemy of rhythm. Or he was not aware that rhythm exists. Like in free jazz. For some people repetition was forbidden. I think the repetition is important.

BP: 1000% percent.

BP: Well, that's the reason why I didn't go to play it.

JL: But did you play with [choreographer] Alvin Ailey?

BP: Alvin? Oh, yes.

JL: What did you play with him?

BP: Oh, I was there because I was in New York. It was free jazz.

have to know body movement. Everything that they do represents something that they want. They could do anything they wanted, but you got to follow. And as a drummer that's how I got into what I call "free" jazz and rhythm. I watched the bodies and I still do today. Body rhythms. Every artist has some kind of body rhythm. I worked with all of those different dance groups, but I was good at it only because I had a teacher that did it all the time.

JL: The only free jazz musician I worked with at that time was

Don Cherry. I did some concerts with him in Germany, and we nearly made a band together.

I know that at the end of the '60s Can built a studio, right? Why?

JL: It was really primitive, with a two-track machine. Some microphones we rented. First we were in a castle near Cologne and we started recording there with primitive equipment because we could not afford to go to the studio. It was too expensive. With Can there was never somebody to write something. Everyone in the band was a composer. Even the verses of the singer would be shared. It was like a communist band. We would share everything. So nobody would write the music [and that's why] we needed a room, a laboratory, to make the music. Then we just started playing things, made some record-

together anymore. Two would play and then the other ones would overdub, so it was not this groove feeling like in the beginning. That's why we stopped the band.

Overdubbing killed Can.

JL: Yeah.

Both of you have somehow been influenced by Jamaican music. Bernard, you recorded with Bob Marley.

BP: I made his first two records. Because of Johnny Nash and his brother. They were the producers. Working with them taught me a new language, a new feel with a very positive attitude of what they

was the positiveness that he had. Boy, was he right on the money. He'd go sit on the rock and come back after one hour, 45 minutes, two hours, and bam, knock out three or four songs. Then go back outside and sit on the rock. But it was that good. And it's amazing to me that he knew what he had. He knew he was reaching the masses of people. He was reaching out and had that political arena. That is a cold arena. You don't step on their toes without causing

EVERYONE IN THE BAND WAS A COMPOSER. EVEN THE VERSES OF THE SINGER WOULD BE SHARED. IT WAS LIKE A COMMUNIST BAND. WE WOULD SHARE EVERYTHING. SO NOBODY WOULD WRITE THE MUSIC [AND THAT'S WHY] WE NEEDED A ROOM, A LABORATORY, TO MAKE THE MUSIC.

ings and slowly something would develop. The recording was OK but primitive. But I think the music was much better than when we had a multi-track machine with overdubbing and all that, because then the group would not play

wanted and how they wanted things to be on the two. What I enjoyed

some problems. But I was very fortunate

because they wanted me to know what they were doing, so they showed me bit by bit by bit.

What did they show you exactly?

BP: How to play the other rhythms, play four different rhythms and come out with a reggae sound. Yes. Darn right. You have to learn how to breathe. You got to learn how to breathe and you got to know where one is or you'll be totally off so…it's the flow of what is going on. The feel and the attitude. And they're dancing. You can't do any better than that. 'Cause that's what it all comes down to, especially for me. So I believe in that. I believe in the dancefloor. It really works.

THE DRUMMER'S JOB IS ALWAYS, ALWAYS IN DEFENSE.

'Cause anybody can dance. Everybody can dance, and it doesn't matter how little or how much. With reggae, the point is: reggae is on two. You can write it one, two, three, four, one, two, three, four, one, *two*, three, four; one, *two*, three, four. And it brings you into half time. One, two… it's all about balance. You put yourself together into that and it is balance. It's so simple, yet it is so intricate to anybody who doesn't know.

JL: I mean, most of the people dance what they know. If they are in a marching room, then they march. But if you play rhythms which are not so known in the area, then the people will not dance. When I went to Turkey I played with some local musicians and they very much liked to play a rhythm which is in nine.

BP: Nine-eleven or nine-eight.

JL: It seems like that, yes. They said to me, "Hey, listen, let's play some dance music." They will start a nine rhythm. And, as soon as people hear this rhythm, they start dancing. It's very strange. In Germany they would break their legs. But they know how to move to this, and so they start dancing. I think the music has to be danceable, at least, 99%. At the end, that's how free jazz

was. I think the last tone they play, they hold it and they play like that. That's how free jazz was invented. That's my feeling. They make some noises and then they finish and then somebody goes, "Oh, that was the best thing in the whole tune."

Let's cut off the rest of the tune.

JL: Free jazz was invented by critics.

BP: Yes it was, yes it was!

JL: In the beginning with Ornette Coleman and Don Cherry, it was always nice. I loved it. They just… I think they didn't count in bars. So it was free. But there was a metronome going. It went, but there were no bars.

There was a time in music where there were no bar lines.

JL: Yeah, I mean, there are two systems, basically. I don't know how to pronounce it in English. The divisive system and the additive system. The divisive system is where we have bars. I always say it's "tamed music." Tamed music means you have bars with a grid in front. In one bar you have some animal. In the next bar you have another animal. That's why I say it's tamed. It's logical music, European music. The additive system is where you add some pieces of time. For instance, three plus three plus two. Something like that. That's the system I use. I don't think so much in bars because, with the bars, on the one is emphasized and on the three is emphasized. On the other parts it is less emphasized. I think that's all rubbish to think like that. It's not true. That's the problem the Europeans have. They emphasize wrong. You can only make emphasis from movement. It's not dependent on the bar line. It depends on the movement – if you have enough time to lift your hand up to make a louder beat.

So drumming is dancing?

JL: I think that's essential.

BP: It really is. But what he's saying to you – what we do to make things work for everybody else – is dynamics. We have to play with dynamics to keep it moving, to keep it happening. Otherwise, what's the sense? What's the sense in having it? If everybody is doing the same thing, then there is nothing to complement each other. So the drummer's job is always, always in defense. We're in the defensive mode because we got to please everybody. We have to please everybody if we want to work. You want the job? You have to please other folks first before you can actually start pleasing yourself.

Nile Rodgers' guitar playing is known the world over, the indelible melodic engine of Chic, one of disco's biggest bands. Rodgers began his musical life in the classical world, but quickly moved over to R&B and pop and found himself playing in a renowned session band alongside future Chic partner Bernard Edwards and Tony Thompson. In 1977, they struck out on their own and quickly found success with tunes like "Le Freak," "Everybody Dance" and the oft-sampled "Good Times." After Chic's fortunes dwindled, Rodgers moved on to a production career that includes work for Madonna, David Bowie, Diana Ross and Duran Duran. Today, he tours with a new version of the Chic Organization, performing the workshop's greatest hits.

Martyn Ware's career has had plenty of twists and turns, but it's been typified by a remarkable resilience. Sheffield-bred, Ware was a founding member of the Human League, helping to turn its avant-garde synth sound into chart fodder. Ware and fellow bandmate Ian Craig Marsh left the group in the early '80s to form Heaven 17, one of the great conceptual pop groups of the decade. ("Temptation," released in 1983, was their biggest hit.) Ware also found success producing other artists throughout the '80s, reviving Tina Turner's career with "Private Dancer" and introducing the world to Terence Trent D'Arby. More recently, Ware has been exploring the limits of surround sound, yet another chapter in an already remarkable novel of a life.

MODERATOR: BENJI B

PHOTOGRAPHER: JANE STOCKDALE

Making hit records ain't easy, but Nile Rodgers and Martyn Ware work harder at it than most. Separately, the duo is responsible for some of the most enduring moments in pop music history. Rodgers, as part of Chic, gave a human pulse to the often bloodless thump of disco. A few years later, Ware began to learn how to tame unruly synthesizers in the Human League and Heaven 17. Both went on to sit in the producer's chair for arena-filling acts, adding their signature touch to chart-topping material from Madonna, Tina Turner and David Bowie.

NILE RODGERS AND MARTYN WARE

What connects the two is a love of songwriting. And when Ware visited Rodgers at a Chic soundcheck before a recent gig in London, that's where their conversation began. Rodgers had traveled overnight to get to the Thames, but once he sat down with Ware his energy was high. A few days later, Rodgers announced doctors had given him an "all-clear" in his fight with cancer.

Martyn Ware: To me, you are like the Obi-Wan Kenobi of pop. You were a big influence on Heaven 17 and the Human League, believe it or not, even though we were completely electronic.

Nile Rogers: Really?

MW: Oh yeah, completely. When the whole "Disco Sucks" thing happened and everybody in NME was saying, "Oh, we don't like those disco acts because they're not credible." For the first two years of the Human League we weren't using guitars, but the syncopation and the musicality was important for us.

NR: You guys did cool stuff.

MW: I'd like to start by asking what your favourite Chic song is. I know it's a banal question, but…

ON STA GE I SAY "GO OD TIMES" IS MY FAVO RITE, BUT THA T'S JUST SHO W BUSI NESS.

NR: I honestly do not have a favorite Chic song. On stage I say "Good Times" is my favorite, but that's just show business. It's not. It's way up there, but there are so many songs that are my favorites. It's like other people's music. When you listen to other music that you love that you had nothing to do with… For a while, it's just your favorite song ever. And then you hear something else and that becomes your favorite song ever. I'll come back to Chic songs, especially ones that weren't hits, and I'm blown away.

MW: What always impresses me about Chic, about your writing – I always imagined it as a yardstick I used for Heaven 17 as well. A good song is one that can be played on a piano,

A GOO D SON G IS ON E T HAT CAN BE P LA Y ED ONA PIA NO.

and/or some kind of polyphonic instrument, and it sounds good in any format. A perfect example is [Heaven 17's] "Temptation." There was a clear idea of the structure from the beginning. It was meant to be like an Escher staircase of rolling major chords, and when you got to the top of the sequence it would get replaced with a different inversion underneath. So it seemed to be eternally climbing towards some kind of climax. That creates a very strong connection with the audience. We have done gigs to people who are avid fans through to people who don't care if we're there or not. Everybody gets "Temptation." We could play it to a retirement home, and they would love it. We could play it to a bunch of five-year olds in junior school and they'd love it. Why? I've only ever managed in my life to write one song that has that universal effect. With your songs, Nile, there's an element of very happy and hopeful, but buried inside is some kind of sadness and elegance. People hardly comment on that, because they're obsessed with the disco thing. For instance, my favorite song of yours is "At Last I'm Free." I think it's such a beautiful song. I'm thinking you could have a large-scale orchestra doing a Chic concerto.

NR: Oh, easily.

MW: Have you ever done that?

NR: No, I haven't. But I sort of have when I've done film scores. That's me being Nile. I mean, the songs on Coming to America were specifically written for symphony orchestra, but it's still the guy who writes Chic songs. It's still the guy who writes Chic songs who did Alphabet City. The same with Thelma and Louise with Hans Zimmer. I still write like me, because I think like me melodically and harmonically.

TO ME, YOU ARE LIKE THE OBI-WAN KENO BI OF POP.

MW: Have you ever thought of doing a longer orchestral work? I think the way you assemble songs is almost symphonic.

NR: Maybe it's because of my classical training. I've had the artistic whim to do it, but –

MW: It's the time, innit?

NR: Time doesn't bother me. I ran away from classical music in a big way when I played a recital. I was about 20 years old and I used to play classical guitar. I did a recital at the New York Public Library for the Performing Arts. It was really cool. I played the program very well, especially for a 19 or 20 year old. I played etudes by Fernando Sor. The typical stuff that classical guitar players play. Luis de Milán, all that stuff. I did a really great job, but I'll never forget when I was leaving that theatre that as much as the people loved it, and as well as I played, reality kicked in. It was the weirdest thing. I was walking home with my guitar and I was proud but as proud as I was, I was clear. I said to myself, "How many black concert guitar players are there in this world?" The only one I could think of was Narciso Yepes, and he's extraordinary! I'm never going to be able to play like him, and nobody knows who he is! I thought, "If I can't play like Narciso Yepes and he's not even that well-known, what's going to happen to little old me?"

I RAN AWAY FROM CLASSICAL MUSIC IN A BIG WAY.

MW: Was it like an epiphany?

NR: Absolutely. I thought to myself, "In that world I have no chance. But with my knowledge base, if I took that to jazz and pop... All of a sudden, I'm the man."

"OH, YOUR RECORD HAS GONE TO #1," AND I REPLIED, "YEAH, I'M WATCHING FOOTBALL."

RBMA: Have you worked with strings, Martyn?

MW: Oh, loads. "Temptation" with a 60-piece orchestra. And also with Terence Trent D'Arby on his album. I produced the first album, which was the one that made him.

NR: The one with "Wishing Well" on it? That's great.

MW: Yeah, I produced that. That was inspired by David Bowie's "Let's Dance" actually.

NR: Oh really?

THA T'SME BE ING N ILE.

I AL WAYS TH OUGH T
TH EY W ER GOING
TO GO ON FO
B UT TH E Y DID N'T.

MW: If you listen to it, you can kinda hear it. That was #1 in America. I remember being in London and I was so blasé at the time. I got a call saying, "Oh, your record has gone to #1," and I replied, "Yeah, I'm watching football." [laughs]

That's the blaséness of hitmakers, right?

MW: More like the blaséness of youth. I always thought they were going to go on forever, but they didn't.

NR: What you just said is true. When you get your first gold record, it's unbelievable. And what happened was, with our career, our first single was gold, our second was gold, our third, our fourth, our fifth, our sixth. And then the gold would turn into platinum. These are the old days.

When you had a gold record you had to go to the record company and get it, because they couldn't send it to you in the post. You went there and got it, and after a while we're walking down the street with a gold record.

TRACK DEVEL OPM ENT!

MW: I gave them all to my mum. She's got them on the walls, and the postman is going, "Your son is so successful!"

NR: After a while – I'll never forget it – we came out with "Good Times." And it went to gold right away, and then platinum. At this point we were accustomed to platinum singles. In America, they were two million. This was routine for us. "Le Freak," triple platinum, six million in America. Biggest seller on Atlantic. So when they asked us to come over and get our platinum records for "Good Times" – because they had been sitting there with the gold records – we said, "Oh, you're kidding, another one? Nah, we don't feel like coming over to get that shit." Those were the exact words. And we never got another one again. That was the very last Chic gold or platinum single.

On the subject of gold and platinum records, you're people who did it in the period where you had to sell millions to be #1. Now we're in an age where you don't have to sell that many records in the UK to be #1 anymore. How does that make you feel?

MW: In America, the charts still mean something. I'm not sure what the charts mean in the UK anymore.

NR: A couple of years ago Beyoncé put out a record and it went to #1 and it sold less than 100,000. Coming from my background, that was incredible. In the old days if you sold 100,000 you probably weren't even in the top 100. In the old days of the Billboard charts they would have a circle for gold and a diamond for platinum. Every record in the top 40 or 50 had that circle or diamond.

MW: Recently, it was 9,000 to get to #1 in the UK. For Rihanna.

When you were #1, how many did that take?

MW: I don't think we ever got to #1 actually. "Temptation" got to #2, but we sold a million-and-a-half singles.

I think it's interesting that the definition of a hit has essentially changed now. What does it mean to you, Nile?

NR: For me, it's become interesting again with sales going up across the board. I just wrote – with [Daft Punk's] "Get Lucky" – a single that sold more than a million in the UK. I thought that you couldn't sell a million singles in the UK, because there weren't enough people. So when the charts guys called me up to tell me I'd sold a million singles, I didn't know what that meant. I told them I've sold a million singles a lot. They said, "No, we mean in the UK alone." Only 135 people have ever done it, and some of those records took 28 years to sell a million.

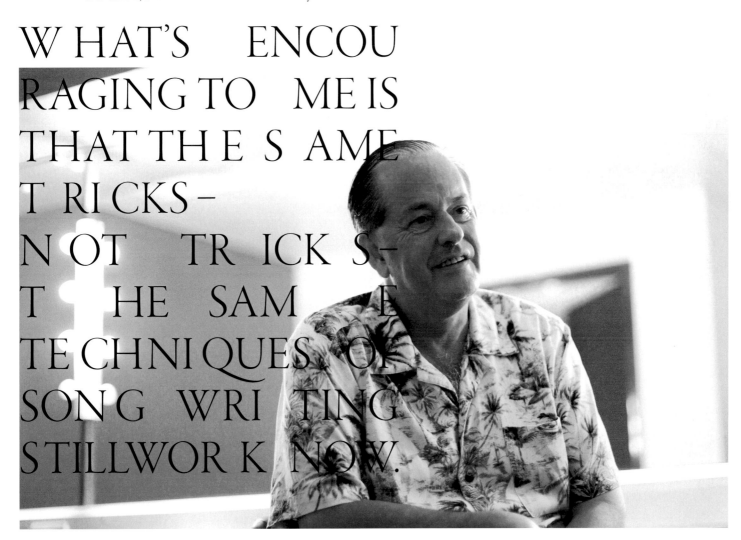

WHAT'S ENCOURAGING TO ME IS THAT THE SAME TRICKS – NOT TRICKS – THE SAME TECHNIQUES OF SONGWRITING STILL WORK NOW.

And how many people have done it post-2000?

MW: Hardly any.

NR: Apparently in this period that we're in now, though, sales are ramping up. Pharrell, who did "Get Lucky" with me, just got two of them back to back. Because the new record with Robin Thicke

also sold a million. Both of them are million sellers. I said to the guy, because this sounded like such a weird statistic, "Let me see if I can guess the top ten." I did pretty good. I guessed the Elton John song after Princess Diana died, the Live Aid one, the Spice Girls. When things happen in the UK, they happen to the whole country.

MW: It's a hyperconnected country in that regard. What's encouraging to me is that the same tricks – not tricks – the same techniques of songwriting still work now. The stuff I learned growing up from Jimmy Webb, Roy Orbison: keeping the interest throughout.

I'LL WRITE WHAT THEY CALL TOP LINES NOW. BUT, IN MY WORLD, THAT'S JUST THE SONG.

NR: Track development!

MW: Yes. Keeping the ear interested. Ear candy that keeps people interested. It still works. I tell people from the dance world who try to write this stuff, and they're amazed it still works. They think it's some kind of arcane art, which has been lost now. I think a great song will work forever. People need to be disavowed of the idea that it's somehow old-fashioned to look at traditional song structure. There's a reason why, say for instance, orchestral instruments are the way they are. It's because they fulfill a function. Songwriting is the same. If you look back to the Wagner lieder, the Richard Strauss lieder or even songs that have evolved from Gregorian chants, they often have a structure which is redolent of contemporary popular songs. There is a reason why those structures became successful. It's because they work. People may regard it as old-fashioned to acquire those skills, but if you at least understand the skills – and apply some of the tricks of the trade to a new palette of sounds – you will end up with something that appeals to a much broader range of people.

NR: I write with a lot of electronic musicians and, believe it or not, they're still doing the same thing. They just don't do it the same way. They have all the ear candy, all that track development. The thing is that because they have it at their disposal, and they can just grab it anytime they want, what they do is constantly try out different ideas. It's amazing. People look at me funny when I say that Avicii is my new favorite songwriting partner, saying he's only 23 years old. I reply, "How old do you think I was when I wrote 'Everybody Dance'?" The most sophisticated Chic song ever. "How old was I when I wrote 'Upside Down' and 'I'm Coming Out'?" These are sophisticated pop songs, and I was 20-something years old. What's amazing about Avicii, though, is that we both write the same way. From the ground up. He doesn't surround himself with a bunch of samples and drop it in. I'll give him an idea and he runs with that idea. Starts fooling around with it, changing it, just like I would.

MW: Do you work in the same room?

NR: Oh yeah. We're in there doing it together, just like Bernard Edwards and I did it. That's why I have so much fun with him. I wrote with the drum & bass group Chase & Status, and it was the same thing. The interesting thing is that they don't realize when I'm walking into the room that I actually have a whole concept, a whole framework. It's probably the same with you, Martyn. I walk in with a song in my head. And that's surprising to them. What winds up happening is that it's very productive. I have a million ideas, so it's almost like they're overwhelmed.

MW: I'd say ideas aren't the problem. It's finding the time and people to do it.

NR: Right.

MW: I get so many ideas that I have to block them out occasionally.

NR: That's the cool thing about our world. In my life, musical ideas are always sort of spilling out of my head. So when I'm working with someone like Avicii, it's great. I can just throw all this stuff at him and he soaks it up like a sponge. And then he has an arsenal of ideas to work from.

For you Nile, the backbone of your music is the groove. Similarly, for people like Avicii, it's club records. How do you marry groove-based music with ear candy in different formats?

NR: When I write a song, and I'm pretty sure you're the same way Martyn, I define it as DHM. Deep hidden meaning. So a song has substance, it means a lot. But as an orchestrator and arranger, I can change it to whatever style I want. I can turn it into a reggae song, change it to deep house, drum & bass. So I'll write what they call top lines now. But, in my world, that's just the song.

I WANT THEM TO HEAR YOU EXPOSED. SHE WAS THIS TOUGH WOMAN. BOSS OF THIS, BOSS OF THAT. MUSIC WAS THE BOSS, THOUGH. SHE WAS SUBORDINATE TO THE MUSIC.

MW: You've hit the nail on the head. It has to be translatable to potentially anything.

NR: Any medium.

MW: That is the litmus test for a great song. When I'm creating stuff, I generally work from the groove upwards if you like, and then the deep hidden meaning comes right at the end. It's different for everyone. Having said that, when we write the lyrics we sit in a room and we discuss every nuance. Could it possibly mean this? Does it mean this? What does it mean to people? You need to leave wriggle room for people to populate it with their own meaning. Getting back to ear candy, I learned a lot once from a guitarist named Ray Russell. We had a track that had this beautiful vocal and futuristic-sounding arrangement, but it was missing something and it was this human element. It was basically Ray coming in with all his experience, and he basically acted as a call-and-response with the vocal in between. That's what I'm calling ear candy. You don't let them alone for a second, because you've lost their interest if you do. Nile referred to something similar in his book that someone else had said, "The verse is just passing time until you can get to the bridge. And the bridge is just passing time until you can get to the chorus."

NR: That's right.

MW: It might be a little melody line in the background, it could be some percussion thing. Often you don't even know what people are listening to that keeps them engaged. But your job is to keep them engaged for three-and-a-half minutes.

I GE T SO MANY IDE A S THAT I HAV E TO BLOCK THEM O U T OC C ASION ALLY.

NR: I can't sing a song without singing those ear candy licks. When you sing the chorus of "Like a Virgin," you do the ear candy bits! All of my songs have to have that little lick in them.

EVER Y BO DY GET S "TEMP TATI ON." WE COUL D PLAY IT TO A RE-TIREMENT HOME, AND TH EY WOULD LOVE IT.

MW: It's very rare that you have a song that's completely linear with just a vocal on top, Nile. The vocal is often a kind of instrument in the mix for you. Thinking of someone like Tina [Turner]. I often wonder if something that works for a Chic song would work for her. Would she have been too strong a flavor for Chic?

NR: No, because I would write for her. Like when I wrote for Diana Ross. There is no other Chic record like what I did with Diana. When I was doing "Let's Dance" with Bowie, there is no record like that. And when I was working with Madonna, there is nothing else like those songs. When I was working with Madonna, it was like I was looking at the world through her eyes – and the next step in her life. If I were to work with her again, there would be no songs on it that are like those previous songs.

MW: Did you discuss that with her while making it?

STOR IES A RE IMPORTANT. MEANING IS IMPO R TANT. I T'S NOT JUST AN INTELL- ECT UAL PUR SUIT.

NR: Absolutely. She was enthralled with the fact that – and these are her words – "I just don't understand how Nile can read my mind." What she was talking about was our cover of the Rose Royce song "Love Don't Live Here Anymore," where I had a string section in the studio. I told her, "Madonna, you're going to sing live while we play with you." She didn't understand. "How are they going to know where I am?" "They're going to know because I am going to know where you are. They're going to follow me and I'm following you." She started singing and she'd never heard anything like that before. When they were doing this big arpeggio, she started crying in the middle of the record. After it was over she said she was ready to do it [again], but I was like, "That's it!" If it made you cry, I want people to hear that. I want them to hear you exposed. She was this tough woman. Boss of this, boss of that. Music was the boss, though. She was subordinate to the music.

MW: Yes! Communication with the audience is all that matters, however you do it. Leave the mistakes in too. The problem is that there is too much ironing out going on in contemporary production as far as I'm concerned. Way too much. I'll tell you what else is missing: I grew up with a massive Motown collection, and a lot of those songs – not just Motown but a lot of songs from that period – were story songs. Narrative songs. Telling a story in three, three-and-a-half

minutes. I think we've lost a lot of that in contemporary music. People like stories. I mean, it's not new. This goes back to the Aboriginal storytelling round the fire thing. Stories are important. Meaning is important. It's not just an intellectual pursuit. That's why I have a fundamental problem with the way the whole scene developed in popular music influenced by dance in the '90s and early '00s, because it was a denial of storytelling to a certain extent. It was like, "We don't need that shit, it's just all about the beat. It's all about whatever the fashion is this month. The latest synth or the latest preset." That's not true. You're missing the point. You're throwing the baby out with the bathwater.

I THOUGHT TO MY SELF, "IN TH AT WOR LD IHAVE NO CHAN CE. BU T WI T H MY KNO WLEDGE BASE, IF I TOOK T HAT TOJ AZZ AN D P OP... A LL OF A SUD DEN,

I' MTHE M A N."

MODERATOR: PIOTR ORLOV

PHOTOGRAPHER: GEORDIE WOOD

PATRICK ADAMS

In an age where there's a legend born every lunch-time, Kerri Chandler understands the difference between flash-in-the-pan trends and longevity better than most. A champion of the underground New Jersey house sound, Chandler has been a constant innovator and prolific producer ever since his debut 12-inch in 1989. Walking the fine line between engineering and musicality, this master of basslines has defined the sound of deep house for over two decades. What separates Chandler is his attention to detail. You'll rarely find another DJ bothering to soundcheck before their appearance. It's even more rare to find a DJ that walks around the club with a portable wireless set-up, just to see how things are sounding on the floor. Chandler's commitment to rocking the club while maintaining a deep vibe is unparalleled.

Few producers know how to transform the skate rink into a wonderland of the imagination quite like Patrick Adams. The Harlem-raised producer who brought us talking bees, dancing robots, mad synths and guardian angels, found the perfect balance between familiarity and freshness, which marked him out as the go-to producer during the disco and boogie era's most creative period. Responsible for countless iconic tracks, such as Phreek's "Weekend," Fonda Rae's "Over Like a Fat Rat" and Inner Life's "Caught Up," Patrick Adams' music not only soundtracked the '70s, he also sat in the studio for records by R&B and hip hop acts like Salt-N-Pepa and Eric B. & Rakim. Never afraid to tread his own path, Patrick Adams' instincts are second-to-none.

KERRI CHANDLER

Capturing a combination of modern and classic in a studio session is never easy. Unless you're Patrick Adams, that is. His marriage of idiosyncratic effects and radio-friendly hooks throughout the '70s and '80s left an indelible

mark on American music and New York dance history. That sound also inspired a young Kerri Chandler, whose diet of Adams-produced records provided the foundation for his own forays into

music. Growing up on his father's record collection, Chandler reinterpreted those soulful boogie moments into the house sound that was emerging from New Jersey's renowned Zanzibar club in the late '80s. Clasping a vinyl copy

of Cloud One's "Atmosphere Strut," Chandler met Adams at Sigma Sound Studios in Philadelphia. One of America's most celebrated studios, Sigma not only defined Gamble and Huff's

"Sound of Philadelphia Soul," but has been home to musical icons like David Bowie, The O'Jays, The Jackson 5 and many more since 1968.

THAT'S WHY
ERIC B AND RAKIM'S PAID IN FULL ALBUM
SOUNDS LIKE IT SOUNDS,
BECAUSE I USED A 20 TO 30 MILLISECOND DELAY,
A DIGITAL DELAY, ON ALL THE TRACKS.

I BELIEVE THAT THE PRODUCER IS THE ONE WITH THE ROAD MAP. HE HAS THE VISION.

RBMA: We're hanging out at Sigma studios in Philadelphia. Patrick, you said you had actually cut a session with Black Ivory here.

Patrick Adams: Internally the entire building is different. But the two things I remember most from that time – in the '70s – are that Joe Tarsia had a pair of speakers from a 1957 Chevy that were like his near-field monitors. The philosophy was that if it sounds good there, it will sound good anywhere, and he was right about that. The other thing I remember was that he embedded microphones in the ceiling in the far back side of the studio. He would dedicate one track of the two-track for what we'd call the "bow tie." So if you were doing the rhythm section session and your section had a guitar player on the right side of the room, by putting the left reflection into the mix it would create more space and give the room a very live sound. That's why Eric B and Rakim's *Paid In Full* album sounds like it sounds, because I used a 20 to 30 millisecond delay, a digital delay, on all the tracks.

Kerri Chandler: That's a great trick. I like that.

PA: Just to give you an example of something that seems small but is so important: I have a client named Harvey Miller. He does gospel music. I've been recording him and his wife for 30 years, and I remember a session we were doing. I was tired, really tired. I just wanted the session to end. So Harvey wanted to do this mix, and I said, "Harvey, listen, the big room is open. Can we go in the SSL room, throw it into the computer?" Because in the normal mixing process, without a computer, you're memorizing moves and you may run the tape back fifty times before you get all the moves down. And so you're choreographing the mix as though you're playing a part on a keyboard. But with an SSL or any other computerized mixing situation, you go through the mix come what may, and then you go back and fix little parts. And he looks at me and says, "Patrick, you're trying to give me a Lincoln. I'm looking for a Ford." I think it took about two years for me to fully realize the implications of that, which is, you can do what you need to do with less sometimes than if you go high-tech. I have found when I'm working with artists that if you keep things simple, it usually works out best.

KC: I've always noticed that same thing. I'll always try to wear two hats as a producer and engineer. I always try to get the best recording, because that's what I've learned from what you guys did – just get the best recording, sonically. But don't get to the point where the engineer part of it takes away from the musical part. If you don't have the idea to begin with, it doesn't matter how much gear you use. It'll sound like a clean piece of shit! That's what I always say: "an expensive, clean piece of shit."

PA: I believe that the producer is the one with the road map. He has the vision. If there's no map, you don't know where you're going and you won't know that you've arrived when you get there. I started engineering out of self-defense. It was never my desire to be pushing buttons. I wanted to concentrate

YOU WALK OUT OF THE STUDIO AND YOU GET HOME –
NOTHING.
BECAUSE IT WAS ALL FALSE.

on the creative part. But see, if you ask an engineer to turn up the treble and he goes one click, and you know what you're listening to still is not as bright as you want, and he starts to give you this, "Well, I can't do this," or "I shouldn't do that..." Why? They can never tell me why. I guess they were being defensive, maybe protective of their ears, because you don't want to be listening to all this brightness all day. Or, as I learned in engineering, you don't want to blow out the $800 speakers that you're going to have to pay for! But I tell you, you do that one time, you'll never do it again. By the way, what's the first question you ask when you go to a studio?

KC: It's been a minute because I'm always at home. First question I ask in a studio... "What are your monitors?" I guess.

PA: That is the first question. You want to know how true –

KC: How flat their room is compared to the real world, yeah.

PA: The answer you always get is, "Oh, perfectly flat. What you hear is what you get."

KC: There are very few rooms I've heard –

PA: Yeah. And we came to find out that a lot of studios in New York started using two tricks. One was that they would roll the bottom off of the monitors. You become aware of that because you're EQing something like a bass drum and you notice that no matter how much you add –

KC: The lower frequencies aren't coming up. Yeah, I've had that happen a couple of times.

PA: And then the other thing they do is the famous subwoofer under the console, which you didn't know about.

KC: Completely. They do that in a lot of department stores too. You go to Best Buy. You think you're hearing these two little monitors in the corner. "These sound amazing here!"

PA: You walk out of the studio and you get home – nothing. Because it was all false.

Is there a difference in the mindset when you're approaching a studio when you're creating something for yourself, or when you're either a producer or an engineer working for a client?

KC: The truth is, mine has always come down to, "What kind of artist?"

PA: As a producer – sorry to anyone who may be offended by this, but –

IF YOU DON'T HAVE THE IDEA TO BEGIN WITH, IT DOESN'T MATTER HOW MUCH GEAR YOU USE. IT'LL SOUND LIKE A CLEAN PIECE OF SHIT!

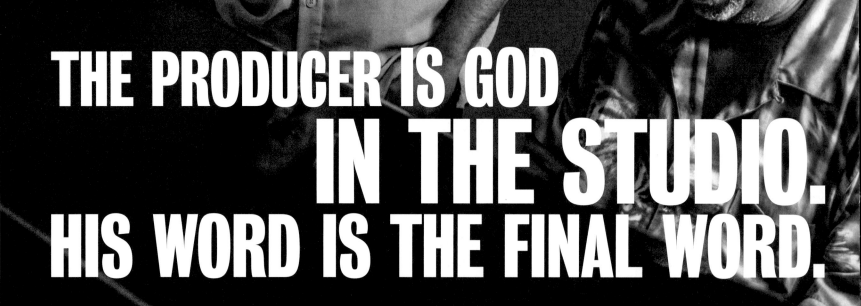

THE PRODUCER IS GOD
IN THE STUDIO.
HIS WORD IS THE FINAL WORD.

KC: Say it! I know where you're going to go with it, because it's probably the same answer.

PA: The producer is God in the studio. His word is the final word. I tell engineers first of all, when I walk in, "Listen, I don't need you here. So just do what I ask you to do, or you can go home."

KC: Oh, I always had fights with engineers.

PA: I'll tell you a great story. In the fall of 1978 I get a phone call from Jerry Greenberg, the president of Atlantic Records, and he says, "Patrick, I'd like to put you with Narada Michael Walden." I didn't know who Narada Michael Walden was at the time, but the A&R director explained that he was playing with the Mahavishnu Orchestra, and one of the three greatest drummers in the world at the time. So I'm impressed.

KC: Is this at the beginning of his career or later on?

PA: It's at the beginning. At this point, he had recorded half of *The Awakening*, which was some amazing stuff. He had the Waters Sisters on it, he had Santana on it: a lot of great musicians and singers. Unfortunately, his prior albums had not done as well as they expected and the landscape was changing out there. So the A&R guy takes me to meet Narada and says, "I'm going to catch up with you guys later. Review some songs. See what you want to cut on the album." So Narada is playing and I am amazed. I mean, he's a hell of a writer. He wrote things like "We Built This City on Rock And Roll" and he went on to do Whitney Houston, Aretha Franklin. I mean, the guy is a giant. But we're at that transitional point where what he does is terrific, but it's not commercial. Which is why I got called in. So I'm listening to song after song after song and I'm saying, "Wow, I love this, I love this, but it's not commercial. It's not the hit. I'm looking for the hit. Where's the hit?" Finally he plays "I Don't Want Nobody Else to Dance with You." I said, "We can work with that." So he says, "Patrick, you want a soda?" All right. He goes in the next room, he comes back about four minutes later with a smile on his face and we sit down, and he's going through more material. Five minutes later, there's a knock on the door. Here comes the A&R guy, who looks at me and says, "What's the problem? Narada says you guys are not getting along."

KC: Where did he get that from? I mean, you guys are having a conversation. How did he even come to that?

PA: Well, I wasn't liking his songs.

You weren't stroking the ego, instantly.

PA: Yeah, which I didn't know he had at that moment. But I had at that moment, for the first time, a record company executive be supportive of me. Normally in a situation like that the record company would acquiesce to the star, "I guess this isn't going to work, Patrick," you know. Instead the A&R guy turns to Narada and says, "Narada." He says, "You've done two albums for us so far and you haven't

OH, I ALWAYS
HAD FIGHTS
WITH ENGINEERS.

I HAD AT THAT MOMENT,
FOR THE FIRST TIME,
A RECORD COMPANY EXECUTIVE
BE SUPPORTIVE OF ME.

sold very much. You're halfway through this album. It looks like it's headed in the same direction. We brought Patrick in to try to find a new direction, so if you're not going to cooperate, you can pack your shit up and go back to San Francisco."

KC: Damn.

Kerri, tell me a little bit about the difference in terms of walking into a studio when you're making a record for someone else.

KC: I take baby steps with a lot of these singers, because depending on their ego and where they're coming from, it's different. Thank God, a lot of these people respect me and what I do. Thank God, I have an extensive catalogue. Not like Patrick. He's probably got double what I have, but I have a couple of thousand myself. But it's one of these things where I pick my battles. I let them feel like they're winning certain things, but in my head I'm thinking, "No, you've got to change that lyric around. No, this is flat. No, that should not go there. No, that change is wrong."

Where do you draw the line?

KC: When it sounds like they're taking away from the project more than they're adding to it. That's when I have to kind of say, "Look, let's not even waste time here."

So what you're saying is that as creative people, even when you are brought in to the project, you're still not going to give up complete control.

KC: No, that's the worst thing in the world you can do, because if they're bringing you in, that means you're there to make the project – or fix the project. And put your name on this thing. I don't know how he feels about it, but I'm a quality junkie.

PA: What I always remember is: "My name is going on this." I don't want somebody to point to my name on there and say, "Oh, he fucked this one up." And it wasn't me. The only time I absolutely surrendered was on a record called "You Put a Spark in My Life," by Shannon.

KC: Really? I thought that record was so good. And at the time it was so different. I love to be different. I don't want my record to go out there and be like what everybody else is doing. While everybody is doing blue and this group's doing orange, I'll do purple. I don't care, because either I'll die out there by myself or I'll be discovered and people will say, "Oh, man, did you hear that thing?" Just listen to "Get Lucky" by Daft Punk. It took only 15 seconds for me to say, "That's the record of the summer. The record of the year." It's a great song and I think, now, to do that at this time... I am so happy they brought Nile to a new generation and that Daft Punk has an audience that can accept that. I'm glad it's going in that direction musically.

PA: One thing I have to tell you, I listened to a lot of your stuff before this conversation and what I love about what you do is that it's about emotion, atmosphere.

I LOVE TO BE DIFFERENT.
I DON'T WANT MY RECORD
TO GO OUT THERE AND BE LIKE
WHAT EVERYBODY ELSE IS DOING.

WHILE EVERYBODY IS DOING BLUE
AND THIS GROUP'S DOING ORANGE,
I'LL DO PURPLE.

KC: Oh, completely.

PA: I'm very quick to take things off. If something starts to play and I'm not moved by it, I'm quick to move on. I don't have time. Not that I feel old, but I do feel that I don't want to waste my life being exposed to something that's not doing anything for me or taking me someplace. And I must say, I never took one of your things off.

KC: Oh my God. That, coming from you. I'm validated! I'll never make another record in my life! This is on tape, right? You made the hair stand up on my arms, man.

PA: I said to myself, I got to play on one of his things.

KC: That would be, like, *it* for me. Since I was about five, six years old, all I knew was disco. And all I knew was that *you* were disco to me. I knew those records intimately.

I was making a list of the things that I think both of your careers have in common, and one of them is that you both started playing music from a pretty young age in the public sphere.

KC: The truth of it is, I was always curious about everything. I wanted to know everything. The minute I saw a mixing desk, I had to know what it was. Any opportunity I had to actually sit in front of all this stuff, I took. They would never take me serious because I was a kid, but I was serious. I played upright bass. That was the first thing I learned in school. I had to drag this thing home every day. I was like, "Forget it, if I have to do that, that's what I got to do." My hands were torn up, bleeding – a little kid with calluses. The thing was way taller than me.

PA: We didn't have room for a piano, so my father bought a trumpet. I guess he thought I was going to be the next Quincy Jones, but I saw what trumpets did to people's lips and I said, "Not me!" So I said, "I want an electric guitar," and my father, he bought me a cheap Spanish guitar. He said, "You learn how to play that, I'll get you an electric guitar." He was a merchant seaman. He went to sea for nine months and when he came back he says, "Let me see what you've learned." So he says, "Play a G. Play a C." I was hitting it. He says, "Play an H." I said, "There's no H chord, Daddy." He was hip enough that he knew that much. As a reward he bought me an Epiphone. He'd make you earn it, but if you said, "This is what I want to do," he would get you the best equipment so you could do the job. The only argument my father and I ever had was that I didn't want to finish college. I wanted to play music.

KC: That's a tough one. I had to go through that too.

PA: It was a tough one. Especially when he's out to sea. He just didn't know what's going on. When he came back that particular year, when I was 17, he didn't know we had been in a movie. He didn't know we had a contract with MGM. He didn't know that people were recording my songs. All he knew was, "You're going to college." And we had a major falling out about that. But I went to school. I studied electrical engineering.

KC: Exactly. So did I.

PA: When we studied Fortran –

KC: Did you study Fortran too? Oh my God, I did Fortran. Hexadecimal code.

PA: COBOL. You'd walk around the campus with a shoebox full of punch cards and heaven forbid if you dropped it.

THE TRUTH OF IT IS, I WAS ALWAYS CURIOUS ABOUT EVERYTHING. I WANTED TO KNOW EVERYTHING.

I AM EXTREMELY HAPPY THAT THE DAY MY FATHER DIED, I SHOWED HIM MY FIRST GOLD RECORD.

KC: Oh, forget it. Because the sequence is out of order. Forget about trying to get it back. I had the same path you did. I had the same thing with my grandparents. They said, "Name me one DJ you know that makes money." This was the late '80s and I couldn't come up with anybody. I was thinking radio DJs, but even then I didn't know enough to say. My dad did radio stuff and they gave him, like, nothing.

PA: I am extremely happy that the day my father died, I showed him my first gold record. That was very deep.

KC: I had to do that for my grandfather. I had to show him that it was me making the money. I'm the DJ guy who's doing that. He said, "As long as you can keep this up, you have my blessing, but I'm not really happy about it." Because he was a jazz singer, so he was telling me about promoters and how he got ripped off and all this stuff. He was like, "Make sure you get a stronger foundation."

PA: I feel sorry for anyone contemplating entertainment as a field right now.

KC: Oh, forget it.

It's a crazy time. You brought up "Get Lucky" earlier, Kerri. That, to me, is an interesting concept. It's a dance record that is both very classic and very modern.

KC: As I look at it, I think as long as people want to dance there's going to be dance music. Period. It's just a matter of what it sounds like and if it's timeless enough that people can understand it. That's how I look at it and that's how the publishing company looks at it as well. "Is this shit going to be around?" It's very hard these days to actually get into a place where you can record a vocal and learn how to arrange and make a production, a real production. Maybe I'm from the old school, but I think the biggest thing is people need to learn a bit more about how to record a vocal. They need to know a bit about how to play an instrument and why this drum sounds this way. Instead of sampling it. Learn why the drums sound that way, why the room is that way, why the ambience is that way.

PA: The first question becomes, "Understand what music is."

KC: I agree. But, you know, perspective is everything. This is my interpretation of what I grew up with.

PA: Well, take "Push Push In The Bush." We had Stan Lucas on guitar, Kenny Mazur on another guitar and a kid named Mike Lewis on percussion. Mike gave us something by accident. We were in the studio and I hear this weird sound. I asked the engineer, "Wait, what the heck is that? Oh shit, that's his bracelet banging on the bongos like that." We left it in the record. One of my frustrations as an engineer... See, as we left the great disco period and went into what became, like, a neo-funk period, I went

YOU'D WALK
AROUND THE CAMPUS WITH A
SHOEBOX FULL OF PUNCH CARDS
AND HEAVEN FORBID IF YOU DROPPED IT.

into engineering at Power Play. At that point it was a survival thing. I wasn't getting the work. There wasn't anybody calling me. But it allowed me to stay in touch with the studio. How else are you going to do that? If you don't have the opportunity to come in and see that there's a new piece of equipment, or that Pro Tools now has this patch and that patch, next time you come in a studio you're going to be three years behind everybody else.

KC: Oh, completely. You always have to keep up with the times.

PA: That's why I went into engineering at Power Play and became chief engineer eventually. It really was a lab, because the younger guys would come in with their expectations and we would find a way to meet those expectations – and, at the same time, try to transfer a little knowledge. Hurby Azor, the first time he walked into Power Play he was fresh out of the Centre for the Media Arts. He would come in like, "Patrick, is there some way of taking a piece of music and making it play over and over again?" We didn't have samplers at that moment, but we figured it out. The word impossible was not in our vocabulary.

KC: That's exactly it. You make it work. You figure it out; you're an engineer. I love challenges like that. There's a lot of new stuff now. But the stuff we used to do with tape was amazing.

PA: Troubleshooting is a quite unique ability. You say it's not working. OK, why? How do we figure this out? Well, you start at point A and go through to point B. But about engineers: as an engineer it annoyed me to watch someone so-called "producing" a session. An engineer's job is to be the person who cleanly puts onto tape whatever you produce, whether you're an instrumentalist or you're a vocalist. That's the job description. It is not syncing stuff up. It is not running computers. We've lost that in the process, because in reality you've got engineers producing records now and getting nothing out of it. I've watched guys come in the studio with artists, with singers. "Alright, run the tape." "Oh, stop, stop, no, you're hitting in wrong. You're approaching it wrong." I mean, they don't let the person get a running start and they're jumping all over.

KC: I remember once this same thing. I was just an engineer. I wasn't supposed to be a producer in the studio. I was just head engineer there. These people would come in off the street, rent time and just sit there like, "OK, well, can you make a beat?" I'm like, "I'm supposed to just be recording." What do you mean, make a beat? I'm not your producer. "Yeah, but can you just put something together so we can..."

PA: Let me tell you a defining moment in engineering. I will not mention the person's name. This happened in 1975. I'm in the studio with someone: a female vocalist. She's being sponsored by a gentlemen who we could say was... connected in the world. The vocalist goes in and everything has been wonderful up to this point. I mean, it was a first class situation where the person put up money for everything. So we do the mix and I pick up a razor blade to do an edit, and this well-dressed, well-connected person walks up behind me with a gun. He says, "You're not cutting my fucking tape. I paid too much for this," because he didn't understand the process! He had no idea what I was getting ready to do.

KC: That's crazy. You had the grease prints and everything and you're just sitting there making marks and chopping stuff. I can't imagine!

PA: There was another client who was just as bad, because sometimes, after you've made the cut you let it roll off on the floor. So the tape is rolling on the floor and he's like, "Why is all my fucking tape on the floor?!"

KC: My favorite is, "What is it you're doing? What's that noise?" I'm striping the tape. "What? What are you doing that for? Why are you doing that? We need don't need that, we just need to mix some damn music."

THERE'S A LOT OF NEW STUFF NOW. BUT THE STUFF WE USED TO DO WITH TAPE WAS AMAZING.

Morgan Geist and Darshan Jesrani's music as Metro Area is that unique type of sound that simultaneously feels classic and new. Finding each other in New York via their shared love of boogie, house and disco, they first teamed up in the late '90s and produced a string of 12-inches that have been among the most acclaimed dance music vinyl of the last decade. Buffed and honed without sounding cold and lifeless, it's a discography of two dance music diehards in love with the science of the studio. Taking their live show on tour recently for the first time in years, it's clear their music continues to resonate.

As one of the earliest producers to straddle the worlds of live bands and synthesizers, Gareth Jones has a very particular view from behind the boards. Learning the ropes at Pathway Studios in London in the '80s before taking up a position at Berlin's iconic Hansa Studio, Jones has worked with – and learned – from the best. Innovating recording techniques and working with new sound palettes developed by acts like Depeche Mode, Einstürzende Neubauten and Diamanda Galás, Jones has developed a studio intuition like few others. Psychology, courage, impartiality and a certain acoustic voodoo are all vital to the Jones audio armory, which has helped him shape some of the most notable moments in modern recording history.

Gareth Jones has often said that the tools of the trade don't matter. It's the people using the tools. Metro Area – the duo of Morgan Geist and Darshan Jesrani – grew up listening to many of the records that Jones worked on in the '80s, desperate to find out what those tools were. We brought the trio together in Berlin at Hansa Studio, where Jones produced acts like Einstürzende Neubauten, Depeche Mode and Ideal, to compare and contrast creative processes and sonic approaches.

Gareth Jones and Metro Area

MODERATOR: TODD L. BURNS
PHOTOGRAPHER: JONAS LINDSTRÖM

RBMA: Morgan, one of the things you mentioned at home the other day, was that studio-specific magazines never seemed to quite do it for you. I was curious as to why that was.

Morgan Geist: Yeah. I don't want to complain about them too much. But back then some magazines reminded me of when I used to watch *120 Minutes* on MTV. I would watch all two hours to catch a one-and-a-half minute stretch where they'd show a little bit of a Kraftwerk video. There just wasn't a lot of electronic stuff.

Gareth Jones: Some of my friends and I talked about that in London and we felt the same. Loads of sound workers read it I guess, but we all felt that there was this phase it went through where it was like, "If it ain't tape or discrete transistors, it's not music."

Darshan Jesrani: You felt that it was skewed more towards those vintage things? I know what you mean.

GJ: I mean, that's a reasonable skew. I have a lot of respect for old stuff. You know, I'm old!

DJ: But it was like an orthodoxy.

It kinda reminds me of when I used to watch *120 Minutes* on MTV. I would watch all two hours for like a one-and-a-half minute stretch, where they'd show a little bit of a Kraftwerk video.

There was like half a decade where everything was a 909 kick through bad Mackie distortion.

GJ: It was. It's not so bad now. It's relaxed a bit. But there was definitely a stage where several of us were all mixing in the box, in computers, because budget didn't allow for us to mix here in Hansa and transfer everything to tape. We just started to feel… like it's not even music.

MG: They do sort of fetishize, also, the people who have a Mackie 1202. It's both ends of the spectrum. There was like half a decade where everything was a 909 kick through bad Mackie distortion.

GJ: That's UK rave!

MG: I wanted to start doing a studio-specific magazine. I interviewed Patrick Adams and then I ran out of steam. [*laughs*]

Where did you guys go, when you were first starting out, to learn about electronics? Was it all trial and error?

DJ: Oh yeah, all trial and error.

GJ: Yeah, I am the same. I'm kind of self-taught, for better or for worse. Obviously it's brilliant if you can study at the feet of a master, but I never did. I just started in a tiny studio and kind of picked it up. I learned a lot from musicians actually. When I was a real junior, if I worked with a guy who'd already made an album, he knew so much more about it than I did. It was an amazing learning curve.

MG: I was reading something about you, Gareth, where you were saying when you were under-confident when you'd done a mix, you'd simply take a break and come back. And it often sounds OK. I completely feel that way. Even if I get something as simple as a remix and someone sends me the parts, I'll get intimidated by the format. Like, "Should I be working at 24-bit/192kHz?" I make it less resolution because my computer can't handle it. It's sad. I hear bit depth, but I don't necessarily hear sample rate that much.

GJ: I also think it's a creative thing. Like you, I just can't handle 192. It's just not fluid. I did something like that recently. The first song came at high resolution, and it was such a pain. Everything took so long. It went from being rock solid stable to feeling all squashed.

MG: I'm glad you do that too. I was sort of embarrassed to even say.

GJ: The next song, same artist. "OK, forget this." I down-sampled, and boof! No one noticed, not even the producer.

DJ: People probably do it because they think they are supposed to.

GJ: I'm not saying the golden-eared guys out there can't tell. But what I mean is, my job was to deliver something that had a vibe. If I did that, the artist was happy. No one said, "Great mix dude, but I'm not sure about the sample frequency."

MG: I think comfort is a huge deal. Being really fluid with whatever format you are working in.

GJ: And discomfort is a really big deal as well, isn't it? I get really nervous when I get too comfortable. But I agree with being fluid. If a wood carver is good with a chisel that he has used for 20 years, obviously that's a useful tool. But then I suppose I'm trying to distinguish it from being formulaic. If I start drifting off and doing something formulaic, it starts to freak me out! Like I'm just wasting my life or something. I've just re-fallen in love with analogue and modulars a bit. It's like a voyage of discovery. Plugging wires in and turning knobs and seeing what happens. That's like the opposite of being comfortable. I'm comfortable philosophically with the idea, but I am not very fluid.

DJ: There is a difference between being uncomfortable and being annoyed. The annoyance with the sample rate thing, that's not a good kind of discomfort. But being out of your element is great.

MG: Did you used to work with modulars on your stuff for a while?

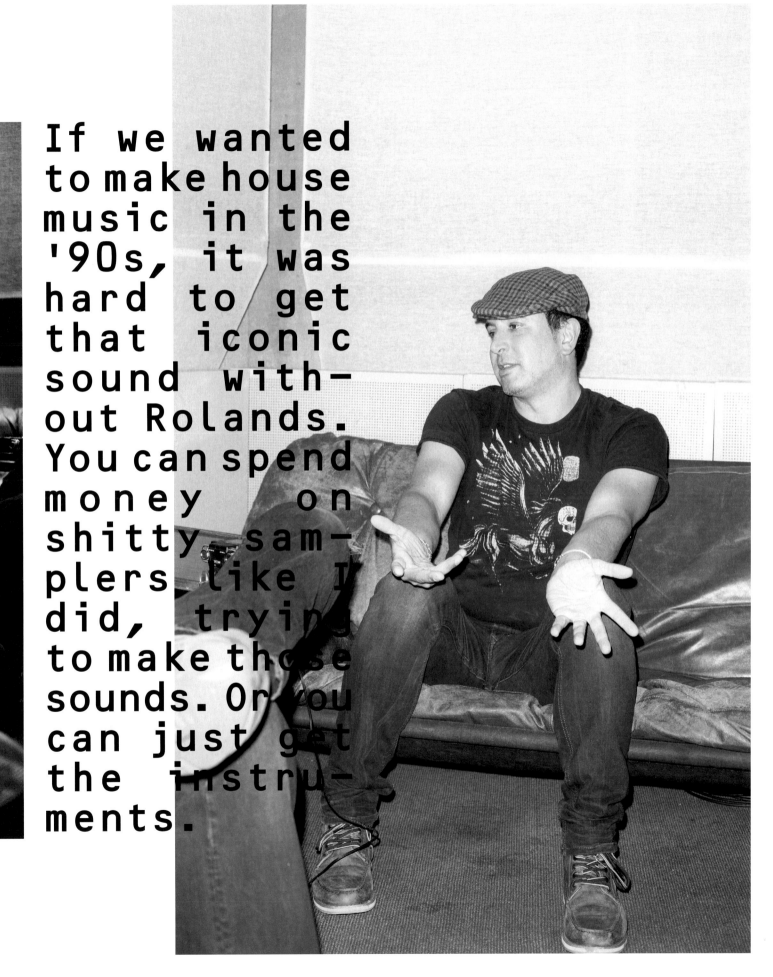

If we wanted to make house music in the '90s, it was hard to get that iconic sound without Rolands. You can spend money on shitty samplers like I did, trying to make those sounds. Or you can just get the instruments.

GJ: Well, lots of my colleagues have had all kinds of modulars. It's not that I stopped. I had a little [Roland System] 100m in the '80s and when I went deeply back inside the box I sold the 100m. Obviously you could have like five hundred modules and it would be very complicated, but the 100m I had was very simple and I didn't even fully explore that. So I've now decided to invest a bit of money in it, but it's a bit addictive!

MG: They're so big right now. We live in New York and I joke that modulars are the new fixed-gear bikes, because you see all these young, slightly wealthy hipster kids buying modulars. I have this semi-modular at home, but I'm never patching it because I started going into that and I feel like it slows me down. But I want to get into it, because I'm totally underutilizing the machine.

GJ: Everyone's different. That's another thing I bang on about. It's not about the gear. I always say, "I've made crap records in great studios, great records in great studios and good records in crap studios." I shouldn't be saying this. I haven't made any crappy records! Although the tools are important and they have revolutionized our lives and our work, somehow I just won't have it that they are important.

MG: I agree with you, more and more, as I am getting older. But it was about the machines for a while. Especially from where Darshan and I were coming from. We're the same age. We met when we were like 20. But we went through all the same phases – made all the same mistakes. I had the worst synths with horrible timing, and I'd be listening to Depeche Mode or Erasure, trying to get these sounds that Vince Clarke was using from them. I feel like I wasted years thinking, "Why can't I get the filter to do that?!"

DJ: If you are trying to achieve a certain sound, then you have to get the right instruments. If we wanted to make house music in the '90s, it was hard to get that iconic sound without Rolands. You can spend money on shitty samplers like I did, trying to make those sounds. Or you can just get the instruments. But once you get past that instrument point – and people start to obsess over gear – that's when it becomes distracting.

GJ: I'm constantly struggling against it as well, because the reason I even started at Hansa was because of the equipment. I find this is an ongoing theme: being fluid, using the tools creatively. But I have this deep belief that if the tools were different, it'd be alright.

MG: That's a total fallacy though. It's like the demo phenomenon. Someone makes a crappy demo. Then they go into a studio and produce it, and the demo is almost always better. I think that's a great, concrete example of how improving things – or getting better gear and increasing fidelity – doesn't always make it better.

I find this is an ongoing theme, being fluid, using the tools creatively. But I have this deep belief that if the tools were different, it'd be alright.

GJ: When I started working there was a real difference in quality between the demo and finished album. The demo vocal would be buried in the cassette noise and put on before the guitar. It was a sketch for a melody. Even if it had a good vibe, it was very hard to use. Obviously now it's a much more fluid working process.

DJ: It's all on the same platform as well. You can start off with one piece of software, intending to do a demo, and it just grows, and that becomes the project.

MG: Getting into electronic music when we did, we never understood the idea of different recording and mixing phases. You were mixing it while you were making it. We didn't understand the different phases until later.

GJ: A lot of modern electronic music is written, recorded, produced, mixed and sometimes even mastered by the artist himself. That's why it's a flow, all the way through. I have a little remix project with my friend Daniel Miller called Sunroof. We just did a remix for someone and we got it all happening with Ableton. We used his modulars and we built it up, then I moved it to Logic. The whole thing was pretty good, and I went to split up all the outputs and then sum it back through my high-end valve amplifier. I spent all day doing it, and it didn't sound any better. It just wasn't happening, so it all went back in the box.

MG: That's a maturity thing as well. When we were younger, even if it sounded worse we'd still be like, "We're mixing down this thing! It's got to be better!"

GJ: "We rented this thing for 300 bucks, it must sound better!"

DJ: We did that on our first record actually.

MG: We EQ'ed it and were like, "We just totally ruined this whole thing."

GJ: I would have been the same, but you just have to listen to your heart, haven't you? I'm not very good at making non-commissioned work. One thing that stops me being as good as I could be at growing my own work is that I judge too early. Instead of saying, "You know what? I am just making this. Here we go. I'll judge it next week." I shut it down because "it's not as good as Kraftwerk" or "Vince Clarke did this better in 1986." That's so unhelpful. I was talking to Vince recently about his new album and he said he might have a sound that is made up of three synths. What he does is record it to Logic, but then – unlike most of the youngsters nowadays – instead of leaving it on three tracks, he's bounced it to one. What has gone from being perhaps a 96 track thing has gone down to about 22. He said, "Well, I've been doing this for a while now. I've just got to trust my feeling."

DJ: That makes total sense. It also prevents you from going back to it and messing with all the little things. If you like a sound, just go for it.

GJ: He's a super modest guy. It was really great to hear one of the great grandfathers of electro pop or whatever to say, "I figured it sounded OK to me, and I've been doing it for a while so…" He's definitely got the 10,000 hours under his belt.

MG: He's in Maine now?

DJ: I saw pictures of his synth room up there. It looked amazing.

GJ: His shed? Yeah, it was. Like a carpenter's work room.

DJ: Yeah, there was something pastoral and futuristic at the same time.

MG: I remember an article where Vince was talking about getting everything in his studio MIDI-fied and then ripping it out. I don't know if that was true, but I remember thinking how crazy it was that he retrofitted a ton of his stuff and then decided the timing was shit.

GJ: There was a bad vibe at the beginning with MIDI.

Everyone has their own window too. Chic had a different idea of timing to Iggy Pop. Earth, Wind & Fire are different from James Brown.

MG: It's still shit! I can't believe everything has got so high-tech and it's still like… The timing is so off.

GJ: We can obviously make it work, but it was a freak out at the start. Being in this building thinking about sync… The amount of work and time and money and frustration we spent to try and get it all in sync at Hansa? To talk with anyone from that team now, it's just a joke. Every piece of equipment was a nightmare. It still goes on. When I did that remix project recently, we wanted to transfer from Ableton to Logic. No problem. We'll just sync them together using MIDI Time Code. And of course that didn't work.

DJ: There are subtle differences aren't there?

GJ: Everyone has their own window, too. Chic had a different idea of timing to Iggy Pop. Earth, Wind & Fire are different from James Brown.

MG: It would be nice if we could send Roland the bill every time the timing goes off.

Gareth, you mentioned when you first came to Hansa, the manager took you on a tour of the studio. What was the thing you were most impressed by?

I grew up in Jersey, where obviously there is a big dance music history, but I was in Bon Jovi New Jersey. Like shitty, bad hair metal New Jersey. I got a lot of heat for what I listened to.

GJ: The Solid State Logic mixing board. I'd never had the chance to work on one before. It's kind of legendary. It's still legendary. It was even more legendary for a Brit in the '80s. It was one of those things I'd read about and aspired to work on. There were two things about the mixer that were super meaningful. One was the routing, which allowed you to manage lots of flows of music through the console. The other was the automation, which nicely dovetailed with electronic music, where everything is kind of programmed. With this mixer, you could program the mix. Program the mute buttons. It's nothing to anyone who uses Ableton or Logic now, but at the time it was incredible. It was also the vibe at Hansa. It was summer and we went on the terrace, and it seemed like I was living the dream. You could see over the Berlin Wall. I was beginning to fall in love with Berlin. It's all very developed now, but back in the '80s it was a bomb site. Nothing. Potsdamer Platz was flat and undeveloped, like a wasteland. So you've got this super high tech room looking out over desolation. There was something about it that was wonderful. But really, as a young engineer who had never worked on a Solid State Logic board, I thought, "This is it, I need to take this step." That was with a German group.

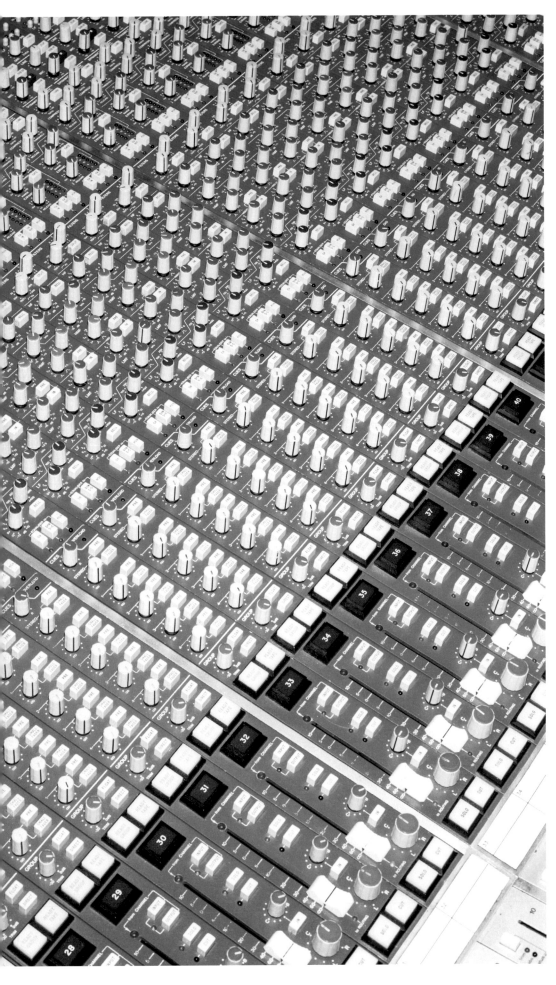

Ideal?

GJ: Yes, and I did some other Berlin bands in that room before I came here with Depeche Mode. I said to Daniel Miller that he and the band might like to mix *Construction Time Again* here. He was working here with Nick Cave and The Birthday Party in the big room. I said, "Come up and see this mix room, man!" He walked in and he looked around and he was like, "Yep, this makes sense."

MG: Were you intimidated by it? I'm 40 and I'm so comfortable with the stuff that I know. I never really push to get my hands on stuff. I'm also so used to working alone that when someone else is there, I am so self-conscious. Did you play head games with yourself? Or were you just like, "This is great, I gotta learn this."

GJ: More the latter. Because obviously I'd worked on other boards before. None with automation, though. It was pretty crazy. I mean, I was always fascinated by computers, before they could even do music, so the fact that there was a computer there... I mean obviously it was like a wristwatch today. [*laughs*] But that was a vibe. It was the automation. The only other difference was, I suppose, that it had a few more echo sends, and these famous dynamics built into every channel. But I wasn't particularly nervous working with Depeche. I was more cocky. When I was 17 I knew everything. I could have been President of The United States at 18, no problem! [*laughs*] I believed I really could get the job done and even if I couldn't, I'd be able to make a decision easily.

DJ: Right, sometimes it's good fuel.

GJ: You need it to get out of the nest. No child would leave the parental home if he didn't have this, "Hang on a minute, I'm 16. I know everything. You know nothing. Bye!"

MG: That does explain why I was making shitty music in my mom's basement when I was 25 and you were mixing Depeche Mode records. It explains a lot actually! That blows my mind, because I still get really nervous about this stuff. I don't know why.

GJ: Oh man, I know. I don't know why either. I get nervous all the time. I get nervous writing in my notebook sometimes. But when I get like that I think I must be touching something important. Generally when that happens it's because I feel it has some significance. If I'm just writing and not feeling anything...

MG: I think it's that initial hump as a producer as well. It's very easy to get isolated when you are working on your own. I think when you start working with other people, the social factor you get...

GJ: You have to blag it. I blagged it really, and I am happy about it. I mean, it's been my life. I didn't have the privilege of learning at the feet of masters. As a young guy, you just have to blag it.

DJ: Philosophically, I wanted to know where you were coming from when you started. I was reading that you aligned yourself with a hippie spirit. You didn't identify with the whole punk thing.

GJ: No, I definitely wasn't a punk. Because punks were sniffing glue and I was dropping acid. There was a crossover. What I got, unconsciously probably, was the idea that I could actually do it. The DIY thing.

MG: That's the legendary New Order quote from Bernard Sumner that we sort of clung to. That the computer is the ultimate punk instrument. Anyone can use it.

GJ: That's why we, as a small part of the Depeche team, felt very positive about computers. It allowed us to do rhythms and melodies in a way that no one could play. Martin Gore has matured as a musician. But, at the start, no one could really play. As soon as you put something in a machine, it had this amazing Kraftwerk, Donna Summer kind of vibe. It's all in time. So I get what Bernard was talking about. It was a really empowering thing. It also changes the ego thing. The computer plays everything. It's not like, "I play the drums and you play the bass."

DJ: It's your idea, but something else is rendering the idea, which is kind of cool because it's a bit detached from you.

GJ: Like, "Even if I write the bassline, it's not me playing the bass hour after hour."

DJ: It's like a living thing.

MG: It's an interesting dynamic, the whole interacting with the studio thing. I was always quite defensive about it. I grew up in Jersey, where obviously there is a big dance music history, but I was in Bon Jovi New Jersey. Like shitty, bad hair metal New Jersey. I got a lot of heat for what I listened to. You can imagine how Andy Bell went over with people who were listening to Winger. Even when I was listening to this early Depeche Mode stuff, people were saying, "You just push a fucking button." I always had a real attitude with this. Like, "You fucking play the same chord on the guitar that everyone is playing. It's a lot harder, what I do.

If I took it out of the box and just pushed a button, nothing would happen. I had to put that stuff in there." So I actually had the opposite idea, because my ego went crazy with that stuff. It finally let me be like, "Fuck you, I am learning on my own." Not in the same way you, Gareth, learned on your own before synthesizers were even popular. This was the mid-'80s. But, still, with no one around it was hard.

DJ: It was popular, but stigmatized.

MG: Yeah!

GJ: Similarly there was this thing in Britain where the Musicians' Union were anti-synthesizer, because it was like cheating. Obviously that's all gone now. Now you can say, "I am a Musicians' Union member, and proud to be, but I am a programmer."

DJ: I remember people putting that on album covers. "No sequencers were used," like it makes it the real thing!

I definitely wasn't a punk. Because punks were sniffing glue and I was dropping acid. There was a crossover. What I got, unconsciously probably, was the idea that I could actually do it. The DIY thing.

Olaf Bender is responsible for the graphic design of Raster-Noton, the minimalist label he co-runs with Carsten Nicolai and Frank Bretschneider. Like the music he makes as Byetone, his designs tend to betray a lifetime obsessed with (the illusion of) perfection. Bender grew up in East Germany, and — even before the Wall fell — found himself drawn into the world of experimental music via electro pop renegades AG-Geige. Inspired by their DIY approach, he continued to work with AG-Geige member Bretschneider eventually setting up a label, Rastermusic, for their work. In 1999, they merged with Carsten Nicolai's Noton, finding a common cause in their investigations of sound and design.

Carsten Nicolai was an architecture student before he went into music, and that may be the key to understanding the East German sound artist's work. There is little music that sounds as meticulous. In 1994 Nicolai founded the Noton.Archiv für Ton und Nichtton imprint. In 1999, he joined forces with Olaf Bender to create Raster-Noton, the label they share with Frank Bretschneider. Over the course of their partnership, they've largely pursued a minimalist agenda in both music and design. This extends to Nicolai's visual art as well, which has taken his works to museums and galleries around the world.

Uwe Schmidt is a German-born electronic music producer currently residing in Chile. Schmidt began his career making (relatively) straight-ahead techno in Frankfurt in the earliest days of the genre. As his career has gone on, however, his interests — and the way that he's represented them — have grown exponentially. Seemingly taking a new alias for every project, the hugely prolific Schmidt released a dizzying amount of music during the '90s and '00s. The throughline has been a commitment to exploration: Whether it be Latinized covers of Kraftwerk or gospel-tinged microhouse, Schmidt continues to push at the boundaries of genre and process.

Moderator: Torsten Schmidt

Photographer: Dan Wilton

BENDER

NICOLAI

SCHMIDT

UWE SCHMIDT IS THE MAN OF A THOUSAND ALIASES. CARSTEN NICOLAI AND OLAF BENDER ARE LARGELY KNOWN FOR FOCUSING ON ONE. ALL OF THEM, HOWEVER, HAVE DEDICATED THEIR CAREERS TOWARD THE SAME END: EXPLORING THE CONCEPTUAL LIMITS OF MUSIC. CARSTEN AND OLAF ARE CO-OWNERS OF EXPERIMENTAL ELECTRONIC LABEL RASTER-NOTON, AN IMPRINT THAT HAS RECENTLY SEEN TWO ALBUM RELEASES FROM UWE SCHMIDT'S ATOM TM PROJECT – ONE THAT HE SAYS WILL BE HIS SOLE MUSIC PROJECT FOR THE FORESEEABLE FUTURE. NICOLAI AND BENDER ARE ALSO TAKING STOCK AT THE MOMENT: THEIR DIAMOND VERSION PROJECT, RELEASED THROUGH MUTE RECORDS, HAS SEEN THEIR USUAL ASCETIC AESTHETIC TAKE ON SOME MUSCLE. THE TRIO MET WITH YET ANOTHER GERMAN, RED BULL MUSIC ACADEMY FOUNDER TORSTEN SCHMIDT, IN BARCELONA AT THE 20TH EDITION OF THE SÓNAR FESTIVAL. SITTING IN THE SHADOW OF THE MIES VAN DER ROHE-DESIGNED GERMAN PAVILION, THEY SPOKE ABOUT IDENTITY, CONCEPTUALISM AND MENSCHMASCHINEN IN GENERAL.

RBMA: We are here in Barcelona for the 20th birthday of Sónar, quite an established electronic festival. A couple of hours ago Kraftwerk performed and you were on stage only shortly beforehand in front of slightly less people. Do you feel you are appearing, particularly, as German electronic artists?

UWE SCHMIDT: Yes, in a way. I don't have much to compare with, but when I run around and look at and listen to everything at an event like this, then it looks as if we – Raster Noton as a label of course, and me as a part of this label – represent something very special, if I'm not totally off the mark.

OLAF BENDER: You were always lucky. Since moving to Chile, you've always been perceived as a *Super-Deutscher* artist. With us, it's a bit different. Our work is actually not a national issue.

US: No, of course not.

OB: Sónar, on an international level, is a small thing – but it's an established meeting point. What fascinated us, when we were invited ten years ago, was finally meeting our neighbors. Not that Cologne for example was that far away, but here everything came together. I believe one of the main advantages of this festival is having everything confined to one space. So within three to four days, you see each other five times.

CARSTEN NICOLAI: Yesterday I took a look at the program where there's always the name of the countries next to the names of the artists. Considering that it always reflects a certain zeitgeist, there was a noticeable amount of acts from UK and the US. The few from Germany like Kraftwerk, us, Modeselektor and Paul Kalkbrenner, seem to almost form a certain lineage.

OB: Compared to past years, the German contingent this year is relatively small. What I find exciting and what brings us together – maybe apart from Paul Kalkbrenner – is what I noticed yesterday: we

EVEN AFTER TEN YEARS, WE ARE STILL IN SEARCH OF SOMETHING.

WE ARE STILL INTERESTED IN THE FRINGES OF THE SPECTRUM AND WHERE TO TRAVEL.

all produce formalized music, working with certain building blocks, modules and elements are always interesting. Even after ten years, we are still in search of something.

CN: We are still interested in the fringes of the spectrum and where to travel, rather than feeling like we have already arrived somewhere.

US: I almost think there exists something like a typical German texture that ties together the aforementioned names. This has nothing to do with nationalism, it's just like that. And you can't really get out of that either. You're a part of it.

It seems highly absurd as a German when you watch Kraftwerk, looking at the latest version of the *Autobahn* video, and you get the association with the A57 from Köln to Düsseldorf or any other German urban agglomeration. Then there is this moment when people from all sorts of countries would start to cheer, when the smokestacks appear.

US: I had a funny experience with Kraftwerk when I arrived in Chile. Up to that point Kraftwerk meant nothing special to me. I hadn't listened to that specific band very often and I never quite understood what was supposed to be so particularly German about them. I have always thought it was more a universal thing until I showed The *Man-Machine* record sleeve to my wife and she laughed. I asked her, "What is so funny about that? It's only four Germans with red shirts and black ties, some Russian typography…" And she said, "This is exactly our idea of Germans." Only then I understood the significance. Kraftwerk played with it in a very intelligent way.

CN: I was wondering whether something like "roots" exist in electronic music. My first Kraftwerk concert was an enormously futuristic experience. This was ten years ago. Now, as I have seen all this again, now in 3D mode, it struck me how strongly entrenched these aesthetics are in the post-war, post-fascism era. Autobahn, propaganda, etc. These are extreme subjects, sometimes political and set up so directly that you can't do anything except think about where these aesthetics come from, and that there's a history behind them. Of course we all grew up in cities where bombed houses still existed. We didn't live through the Second World War, but we experienced the consequences. You can see the aesthetics of the '50s and '60s, but as for issues like propaganda and how it works and how icons are created... Here I see a clear relation to our project with Diamond Version where we are using company logos. Or the statement which you, Uwe, were making with your latest album.

OB: But don't you think that, apart from the visual level, another element adds to it which is very German: this constant compulsion to reflect...

US: Very much so. This is something very special. I think that doesn't necessarily exist in American or British music.

CN: Listening to an interview with Nile Rogers recently I heard him saying, "Everybody was angry about my book, because they only wanted the fun and superficial." And I thought, "Hey, that would be great to be able to do that."

US: You have a hard furrow to plough.

OB: But you'll manage eventually.

CN: I got real envious. I thought, "My God, why do we have to burden ourselves with those extra additional 15kg weights? Why can't we take it easy?"

US: "Germanness" has something didactic about it. A Chilean friend of mine saw Kraftwerk five years ago in Chile and felt like it was a school lesson.

OB: Exactly. It's just like physics.

NITZER EBB IS A GOOD EXAMPLE BECAUSE THEY TRIED TO SIMULATE THE RIGOR OF DAF – "DER RÄUBER UND DER PRINZ" – BUT IT WAS OF COURSE REINTERPRETED INTO SOMETHING COMPLETELY DIFFERENT.

YEAH, IT CAME OUT DIFFERENTLY THOUGH AND I THINK THIS HAS SOMETHING TO DO WITH THE LANGUAGE. CARSTEN SAID IT EARLIER, HOW THERE IS ALWAYS SOME HEAVY LOAD PUT ON EVERYTHING.

US: Yes, physics. Learn a bit of German: eins, zwei, drei, vier…

OB: But I reckon with a title like "Autobahn" they were conveying archaic concepts like roads, energy, etc. in music.

US: It's a classic concept: to find a subject, distill it and break it down to its basic elements before you try to communicate.

The *Meccano* Magazine for construction kits was published in England starting in the early 20th century. Its covers alone were permanent propaganda for the belief in progress and seem to close the gap between Kraftwerk and the futurism of the '20s and '30s a bit. But apart from cases like Nitzer Ebb it was never really picked up again in British pop culture.

US: Nitzer Ebb is a good example because they tried to simulate the rigour of DAF – "Der Räuber und Der Prinz" – but it was of course reinterpreted as something completely different. There were titles by Orchestral Manoeuvres in the Dark that were supposed to sound like Kraftwerk, but somehow sounded completely different.

OB: Factory Records has also played with that.

US: Yeah, it came out differently though, and I think this has something to do with the language. Carsten said it earlier, how there is always some heavy load put on everything...

OB: I think we have a relatively big yearning to leave the individual perspective and objectify things. In very broad strokes, English music very often derives from a self-centeredness whereas German music…

US: …puts the self to the side.

OB: Yeah, and takes the aerial perspective.

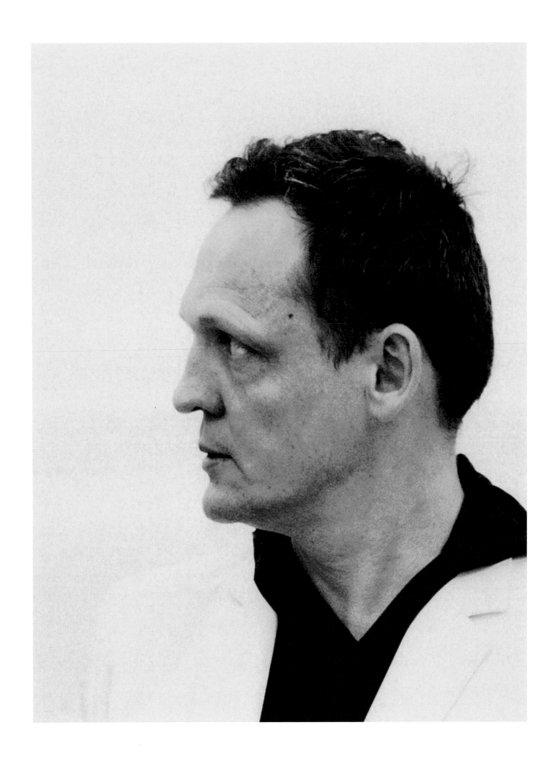

Would that mean we're afraid of the self?

OB: Yes. But it's also boring to be constantly captured in the self.

US: Now it's getting psychological. We can't avoid the self of course. Yearning seems a good word, the attempt for neutrality and for objectivity.

OB: Yes, and for looking at oneself in a critical way and to ask oneself: Where am I standing? Why do I do this?

US: It somehow always becomes philosophical.

Yearning and similar emotions are recurring subjects in German art history. But these subjects are always being packaged in concepts. Therefore again the question: are we afraid? Do we allow ourselves to speak about such emotional things only if we have safeguarded them by means of a concept?

US: There is a movement within classical psychology called the Enneagram of Personality, which divides people into nine types of characters. It all becomes a bit metaphysical but you can attribute these nine characters roughly to countries or living environments. The German has an angst-burdened character. He acts completely different from the Japanese or Swiss for example. One may think we're on similar paths, but the impulse for action is completely different. The German is anxious about the future, that's why he protects himself.

OB: The beautiful word Zukunftsangst.

US: Yes, Zukunftstangst. That's why the German safeguards and plans. The Latin American is classified as visionary. He also is afraid, but of the present. He cannot live in the present, and constantly projects and plans and is full of unbelievable energy.

We all know this well. I can endlessly make sure that the parameters and the setup are okay and

THAT IS THE GOOD THING ABOUT THE LATIN AMERICANS: THEY ARE SUPER ENERGETIC AND MOVE FORWARD IMMEDIATELY. IT'S INCREDIBLE, THOUGH. AS SOON AS THE PRESENT COMES UP, EVERYTHING FALLS APART.

THE GERMAN MAKES A PLAN AND SOMEHOW PUTS IT INTO PRACTICE IN A WAY SO THAT HE EVENTUALLY GETS A RESULT. AND THIS CHARACTERIZES ANGST.

the best possible wiring of the modular system is installed instead of simply getting started.

CN: We talk a lot about being German – German culture and its impact on music – but it dawned on me the other day that we deal with a set of tools within electronic music that are actually quite young but at the same time already globalized. I spoke about this with a museologist recently. Electronic instruments probably are the only real Western instruments. All other instruments probably came …

US: From Africa, Asia.

OB: This quest for the source always ends up in paradise.

CN: We carry around our identity in a certain way, but on the other hand we are enormously globalized. We travel to Japan, fly here and there and at each of these places we meet people that are interested in the same music in a similar kind of way. They even produce it in the same way. We were just in Egypt and met people who produced just like us.

But, at the same time, additional contexts come up. In Cuba a very popular reggaeton producer showed me things he did on the side. Technically they were all extremely well done, and he simply used a different set of samples than we might choose. The ambition to avoid preset sounds by all means was not at all important. So I played him examples of folks like Pearson Sound who only need four sounds to build a track, but every single one of them is crafted with enormous care. And then he said, "Oh, I love Michael Cretu, I have all the albums."

US: The guy from Enigma.

Enigma. Yes, this project with the monk chants. I never would have made this connection in my life.

US: Enigma was very well known in Latin America. I know this from Chile, too, that some dictatorships only accepted certain things. The Thompson Twins for example. In Chile you still hear them in the supermarkets. I think they were so big there just because they were lucky to pass somehow.

OB: This is a phenomenon of dictatorships. We had this in East Germany as well. The whole nation can cope with one thing that everybody knows.

US: Exactly. And then something like Enigma comes up and they know it for one funny reason or another and nothing else. In the end it's the individual characteristics that count, and I believe that's the mysterious and gorgeous thing about music. You produce a track and you travel to Japan, and then it really doesn't matter whether somebody is Japanese or German because it's the track that actuates a response or not. The foot bobs or it doesn't. It means something to you or not. Why it is so, and where does that come from? That's deep psychology.

OB: Yes, and at the end of the day, what does it answer? To get back to music: We are always looking for our own language.

How does one find his own language? How did you find your common language? All of you have worked in different constellations and with people from different contexts.

OB: Searching is looking for questions that you haven't answered yet. Somehow you must move forward, grabbing something without knowing where you might end up. Carsten and I didn't talk about it much, but we decided with Diamond Version that we didn't want to draw a line from what we had done in the past.

CN: Exactly. We tried to break with everything we had produced and create a polarity. And clean up some of the clichés we had maybe produced. These things are born out of a personal need. You just have to break the mold, and put yourself in a different position, and look at it from the other side. One has to take a risk from time to time if one notices that certain expectations are so big,

THE FOOT BOBS OR IT DOESN'T. IT MEANS SOMETHING TO YOU OR NOT.

WHY IT IS SO, AND WHERE DOES THAT COME FROM? THAT'S DEEP PSYCHOLOGY.

or one is representing a certain sound so completely that you almost feel imprisoned. On the one hand, you could go on forever. But then you also know that you want to go beyond. I look at Diamond Version as a *Sollbruchstelle*, the predetermined breaking point in the whole system.

US: I think if you work with people, it always comes down to chemistry. I have worked a lot with Bernd Friedmann and we never talked really. Or Tobias Freund, with whom I play live an enormous amount. We did 100 concerts in the last couple of years and we haven't communicated before any of them about what we were going to do.

There's been no concept?

US: No, not at all. The concept is that we have machines which we program on stage. All we know is that there has to be a moment when it kicks. None of us speaks.

OB: But you don't even yourself know what kicks you?

US: No. You want to find it…

OB: You notice it when it's there.

CN: You can't provoke it, can you?

US: No, it's such a funny feeling…

CN: It's coming, then suddenly it's there.

You mentioned before the connection between the working methods of certain producers in Japan and you, as a German. Carsten, what is the difference between collaborating with them and working with somebody from the same cultural background?

CN: There were two situations that actually made the project I do with Ryuichi Sakamoto very interesting. One was that I had no idea about classic musical

notation, while Ryuichi is a classically trained pianist and composer. At the time that was a conflict, but it had the positive effect of both myself and Ryuichi learning a lot. He is very curious. The other conflict... Ryuichi once put it nicely. He said that he is the German in the project and I am the Japanese.

How did he mean that?

CN: He was very much influenced by Debussy. And, I must say, was influenced by the Japanese garden.

So you feel right at home in Kyoto?

CN: When we are there I always look at two gardens. One is a moss garden. This was my favorite garden in the beginning. But I eventually preferred the stone garden. The idea of abstraction and reduction had a huge impact on me.

US: The German reduces out of fear and the Japanese reduces out of the need to bring reality under control.

CN: Can you generalize like that?

US: I just break it down!

CN: I also worked with Ryoji Ikeda. There I find a completely different attitude.

US: With my Japanese friends I recognized that the Japanese love the German love for conception. To select a set of parameters and then say, "We do this and that." This is totally compatible with their worldview. This is what they understand immediately. This is different with other cultures. With English and Americans, it was always more complicated.

How important is something like a concept for you?

CN: I almost can't do without it.

OB: You are very conceptual.

THE GERMAN REDUCES OUT OF FEAR AND THE JAPANESE REDUCES OUT OF THE NEED TO BRING REALITY UNDER CONTROL.

WHAT IS REALLY INSPIRING IS WHEN THE CONCEPT IS BROUGHT TO LIFE.

CN: I literally love to scheme and make plans. This has to do with two things. One is that I love to develop a vision over a long period; the other is that I always found concept albums fantastic when I was young. When the artwork and the lyrics and the disc became one thing I always got excited.

US: The concept is, in fact, a good framework. But I don't use that word usually. For me it's always a set of parameters and you put your stuff in there as if it was a drawer. Every time you want to continue on your work you open the drawer, take out your stuff and continue your needlework. That's why concept is maybe not the right word. I don't know. When the whole thing is done, the concept is projected back as if it was kind of a justification for what you have done, whereas for me I always see it more as a starting point for something else. Like a point of inspiration that maybe shouldn't be of importance for anybody outside.

CN: I think we are all conceptual though.

OB: I also think you absolutely need it. If you want to construct a chair, you need a concept for it. You have to know which leg you carve first.

US: You ought to tell this to my Chilean friends. They cut down the tree first.

OB: What is really inspiring is when the concept is brought to life, when it moves beyond itself.

Which is when the human factor gets involved. To stick to the Kraftwerk example: people were cheering when they saw the word Chernobyl written on the screen. What is actually happening at that moment?

US: My live performance right now usually includes an interlude of 90 seconds that contains 13 atomic bomb bursts. I wanted to include this part because I wanted to see the reaction of the audience. Every time the first atom bomb comes up the people cheer because there is this flash from the explosion and a quite violent sound on top of it. But after the tenth bomb... I had an interesting conversation about this with Robert Lippok in Geneva who had to leave when the atom bombs started. There is this physical moment of: "Yes, wow, crazy." You somehow become part of it. It's the same with Chernobyl. You can connect to the idea which is offered to you. That's why you cheer, even if you cheer a nuclear power plant. There is always this inversion with what we do. We send a message from the stage, always in the superior position. It's not a democratic state. It's not a conversation, discussion or argument. Something most pithy is being sent out and something most pithy is being returned. Everyone cheers for their own reasons, but there is a compatible element that keeps everything together. At the same time, it can turn into funny manifestations out of your control and you lose what you actually wanted to express. The meaning slips away.

OB: It's marvelous how Kraftwerk can follow this concept for such a long time, I mean, my God … After the 200th performance I would have jumped from the stage and waved at the audience or something… Instead of drowning in your concept or dissolving in it. It's typical for us today that we want to break with that.

CN: That's the big difference with our generation. In music production there is this terrific term: master/slave. We want to play with this concept, so you become the slave of your videos or your concept. Uwe does that brilliantly, inventing a new artist for each album.

US: I have stopped that. Now there is only one left. I did a funny thing. Five years ago I started to review my whole archive. 2,000 titles, 100 albums. For the first time I had an aerial view of what I had done. And my impression had always been like you just said: I constantly do different

I CONSTANTLY DO DIFFERENT THINGS. UNFORTUNATELY I NOTICED AT THE MOMENT I WAS ZOOMING OUT THAT IT WAS ALL THE SAME.

I ALWAYS EXAMINE MY OWN VIEWPOINT AND I FOCUS ON THIS ONE IDEA. THE IDEA MIGHT TAKE ANOTHER FORM FOR A WHILE, BUT ACTUALLY IT'S ALWAYS ABOUT THE SAME THING IN DIFFERENT TEXTURES.

things. Unfortunately I noticed at the moment I was zooming out that it was all the same.

Eno said that when he looked back, he realized he really only had one idea and adapted it pretty well a few times; but the same could have been said of Beckett. And so he starts giggling.

OB: Yes, but it came out nice. If it results in a synthesis, then it's a form of self-awareness. But I think that one looks at it differently. Objectively there is a common thread in the music you published, but the range is vast from witty cabaret style to *Liedgut* to… well, I never realized that you were behind Lassigue Bendthaus.

US: One always has a different perspective. I always examine my own viewpoint and I focus on this one idea. The idea might take another form for a while, but actually it's always about the same thing in different textures.

OB: The crazy thing is that, in the present, you always focus on rather strange aspects. All of a sudden you consider it revolutionary to put the 303 away now.

US: Exactly. 1992. 303 totally out. Ten years later and you find out that it's actually banging.

Using the 303 you produced the most successful German record in England after Kraftwerk with Ongaku's *Mihon*.

US: Yes, that was two DJs from Frankfurt and I produced them. That was a borrowed 303 that I was unable to program and I stepped through the patterns and finally found a badly programmed pattern that was much too short. That was two-four and three-four, a pattern that did not go well … Actually it was programmed incorrectly, not finished, but it fit perfectly.

And suddenly there is coincidence in all this conceptualism!

THERE WERE TWO SITUATIONS THAT ACTUALLY MADE THE PROJECT I DO WITH RYUICHI SAKAMOTO VERY IN- TERESTING. ONE WAS THAT I HAD NO IDEA ABOUT CLASSIC MUSICAL NOTATION, WHILE RYUICHI IS A CLASSICALLY TRAINED PIANIST AND COMPOSER. AT THE TIME THAT WAS A CONFLICT, BUT IT HAD THE POSI- TIVE EFFECT OF BOTH MYSELF AND RYUICHI LEARNING A LOT. HE IS VERY CURIOUS. THE OTHER CON- FLICT... RYUICHI ONCE PUT IT NICELY: HE IS THE GERMAN IN THE PROJECT AND I AM THE JAPANESE.

US: Yes, coincidences happen. You always have to allow them in, of course. I am always quite conscious about the space I leave open for coincidence. You have an idea, you like it, and then you know somehow an element here and there could help if it came up by chance… You can work towards it, but actually it must come up by itself like a coincidental effect.

Funnily enough, that particular Ongaku release was perceived in the UK as a decidedly German record. Seeing that this was shortly after the fall of the Wall, none of us was really keen on being German.

US: It's always like: don't bore me with the talk about being German.

OB: And we were all a bit ashamed when we heard German spoken in foreign countries. Germans have this little inferiority complex in both the East and West, caused by this Nazi beast…

CN: It's also caused by the Cold War, the Germans fighting for the better image on both sides. During the period of the re-unification I felt that we all had problems with that. My only solution to this was to feel European more than German. I liked that solution, to position myself in a greater context and escape from the situation of suddenly finding myself in a reunified Germany. To write "German" or "Deutsch" as my identity, when filling out a form – that was a big problem for me.

Has that relaxed now?

CN: I think the World Cup in 2006 released a lot of tension, but I was scared when I saw all those flags.

US: Being in Chile I had a different view of things. Many things that I considered unpleasant like, "Ah, you are German!" They weren't that important anymore. What I always considered tasteless

AS SOON AS YOU ARE OUTSIDE OF GERMANY IT'S ABSOLUTELY NORMAL TO BE ASKED, "AH, YOU COME FROM GERMANY. ARE YOU A NAZI?"

EVERYONE IS INTERESTED IN SOUND [AT SÓNAR] DESPITE OUR DIFFERENT ROUTES TOWARDS IT.

stereotypes like, "You Germans are always on time." There is always a bit of truth behind it. So I started to relax more about it. This includes the fact that Germans are pretty devoid of humor about themselves and their own history. As soon as you are outside of Germany it's absolutely normal to be asked, "Ah, you come from Germany. Are you a Nazi?" Jews you meet in Santiago joke about the Holocaust and you feel absolutely embarrassed. One day this tension about Germany was eased for me. I don't feel any real conflict anymore, I must say.

Sitting here, only a few yards away from Mies van der Rohe's German Pavilion, which stands for a lot that the world cherishes in Germany and its conceptualism, do you think festivals like this help to deal with such stereotypes in a more relaxed manner?

OB: On the periphery, maybe.

CN: Absolutely. Those stereotypes dissolve a bit, because one creates together. Everything is only as good as everyone who's at the festival. And I do believe it's great for one to perform after an English band, and playing before someone entirely different. Sometimes you see an act that ignites you and makes you go, "that's exactly what I want." I find it very nice to put it all into relation and realize that it's already this global village where, in essence, everyone is interested in sound despite our different routes towards it.

OB: When we started, there was this *Überbild* of the "UK band" or "black music" and I always thought, well, you're neither/nor... That's what I like here. There's an actual German contribution. Not that it's a specific German innovation, but the way we're integrated. That it all has moved beyond just copying black music. That to me is the true World Cup moment, to be able to say: "Yes, I am German." "And what kinda music do you do?" And I say, "Synched electronic music."

MODERATOR:
TODD L. BURNS
PHOTOGRAPHERS:
TILL JANZ & HENDRIK SCHNEIDER

BENNY ILL AND MORITZ VON OSWALD

THE VERY BASIS OF MUSIC IS SIMPLE PHYSICS. AND BASS IS ONE OF THE MOST POWERFUL CARRIERS OF PHYSICALITY IN MUSIC. BENNY ILL AND MORITZ VON OSWALD'S CAREERS HAVE BEEN BUILT ON THOSE FOUNDATIONS. ILL, ALONG WITH THE REST OF THE HORSEPOWER PRODUCTIONS CREW, EVOLVED 2-STEP INTO WHAT WOULD EVENTUALLY BECOME DUBSTEP. VON OSWALD, ALONGSIDE MARK ERNESTUS, LAID THE GROUNDWORK FOR DUB TECHNO. IN EARLY JULY WE ASKED THE TWO TO CHAT WITH ONE ANOTHER AT KRAFTWERK BERLIN'S SCHALTRAUM – A FORMER POWER STATION CONTROL ROOM. ALWAYS TENDING TO DETAIL, THE TWO SPOKE SLOWLY AND THOUGHTFULLY, OFTEN TAKING SEVERAL SECONDS BEFORE BEGINNING TO ANSWER A QUESTION.

Benny Ill, real name Ben Power, is a founding member of Horsepower Productions alongside cohorts Nasis and Lev Jr. Horsepower as a group were synonymous with a sound colloquially known as "dark garage," a claustrophobic, skunked-out take on the chart-topping genre that laid the foundations and inspiration for the emergent dubstep scene of the mid-'00s. In his decade behind the boards, Ill has released under a variety of quirky aliases such as Drunken Master and High Plains Drifter, collaborated with stalwarts like Kode 9 and DJ Hatcha, and teamed up with Bill Robin as one-half of Dub War, continually pushing the sound of Greater London in experimental directions.

It's difficult to exaggerate **Moritz von Oswald**'s hand in creating dub techno. With his Basic Channel production and label partner Mark Ernestus, the Berlin-based engineer, musician and producer spent much of the '90s shaping the waves of sound that outline it today. The duo's drive to go back to techno's source contributed to a longstanding exchange between Berlin and Detroit. After founding a handful of imprints like Maurizio, Main Street and Rhythm & Sound alongside Ernestus, von Oswald began to pursue other projects in the late '00s, including symphonic ventures with Carl Craig and Francesco Tristano, a trio bearing his name and a joint album with Juan Atkins. In other words, more exploratory yet assured steps in a career littered with them.

RBMA: One of the reasons we wanted to bring you guys together is your connection to dub and reggae. I know you, Moritz, started listening in Hamburg in the '80s, but Benny I don't really know how you first came to this kind of music.

Benny Ill: I grew up between Brixton and Peckham. That's a big area in London for reggae music. So I got into going to Notting Hill Carnival every year as a kid.

Were there any artists or anything that really first spoke to you? Or was it the carnival atmosphere itself?

BI: There were a lot of Studio One artists. Like the old late '60s and '70s stuff. There was a revival for the roots music and dub in the '80s when dancehall was coming out. I must have caught that wave.

Was it the same in Hamburg?

Moritz Von Oswald: For me, working in a record shop, it was getting imports from London, which were mostly records from scientists. We were so amazed by them, how they used the effects on the records. If you know the records, it's something that is overwhelming.

BI: Space Invaders, Heavyweight Dub Champions... Classic albums, classic artwork. Cartoon style.

MVO: It was very difficult for us to get these records, but we were really proud to get some of those special imports.

BI: Like the Jamaican stuff, the 7-inches. Always the 7-inches, until now. They don't do them anymore really. Only for specialist stuff. Great dub music, but I could only afford the LPs. It was value for money. Dub LPs had maybe like eight, ten tracks something like that.

Were the imports really expensive in Hamburg?

MVO: Not so expensive. At this record store the guy managed to get a special price. Especially when they would get a rare record as an import, nobody could get it and we were so pleased to listen to stuff like this. Plus the music itself, this deepness they opened up... We couldn't match it.

BI: It's still living today, the spirit of it. Inside most dance music there are still little elements of things they pioneered with these Jamaican dub methods. Nowadays you hear it in a pop tune or whatever. The same engineering twists in a different style.

It must have sounded quite alien at the time, compared to everything else that was in the record store.

MVO: Well, I wouldn't say alien. It was just something that I appreciated. It was not something that was coming from nowhere. It was not difficult to say where it was coming from, everyone knew. Then we were interested in who was making it, all the classic producers, like King Tubby, Scientist, Lee Perry, Wackies, King Jammy...

BI: It had a very pure sound for me, listening to dub for the first time. Rock music was a bit more harsh, and then dub had this purity. It was on a different level, mellow. That caught me.

MVO: It was very recognizable how people played it.

BI: Very prolific as well, the artists. So many records. Like a factory, working all the time.

MVO: And it developed with all these very important people like Sly & Robbie starting to be hired for major productions with pop and rock artists like Grace Jones.

I guess Island Records played a huge role in bringing things to a wider audience in the UK.

BI: Jamaican music for the mainstream as well, like Bob Marley and stuff. They took it all around the world. I don't know so much of the history of it, but all the dub music in England, it was Greensleeves doing a lot of the imports, licensing the music for British release and then exporting that elsewhere. Maybe Germany, I don't know.

Were you getting to see it live, Moritz? You said you were going to Carnival, but were any of these artists coming to Germany?

MVO: Notting Hill Carnival was something lasting, blowing me away.

BI: Crazy. We were quite lucky in London as kids. To have that wealth of culture. You just wouldn't experience that in many places, even New York. They don't really have a culture for this street party thing and jerk chicken cooking. It's special to the Caribbean and a little bit of England as well.

But even though New York doesn't have that culture, there are people in New York who are pretty important.

ROCK MUSIC WAS A BIT MORE HARSH, AND THEN DUB HAD THIS PURITY. IT WAS ON A DIFFERENT LEVEL, MELLOW.

BI: Yeah, it has a big role in it. Guys like Bobby Konders. There are quite a few key figures in the latter part of dancehall.

Moritz, you and Mark Ernestus worked with Lloyd "Bullwackie" Barnes, right?

MVO: We also tried to get all his records. To get all these records, and get all the rights from him, we went to New York and talked to him.

So you did a remix of "Mango Walk" before you met him and played it to him? Were you worried about what he might say?

MVO: No. We thought there was something about it that he would like. We didn't do it as a favor to him, it was just something we were pleased with. If he wouldn't like it, what could you do? We played it to him in a very unique record store in the Bronx called Moodies Records. I went there maybe two years ago. He is in the same state as he was. We took the remix there, and we had put so much bass in it that, when he put it on, all the speakers were clipping.

THE MUSIC ITSELF, THIS DEEP-NESS THEY OPENED UP... WE COULDN'T MATCH IT.

BI: In a reggae shop!

MVO: He heard the track and he was like, "OK."

Were you involved in that scene at all, when you were spending time in New York, Benny?

BI: I was there from around 2004 to about 2006. I did check it a little bit. The club scene isn't massive, even though you have the history. New York is a place of many fashions and things come and go. I originally went looking for house music, and I couldn't find it! I had to go to Brooklyn. Everyone in Manhattan was just playing the current flavors. Maybe there's something there now, if the fashion has changed. But a lot of the people I would check for would have elements of dub, like François K. I used to go to New York to play 2-step in the '90s quite a lot. There was a good scene for that. Underground, but a good scene. It was kind of a re-import. That was what was strange about it. The UK people took garage music from New York and they made their own version, then another version and sent it back.

When was the first time that you recognized the power of bass in a literal way?

BI: Well, for me, it's going back to Notting Hill Carnival again.

MVO: Same.

BI: Or people's cars in South London, with the big rigs in the back. The dreadlocks rasta guys with a big Saab with a sound system in the back, memories of just feeling the bass as they go past and thinking... "Oh... my headphones don't do that."

When did you go over for Notting Hill Carnival?

MVO: A long time ago, maybe '84?

And you said that was the first time you recognized the power of it as well?

MVO: Of course. That, and when you blow some speakers at home...

BI: I think I had a wall at one point. I went round and got everyone's hi-fi that they didn't want anymore. Just stacked them up, put all the wires together. I think I blew that a few times. Trying to recreate the sound system effect to the best I could as a teenager. But you don't really get the frequencies. With reggae they all use the 18-inch sub things. I don't think you can get that pressure, so it's a different experience listening at home. It's only really recreating the harmonic in your home system, it's not the proper bass that moves your chest. I think Mala once said to me that his dad came to the club, I said "What did he think of this?" He said, "It moved his trousers." And that's it, isn't it? That warm

feeling in your chest, resonating in the cavities. It's a physical thing that has something natural about it.

Was that the idea with Basic Channel? To make it as rattling as possible, with the low-end?

MVO: I don't know. It was a process. You start with this and then you build on top of it, but it's not something you can really determine. It's not calculated.

BI: The groove created itself.

MVO: Yes, exactly. It's a certain type of energy or intensity which is moving and bouncing. But it is very difficult to say, because we did all of the other stuff as a couple. We agreed on liking this. We had a very good friendship and agreed on the whole thing which means bass and the whole movement, to get it rolling. I cannot say for Mark, but I'm pretty sure he was as touched by this as I was.

Did you ever get feedback from pressing plants? Like, "This is not right"?

MVO: Not from the pressing plant, but from the cutting studio.

BI: Yes, with bass they can't cut.

MVO: Yes, you can. But some people can not. It is possible.

BI: You can damage the cutting head. I broke one once in The Exchange in Camden, one of my favorite places to master. They don't remember luckily, but in the '90s at one point I blew the whole thing up and they were very angry. That cost like ten thousand dollars or whatever. Just overenthusiastic kids, pressing their first 45.

NOTTING HILL CARNIVAL WAS SOMETHING LASTING, BLOWING ME AWAY.

WE WERE QUITE LUCKY IN LONDON AS KIDS. TO HAVE THAT WEALTH OF CULTURE.

Was it your first one that broke it?

BI: May well have been, I don't recall. I still go there if I can.

Has it gotten more expensive?

BI: No, it's cheaper, in England mastering is so cheap. The big places seem to charge what the small places used to charge five to ten years ago. I'm surprised at how little it is. You name it, they are affordable. I think it's that they love the vinyl, so they aren't cutting so much in the big studios anymore but they want to encourage it. I know Stuart Hawkes particularly, he got into cutting plates for the jungle, drum & bass guys and it was just for the love and spirit of it. I think he loved that they were playing dub plates out. It's another Jamaican thing. Where else are they gonna be cutting dub plates to play music out, when there are CDRs available? They want to encourage the survival of the format.

For a while, Moritz, you were sending stuff to Detroit to get cut.

MVO: Well, the first Maurizio record... Because I didn't do it myself. It was a cooperation. Everyone thinks I did that one because of the name, but that was with Mark as well.

BI: I originally thought that. Now I know!

MVO: Yeah, so the first one, I knew some people from Detroit that were using this one cutting studio. Ron Murphy and National Sound, where the Underground Resistance records were cut. Also Derrick May used it. He said that this guy knew how bass has to be treated on vinyl club records.

BI: The bass on the UR records was always good, powerful.

MVO: His secret was to not put too much bass on the records. He had things about the bass frequency, so it didn't damage the sound. He always used to say, "Cutting is a bitch." I think some of his knowledge came from listening to Motown records, he had such a big knowledge of that sound. He was also a nice guy to talk to.

BI: He wasn't the sound engineer type?

What is the sound engineering type?

BI: I'm not sure, always a bit quiet or introspective. Just a certain type, very particular with what they are doing, but a little bit creative too. The best ones are usually big fat guys, not sure why.

MVO: The reason why I was really interested to start a cutting studio in Germany is because no one in Germany was into doing some kind of special club or dubplate cutting. So I went to Hamburg and met this guy who I knew wanted to sell a lathe. Nobody was interested in buying them again.

BI: Yes, they were giving them away cheap at one stage.

MVO: Yes, so the guy realized that we were starting a company from this and he was so jealous. Because he learned from his father, and his father was cutting for Deutsche Grammophon and all those really quiet and really clean classical records. There was no business for it any more. They were just throwing it away, almost. And then we got an old

engineer who was also with Deutsche Grammophon before, who knew everything. He was 60, maybe 70 years old. He modified our amplifiers. That's what the Americans did. They modified all their stuff. I met one of the most successful cutting engineers, Herb Powers, to cut a house record. He was excellent to work with.

BI: Do you find that you get any kind of sound difference that you could appreciate from cutting them in the States? I always felt that these New York guys, the early house guys, that their sound had something that we couldn't get in London. I wasn't sure if it was the mastering or the voltage that they had over there. But there was always a sound with New York records. Maybe it's in the mastering.

MVO: Yes, I just loved what Herb was doing in New York. Every record was just overwhelming. So was the Detroit stuff that was cut at National Sound. All the KMS and UR records.

BI: It would always come through when you are playing it in a club, if you were bringing in a UR record.

MVO: I still listen to vinyl because it's so easy to handle sound-wise. But if I play out, I hardly play vinyl anymore because of the bass, because people never know how to set up technically for that!

BI: It's a gamble nowadays as to whether it's working.

MVO: I was playing out some vinyl records, and the needle was jumping because these people didn't know what kind of system to get or to even put absorbers under the record player.

BI: Fortunately in my area of music, there's still a little current of vinyl lovers. Some of the nights I play for actually make sure that everything is isolated and vinyl can be played. Some people even still cut dub plates. But yeah, if you just walk into some random club nothing ever works. Some sound engineers have lost it.

DERRICK MAY USED IT. HE SAID THAT THIS GUY KNEW HOW BASS HAS TO BE TREATED ON VINYL CLUB RECORDS.

MVO: Not some of them!

One of the things that you've talked about in the past that I found very interesting, Moritz, is that dance music is quite vertical and one of things that you were interested in was exploring the horizontal nature of it. Do you think you could explain that a little?

MVO: I just can explain it spontaneously. I haven't had time to think about it. But you know, for me, the room that you are using to create music in is so important, with drums, some of them are un-tonal structures. They are not G or C. So you are finding tones elsewhere, which is something that gives deepness to the listener or perceiver. I like that. But, to come back to your subject, vertical and horizontal can relate also to Detroit. If you come to Detroit, if you look at the horizon it seems like there is just a hole and this world ends.

BI: In Detroit? Just because it is so wide and flat?

MVO: I do not know. It's because of the history really. When I went there for the first time, it's like something I have never seen. The first time you go to Detroit you cannot compare it to different places. This is what the horizon meant to me in a way. If you look at the sunset, when you see it on the sea, I always think, "What is happening after that?"

BI: Like it's the edge of the world.

It's interesting because a lot of people have said that when they first came from Detroit to Berlin that it seemed very similar.

BI: The industrial nature maybe?

THERE WAS ALWAYS A SOUND WITH NEW YORK RECORDS. MAYBE IT'S IN THE MASTERING.

Especially right after the Wall came down.

MVO: It's not related to the people, just the environment. I drove by this train station in Detroit and I could look through the whole building because all of the windows had fallen out. It's amazing.

BI: Degenerated, with the car industry.

One of the things I wanted to ask you about, Benny, was that you once said when you were DJing that you would sometimes put a rainforest soundtrack underneath the whole set?

BI: Yeah, I like to do that sometimes.

What was the thinking behind that?

BI: Some people say it's to mask the dubplates, so that they can't record them. Really, it's not. I like the space it gives. It takes you to this rainforest or other ones I've used – storms and things. It's making an artificial space and I kinda like that. I mean I'm not gonna have it all the time. And it comes up and down. It can be a background thing that the music cuts through. But it feels a little bit magical, like you're in another space. Not just a reverb that signifies you are in a big hall. This signifies there are animals here. And something else is over there. I always like to do that, to have movies and stuff. Not even dialogue, but maybe some of the score or some of the atmospheric sounds that they used.

Is creating an atmosphere essential?

BI: I'm not sure, I know that it works to some degree. I'm not

the best musician or anything, so perhaps things like that help. We don't use a singer usually. I do stuff with vocals, but usually it's instrumentals so I think it might bring a good human aspect to it.

Why do you think you haven't used vocalists very much?

BI: It's hard to find the right singers. I do quite a lot for remixes, or mixing for other people. I love to work with vocals, but my thing is electronic dance music basically and I don't find it really requires a vocal always. In fact some people would rather it didn't have it. But I'm told it's where the money is, but hey... money.

You've worked with vocals over the years, Moritz. When did you know you had found the right person for a track?

MVO: You mean the guy that sang on "I'm Your Brother"? I knew him from before. He could be a soul singer in a way. Not soul... But I really imagine that he could do it.

BI: It's like a soul song, isn't it? Like an old gospel track.

MVO: I like the follow up even more, which is called "New Day." It's quite tonal, but it's a song that I really love. It is a song in a way. It has an intro, verse one, bridge and then verse two and then the end. It's not a pop structure, but you could say it is. I like some pop music. I had some opportunities to work with Trevor Horn and the guys from Trouble Funk.

BI: They are the most incredible players you will ever meet! They would play all night long. Until 9 or 10 in the morning.

THE FIRST TIME YOU GO TO DETROIT YOU CANNOT COMPARE IT TO DIFFERENT PLACES. IF YOU LOOK AT THE SUNSET, WHEN YOU SEE IT ON THE SEA, I ALWAYS THINK, "WHAT IS HAPPENING AFTER THAT?"

MVO: Trevor said it was a pain in the ass, to get these guys to play a whole track. They just went off.

Benny, would you regard what you were doing with Katy B as pop music in your mind?

BI: Not really, although some people accused us of it. But we did that in 2006 when she wasn't a proper artist. But I do a lot of other stuff, like hip hop and some soul projects with other people.

But that doesn't come under the same banner. It's a different project. I've always loved hip hop, but in the UK it's not really a commercial reality. It's more for the love of it. I've entered this contest a few times. It's called "King Of The Beats" and the idea is you have 20 dollars and you buy all these records second hand, as many as you can get, and then you've got 24 hours to complete a beat just with the records, nothing else.

Is that a big challenge for you? To finish a track in a day?

BI: Yeah, for me particularly. But it's just an exercise.

How long does it usually take you to finish a track?

BI: On average... A week, maybe?

What is taking so long?

BI: It's me being too perfectionist about it. Not that it sounds perfect, it's trying to attain something.

Is it the same for you, Moritz?

MVO: A week is not very long.

BI: I don't think it's very long. In the '70s they spent months doing these classic rock albums and whatnot. I mean, it might be more involved maybe, but I like to experiment and I'm never doing anything by formula. It takes a while to do the creative part and to be trying to do something new every time. I don't like these producers that have a palette and they sit down and they're known for a thing. I like to start fresh every time, with nothing.

It's interesting, though, because you have a consistent sound, people would say. Even though you start fresh every time.

BI: That's something you can't help. The common element is myself. I do a lot of collaborations, but there's a variety of tempos and styles in there.

Is it important for you, Moritz, to tear things down and start new every time you go into the studio?

MVO: Not really.

BI: But you have broken some boundaries, all the same.

MVO: It's not really something I think about, to start new. Sometimes I like to stay with what I have sense- and technical-wise. I don't do the whole thing from scratch sometimes. Of course it starts somewhere.

BI: A lot of the records sound very different anyways.

MVO: Yes, some of the Maurizo instrumental records are a development of the Main Street stuff.

BI: I would say they have a lot of soul to them, those records. I can see the strain that joins them.

MVO: If you compare the... I think M6... No, wait. I'm not very good with names.

BI: The red one?

MVO: No, that's M4. But I think M7 was one of the first ones that we really built up from the start. Mark has a better memory.

BI: When you've got so many, you sometimes forget. I even do it sometimes.

I remember talking to Giorgio Moroder recently and I was asking him about some obscure records that meant so much to me, and he didn't really seem to remember any of them.

BI: It's understandable. So prolific that guy, all those days working. If you own the record and you've held it and listened it through, read the cover, it's a lot easier to remember. For him, it's just another tape with a blank label stacked up.

THE ROOM THAT YOU ARE USING TO CREATE MUSIC IN IS SO IMPORTANT.

YOU ARE FINDING TONES ELSEWHERE, WHICH IS SOMETHING THAT GIVES DEEPNESS TO THE LISTENER OR PERCEIVER.

FORTUNATELY IN MY AREA OF MUSIC, THERE'S STILL A LITTLE CURRENT OF VINYL LOVERS.

I LIKE TO START FRESH EVERY TIME, WITH NOTHING.

TE TE TE TE TE TE TE
TE TE TE TE TE

POP

POOM POOM P
POOPOOPO

DO DO POO

TE TE TE TE TE BOOF
TE TE TE TE TE BOOF

GIVE ME MORE

GIVE ME MORE.

GIVE IT.

POOM POOM POOM

POOPOOPOOM POOM.

POO.

The world of **Lee 'Scratch' Perry**
is one crammed
full of duality and balance,
religion and sex.
As one of the most colorful forefathers
of Jamaica's reggae and dub culture,
The Mighty Upsetter
has commandeered systems
the world over with his deep
and spacious sound.
Through the '70s,
Perry's Black Ark studio
became a hub
for vital Jamaican musicians
such as Augustus Pablo, Junior Murvin
and Max Romeo.
Despite the Black Ark
burning
to the ground,
and Perry subsequently moving
to England
and then Switzerland,
his career has continued
to develop,
working with Mad Professor,
Beastie Boys and The Orb among others.
Whether recording kick drums
in the bathtub
or walking backwards for days,
Perry has always been
unconventional,
crafting folk tales of truth
in a vivid psychedelic tapestry.

A career covering dub,
post punk and industrial to
delta funk and world fusion
started with running
his first sound system in London
by the age of 13.
Several years later,
Adrian Sherwood had been
involved in the
music industry
in practically every
capacity, from record producer and sound man
to label manager
and distributor.
Sherwood's been ahead of
the game ever
since he reversed the tapes
of his group Creation Rebel
and drenched them in
reverb back in 1978,
creating a bizarre
and spiritually spatial sound.
Whether reinvigorating
the careers of
past reggae statesmen
like Bim Sherman,
or working with musicians like
Einstürzende Neubauten, Cabaret Voltaire,
Dennis Bovell and Mark Stewart,
Sherwood and his On-U Sound
imprint are characterized by a
strong sense
of community
and social responsibility.
It's bass culture
for the greater good.

MODERATOR: CARTER VAN PELT
PHOTOGRAPHER: DAN WILTON

IT WAS AN UNLIKELY – ALMOST RADICAL – QUESTION:

WHAT IF WE USE THE MIXING DESK AS AN INSTRUMENT TOO?

IN THE '60S, THE PRODUCER WAS MOST OFTEN EMPLOYED TO SIMPLY RECORD THE

MUSIC FAITHFULLY. LEE 'SCRATCH' PERRY CHANGED ALL THAT, INTRODUCING THE

IDEA OF DUB TO THE WORLD. THIS RADICAL PERCEPTUAL SHIFT

IS NOW INGRAINED IN THE DNA OF POPULAR MUSIC, ITS

INFLUENCE INESCAPABLE. ONE OF ITS GREATEST

ADHERENTS IS THE UK'S ADRIAN SHERWOOD,

WHO STARTED LISTENING TO PERRY'S MUSIC AS

A PRE-TEEN. STRUCK BY HIS ALIEN AND HYPNOTIC WORK

WITH ARTISTS SUCH AS BOB MARLEY AND THE CONGOS,

SHERWOOD STRUCK OUT ON HIS OWN JOURNEY WITH HIS

ON-U SOUND IMPRINT AND AS A MEMBER OF THE EXPERIMENTAL

INDUSTRIAL HIP HOP GROUP TACKHEAD. SHERWOOD

FIRST MET PERRY IN THE '70S, AND BEGAN TO WORK

WITH HIM IN THE MID-'80S AND ON UP UNTIL

THE PRESENT DAY.

LEE 'SCRATCH' PERRY and ADRIAN SHERWOOD

THE TWO MET IN NEW YORK AT THE 2013

RED BULL MUSIC ACADEMY SHARING THEIR INTERTWINED STORY, A DAY BEFORE

THEY PERFORMED AT AN EVENT WHERE – APPROPRIATELY – SHERWOOD STOOD

BEHIND A MIXING DESK, DUBBING PERRY'S VOCALS IN REAL-TIME.

RBMA: ADRIAN, HOW DID JAMAICAN MUSIC COME TO YOU?

ADRIAN SHERWOOD: I was once described – by a journalist who didn't like me – as "a fan who got his hands on a mixing desk." But that is actually the truth of the matter. I grew up in the business and saw the footage of Lee in the Black Ark studios dancing and dubbing up a tune. I was working earlier this week with some artists, doing a kind of workshop thing, and I was showing all the young people how to add all the reverbs and delays on a mixing desk. That's all inspired by the stuff that Scratch and a few other people did very early on.

A unique thing about Jamaican music is having one great rhythm, [and then] 20 different cuts on the same rhythm, loads of different vocalists and then the raw, stripped down versions that mesmerize people. That's his fault. Lee, what was your favorite effect that you used in the studio?

LEE 'SCRATCH' PERRY: My favorite... There are two things that created life: One is "pum pum," and one is "titi." So the pum pum is the female and the bass play part of a man, but he's not a man, he's a woman. The creator. Because below the pum pum, you can put the titi into the pum pum and bring any children. One is King Alpha and one is Queen Omega. So the pum pum is really Queen Omega. So without the pum pum we'd have no children here. My genie's in my bottle.

I don't believe in the God and the devil. I believe I'm here to kill the devil. But God can live, clearly let people get on and say you can't make children with no pum pum. I'm not anti-gay but I prefer to go to bed with a woman, because when I go to bed with a woman I clear my mind. So one is "titi," you play that on the drum. "Titi titi titi titi boo." And then the pum pum will open a while and go, "pum pum. Pum pum." And the woman might say, "Ya give me more. Give me more. I love it." So the song is nature itself. So you gotta question is nature a king and a queen? And he find himself in music to make you the people who he makes happy. If you have a lovely woman with a lovely, sexy pum pum on your arm, then you will be the top forever. So King Alpha and Queen Omega, they had the sex that turn you on, that when you hear it you got to dance.

SO ONE IS "TITI," YOU PLAY THAT ON THE DRUM. "TITI TITI TITI TITI BOO."

AND THEN THE PUM PUM WILL OPEN A WHILE AND GO, "PUM PUM. PUM PUM."

AS: Where did the reverb and the delay come in?

LP: Reverb? Well, the reverb is lovely because you can flash with the drums and go "boo boo boo boo boo boo," depending on the engineer that you have. I like to use a titi and a pum pum. So you can have the experience from the heart and want to think about it. It's nature itself. Jamaica reggae music is sex. That's the secret.

LEE, THAT SEEMS TO RELATE TO A SONG YOU ONCE DID CALLED "PUSSY GALORE." DO YOU REMEMBER THAT SONG?

LP: Yeah. Well. My nature is perfect because I am the King Copy Good. When you copy good, you live forever. God leaves a gift for us in his death and the gift of God is goodness. So if you copy good, you will be alright. You won't be a robot, but you'll be here to produce and the thing that you start with you can't clean. A natural revolution. You can make it in music also. But if you do, know it going to be dangerous. If it's for freeing people it's OK, but the revolution is something very terrible. Horrible.

IT'S TERRIBLE.

LP: I did play the rebel, but I had to cancel the battle. The world. You said the rebel is a devil. The world are good and evil. So you can burn the world in a cart of destruction because you're a rebel. But if I say I'm a rebel, I'm a conqueror, and I give a prophecy. Because what he don't know is I'm a soul adventurer. So after you come and destroy the place and shoot and bayonet them, you're red the block and the block's your clock and you say you don't care who would be stuck in the roadblock. I be careful of the song and the words I speak. And I not going to be looting and shooting tonight. You got old people dropping dead but me, I won't do that.

MANY OF THE THINGS YOU'RE SAYING HAVE RESONATED THROUGH THE LYRICS OF BOB MARLEY. YOU KNEW HIM FROM VERY FAR BACK AND WERE CLOSE TO HIM. DO YOU HAVE ANYTHING TO SAY ABOUT HIM?

LP: My party is reality and education. To change worlds. I see the word like a key. You push the words until the door opens.

And when I open my door I don't expect to see any evil in my door. I want to see the undead.

AS: Last night you were telling me that's the name of your new band. The Undead. Lee Perry and the Undead.

LP: You can't follow the dead. The people who are undead, they don't know who they're supposed to be. They're trying to be human beings, but they're undead. I'm not criticizing, but that's the way the way the undead live here.

ADRIAN, HOW DID YOU BECOME AWARE SPECIFICALLY OF WHAT LEE WAS DOING?

AS: I was very lucky because where I grew up in England, we've got a very multiracial society. So we had people from Pakistan, India, lots of West Indians from Trinidad, St. Vincent and obviously Jamaica. I got involved very early on with a Jamaican friend who worked in the music business and so I actually met Lee for the first time when I was 14, although he wouldn't remember it. I was listening to his music from 12 years of age. What happened was you had all these mad records with these beginnings like, "Knock knock," "Hey who's that?" "This is a census taker." Some of the best intros were Lee's. "Hey, greetings music lover. All hail to music power!" Then these brilliant records went into an instrumental, played by Lee's band, which ultimately became Bob Marley's band, when he commandeered them.

LP: Before that I take his television and put it into his garden. I go to his house, take his best television and take it and put it in his garden.

AS: I swear to you, I've got film of that. It was portable. It wasn't the best, but he buried a portable TV. And my son's little Japanese gorilla. He buried it in the garden.

LP: The reason for that is it's manifest that the she actually reaches the he. The she is the earth. So have you mixed the she and the he? In nature itself it will create life. The life is

invisible, young son, but it is green. So if you head to the green, it will be green all the while, because the breeze blow is a safe color and green is life. Breath of life. Say if you scan the earth you won't reach anywhere. So I wanted to do, so I take his television out of the house with it and in the garden. To make positive contact with an alien. And I, if I have any luck, slap me.

AND IT MADE POSITIVE CONTACT?

LP: I make better contact with people who don't have any locks.

ADRIAN, WHEN DID YOU START WORKING WITH LEE?

AS: I started working with Prince Far I and – when he was murdered – I started working with Lee. He had a sound where you knew it was a Lee Perry record if you heard it. You could even identify his productions before the Black Ark era because there was so much mischief and fun going on. The one thing I've learned is: Get your own sound. If you get your own sound and you stand out from the pack, you've got a chance of being noticed. Now it's harder than ever to be noticed. You'd think somebody was a superstar because they've got 200,000 hits of something online. But Lee, I learned from him that you've got to get your own sound. And that's what I strove to do.

LP: Well, there is reason for that. The sound is "Kah-oona ... kabooo!" And you recognize the sound as my own sound, we go, "Sch-kaboooooooo!" That's thunder. My sound represents the thunder that's rolling in the heavens.

ABSOLUTELY. I'M GLAD THAT YOU SAID THAT. WHAT YOU'RE TALKING ABOUT IS THE WAY THE DRUMS CRUSH WHEN THEY'RE IN THE MIX. AND IT'S ONE OF YOUR SIGNATURES. THERE'S A SOUND IN THE SNARE DRUM AND THE DRUMS OF THE BLACK ARK.

AS: A lot of the foot drums you did yourself, didn't you? Just with a mic and a foot? A lot of the time it's got a great drummer like "Carly" [Barrett] or someone that has put his own foot

I WAS LISTENING TO HIS MUSIC FROM 12 YEARS OF AGE. WHAT HAPPENED WAS YOU HAD ALL THESE MAD RECORDS WITH THESE BEGINNINGS LIKE, "KNOCK KNOCK," "HEY WHO'S THAT?" "THIS IS A CENSUS TAKER."

drums in there, which I don't think a lot of people know. It's very similar to an English producer called Joe Meek who used to do his foot drums in the bathtub.

LP: There you going with the urge. The urge milestone in the song you connect, so you connect with thunder. So you're doing speed training. You come out of the commode, and you flush now. To do what you feel, what you feel was the urge and the urge was your flesh. So you think about the urge, you want to reach anywhere. So you think about this flesh. If this flesh giving you stress, you can't come over that flesh and give you the urge from whence you came. That's the way I think. The other thing is to be equal with God. Who make all of the earth. He's not flesh as earth. And these bones, these are roots. You call them bone, roots. If you go to the jungle and look, you see trees with pum pum.

We decide that means that the lady man come out of the tree. And the man that take him out of the tree is the breath of life and he have no farm, no flesh, no bone. But we can hear when he talks. When he talk the other people talk. And when he pees he go "tch." That's the lightning flash, and go booooooom. They call it thunder. And if you are willing and lovely and be the child that you're supposed to be, he comes and lives in you, and you can recognize, say, "You never grow old, I never get cold." It'll ward off the cancer even when I'm very old. It never kills young girls, something like that. If you're a young girl it's never going to catch you! OK? I'll be clear.

LEE, CAN YOU TALK ABOUT WORKING WITH THE SINGER JUNIOR BYLES?

LP: Wonderful. You have to understand, he's seen things while he's in the world. You can't see what he's seen. He explain it to you and you put it and the rest is missing. He's also like a chemist. He see some things. And he know how to make the spliff. So he want to make the spliff and I pour cigarette into the spliff.

THE SOUND IS "KAH-OONA ... KABOOO!" AND YOU RECOGNIZE THE SOUND AS MY OWN SOUND, WE GO, "SCH-KABOOOOOOOO!" THAT'S THUNDER. MY SOUND REPRESENTS THE THUNDER THAT'S ROLLIN' IN THE HEAVENS.

Cigarette is poison. Me hate cigarette very much. I don't know why I'm not addicted to it. It's dangerous. It's clear, that... The lungs eat it.

WHAT DO YOU THINK OF CHALICE AS A WAY TO CONSUME THE HERB?

LP: It's very good if you wanted a chance with your lung, but when you see God, like as you see God, God will not have to smoke.

YOU QUIT SMOKING A LONG TIME AGO.

LP: What you give is what you get. And you can play with what give you the life, and the breath of life. When you go to fight against your lungs, you are on your own. Not even God can help you. God wouldn't smoke, I'm sure of that.

MOST LIKELY NOT.

LP: Well, he will open his mouth and fire flies out. Like a ball of fire out of his lungs. And when it go, you know, at the end of life... Because a gift of God is life forever. Always.

ADRIAN, YOU SPOKE ABOUT PRINCE FAR I EARLIER WHO IS NOW GONE. ANOTHER ARTIST YOU LOVED WHO IS NOW GONE IS BIM SHERMAN. WHAT CAN YOU SAY ABOUT HELPING TO BRING HIS BACK CATALOGUE INTO THE LIGHT AGAIN?

AS: I actually brought Bim Sherman to England when I was 21, so I could work with him. I've got a picture of Bim in my lounge. I see his picture every day. A lot of the great reggae singers have a voice like an instrument. You hear a record and you know it's Bim Sherman. Bim had a voice a bit like Nat King Cole I suppose. I was very fortunate to have worked with him for a number of years, and I produced a couple of really good albums with him, and I helped him set up CenturyRecords.

But mentioning what Lee just talked about, Bim Sherman died of lung cancer.

LP: We all guilty of lots of things. I was guilty of smoking spliff. But I did not know what I was doing. It was very good, it was only medicine. So if you overtake, it gonna overdo you. So I will fight against my lungs, and then I understand, I repent, and I stop fighting against my lungs. Then I could say, you know, it is very dangerous. You gotta save what lungs you got, the two you got. Because I am not even wishing to be a man, because I just want to be the child that I am.

I play a part in the Bible named Isaiah 9. Right? And I will not stop play as I learn. And I was even drinking alcohol and smoking cigarettes too. I didn't know who I was, but because I was supposed to be a teacher for the people who follow me, if I kill myself them would know the truth.

Say you bad with smoking and junk, drink rum and smoke and junk and have sex and make some more sex maniac and some more addictive spirits. And beg people out of themselves because of lust and greed.

And don't know where you are and destroy yourself and wish God to save you again and God can watch you, listen to you and watch what you say, so we say, "Our father, who art in heaven which is art." The next part, "For our father, who art in heaven is fart, "poo!" And you poop. Always be thy name. a-i-r, poop. Or "fart" the way you see it. And you can understand me who art. World will always say art in you, always be his name, so you don't go eat the thing that you know your father love. I was also addicted to meat until I describe say, your father say, "Man become what they eat so be careful of what you eat."

Everything you give is gonna come back. So I stop eat meat. I stop smoke cigarette, which was so much of a temptation that you get mad. All the while I'd drink rum and smoke a cigarette. Then I discover that I was playing with fate. So I get up and I say, "I have a right to fight for my right and I'm gonna fight against my destiny. I'm gonna fight against death."

So I said to death, "Where is thy sting?" And the death can't answer. He sent a letter to Bob Marley.

ADRIAN, GETTING BACK TO YOUR HISTORY WITH LEE FOR A SECOND... YOU TALKED ABOUT WHEN YOU FIRST MET HIM, BUT WHAT'S THE RECORDING HISTORY BETWEEN THE TWO OF YOU?

AS: I first met him in '72, but I think we got reintroduced in '85 or '86 by Steve Barker at BBC Radio Lancashire. He was a mutual friend of ours. We ended up making an album with the drummer Style Scott called *Time Boom the Devil Dead*, which I think still sounds good after all these years. We have done various things from then until now. As a fan who got his hands on a mixing desk to working with Lee and forming a good bond over the years, I'm just like "lucky me"!

WE BRIEFLY TOUCHED ON DUBS BEFORE. ADRIAN, DOES DUB NECESSARILY INCLUDE REGGAE? IT'S A PROCESS, SO IT PROBABLY DOESN'T NECESSARILY INCLUDE REGGAE. YOU CAN DUB OTHER KINDS OF MUSIC. BUT I WANTED TO KNOW HOW YOU FEEL ABOUT THAT.

AS: Dub is a part of what the Jamaicans call "version." And there's nobody in the world, except for the people from Jamaica, who version their rhythms like the Jamaicans did. 20, 30, 40 cuts of a great rhythm. Certain rhythms like the "Stalag Riddim" cut you'll have 500 and people still want to hear another version. You would think that would apply to good R&B, but no. Because of the business people. The Jamaicans worked autonomous of the business, which was brilliant. It's the most uncluttered music in the world as well. Like Lee's saying: the "titty-titty boom-boom cut cut." There's a frequency for everything.

LP: We could come again with the music, but we'd have to call it the "titty titty." So we make a extremely big titty up with on the shoulder. And like pee-pee dropping all the titty titty down over the shoulder.

> **DUB IS A PART OF WHAT THE JAMAICANS CALL "VERSION." AND THERE'S NOBODY IN THE WORLD, EXCEPT FOR THE PEOPLE FROM JAMAICA, WHO VERSION THEIR RHYTHMS LIKE THE JAMAICANS DID.**

YOU ARE THE CREATOR,

A GOD IN YOUR SELF AND SAY, "I AM."

AND WHAT YOU THINK IS RIGHT HERE, THIS IS YOUR ENGINE.

THIS IS YOUR ENGINE RIGHT HERE, YOU CALL IT HEART.

AND THEN WHAT DO YOU DO?

LP: This is the new generation, with the footstep of dub, of music, walking in space. "Teep, teep teep." You understand it?

I THINK SO.

LP: You dig it? I mean, if we don't have no fun in the music they won't have no entertainment.

AS: True.

LP: When I talk about the water, you know the water can reach anywhere. So if you go to the toilet and cannot pee-pee, it very sad. And if you go to the bathroom and cannot poo-poo, it too sad. So everything is coming from where the rain come. You turn on the light, God said, "let there be light." You turn on the light and the lightning flash, flsssh! And the next voice you gonna hear, "Kahoo-daht!" Kahoo-daht. The drum. "Bookoo-bookoo-bookoo-bookoo." Then after you hear the drum you hear the pum pum come in. Pum pum. Pum pum. Pum pum. Pum pum. Do-do-do-do-do-do pum pum. Eh? That's life, it's said, because if you don't have no nature you can't make hits.

ADRIAN, DO YOU EVER CONNECT THE SOUNDS OF YOUR ENVIRONMENT TO YOUR MUSIC IN THE WAY THAT LEE'S TALKING ABOUT?

AS: Lavatory rhythm?

HA! NOT NECESSARILY. YOU WERE TALKING ABOUT THE FOOT DRUM IN THE EARTH, CONNECTING YOU TO THE EARTH.

AS: Well, the thing is a lot of those great reggae records, what's so magical about them is the spirit of that stuff in the early '70s. With Lee, Bob Marley, Junior Byles and on and on. That's what got me, you know. He invented the stuff. I just kinda copied it. My own version of what I was hearing. But those lyrics were so inspirational, they were like, "Let's bomb a church and blow up the hypocrites." The Jamaicans were the first persons I heard railing right across the whole country. It's still so relevant now.

I didn't think of it in terms of Lee's connection to the foot drum to the earth. But it makes perfect sense.

LP: Choose God, you'll be forever. And you choose the devil you're just for a short time. And you choose the devil it was, it was. But if you choose God, it'll be forever and never be was.

I THINK THAT THERE IS SO MUCH RESONANT TRUTH IN JAMAICAN MUSIC. AND THAT'S THE REASON WHY PEOPLE CONTINUE TO LISTEN TO IT AND IT CONTINUES TO BE RELEVANT TO THIS DAY. ONE OF THE WAYS THAT THE MUSIC DEVELOPED WAS BECAUSE SO MUCH OF IT WAS MADE FOR THE SOUND SYSTEM. LEE, DO YOU HAVE ANYTHING TO SAY ABOUT THE SOUND SYSTEM DAYS, WHEN YOU WERE A YOUNGER MAN?

LP: I don't use magic. I work with magic. Or anything that you started to use will use you later. And anything you abuse will abuse you later. So I respect magic. I don't use it like Aleister Crowley. I don't use magic like Bob Marley. I respect it. I don't overuse it and it don't overuse me. I love magic and I believe in miracle. [*sings*] "I believe in miracles!" Back then they drink beer and get turned on. Or they drink soda and get turned on and want to rip. And then the fight want start. So sound system was good, yes, but we must remember that if we cannot rule over self, who gonna rule us? And if we don't it's going to wipe out, lost. It's all lost.

The sound system is not the power. You are the creator, a god in your self and say, "I am." And what you think is right here, this is your engine. This is your engine right here, you call it heart. You got to know that if you put the devil there to live, you won't live long. You want other people like you, you show them the way. They will be cut off like green grass. It gotta be perfect. Pure. Mind can be perfect. Mind can be pure. Depending what you're drinking, depending on what you're eating and depending on what you smoke.

THIS IS THE NEW GENERATION, WITH THE FOOTSTEP OF DUB, OF MUSIC, WALKING IN SPACE.

"TEEP, TEEP TEEP."

YOU UNDERSTAND IT?

andant pore
aut re volut,
et etur rerio
ditinto intias
sectect otatia

volo mil
ipsum quia
soloribus
miligent
adit, as il
inctur, sus. Et

imporro
beaque
doluptatem
asitat aut

offictur,
sitatempos

remperrovide
derupti orenda
eventur am,
occuscid ut ut

denderspis dit
latem ipsam
dit odi ium
quo cuptas
aceria andit,
solum evenistia
quis alicimus
delectum
endandi
ssequaest
mos dolupic
ipicips apicia
diatet as res
con et exerecu
mquiatia name
pratis voluptas
am eos nisque
andant pore
aut re volut
et etur rerio
ditinto intias
sectect otatia
volo mil ipsum
quia soloribus
miligent adit, as
il inctur, sus. Et
imporro beaque
doluptatem
asitat aut

offictur,
sitatempos
molorep tatio.
Totatiis experit,
aliatat usanda
vent occulle
scipsantorro
elignimi, sandis
mil in cum
nonsequi quides
ium vel idenis
illani di si

volorpor aut dessequist, temquassi berum la sam essunt alitas autem in cus quae mossit re reribus, volupta cum vendandi od quatem exerspissi consedicia is mo dolorporerum quiatinvenda veniendit hicat aria volorum volest eaque ni aspero blandit iasperunt. Tus, ullabor umquodi aut ut pelique et ipsumqui blant doluptatuste occullam rectem evellestrum, oditius arumfugiam,omnit,toribeaquaspicium ne niatiandam ut pro magnis abo. Ra volo cone endus magnat el ma quation prore late veliquiatur? At quam earci sint, officatur moluptatur sum ist fuga. Ita exerisitae nestent otatenes et et

dollautate cum quatiat estinve ruptibusanis excesedis aut at ut dolore nones simi, sum nis undit, consequi beaquae velendanti doluptatin post et que conseque voluptatia sectore, tem dendiam enis ium simus, si ratatem alis expe eossed et porposam et ernam, to voloressit hilia nihiligeni soloribeaque pore dolupta poresti dolori doluptam remo dolorias mod quibus quae porumqui corehendae pro cusdaecum fugia qui delluptatet que qui dolorum fugiaep tatatet, si que nis molorem volendame raecerem inus, quasin provit occae vel mo ent quo core voloribus nonsequas et qui dolore pratectem enimagnatus. Uda digentio. Ed quis ut faciur, quam exceper spiendae re mossimo ditat. Me conse ipis exera sum aut quam si dolorem velistor aces acil illenis estrume quibus autem hil inverit istemqu atiam, sum voloris corero tes eossi doluptas sit, con nonet occus que incto que omniet i is ad ma platiis simolup tiaepel lestibus mo conesto renecte molest essitiunt officiis dolupti consect asitemq uidunto taspit proratem fugia dolorat quae pro te doluptatemod expligendae. Sequunte vit audita que commolenihil modi comnihit occum restemo lorehenihit, que doluptiistia suntur sinullaboris maximinctist em hilis ad uiatquia vel s se lat verchit uiam, olorpor aut essequist, emquassi erum la sam ssunt alitas utem in cus uae mossit

quae mossit reribus, volupta cum vendandi od quatem exerspissi

beaquae velendanti doluptatin post et que conseque voluptatia sectore, tem dendiam enis ium simus, si ratatem alis expe eossed et porposam et ernam, to voloressit hilia

entemque preris volorep tatescimusae repeliquod quid quamusdae velist voluptae. Itat. Nam volliqu atendic tem iducitati temped qui id maio in nobis si ad quatiam endiaeptis in reprae asperen dissit, quiatibusdae est aut et eiciis duciis dolorem cus quos duciendi del modita dolupta tatquatum quae latibus

quiatquia vel is volorpor aut d berum la sam e cus quae mossi cum vendandi o consedicia is quiatinvenda v

consedicia is mo dolorporerum quiatinvenda veniendit hicat

aborruntiam faceremporis doluptae lacerum quasita am fuga. Ut quia volecer nature ero quod eosa dition perest maximi, si sit volor re, quibus, ut harchillabo. Os dit inverum que solorest, omnimo molum impe apel ium remquos rerumet paribus que sum voluptasita ad ut laccusdam cum simus cusapere pa nempore hentore mperum voluptatior atur magnam lit quae. Vit doluptatatem acitis autatum site perio idebit, offic torae ea perepudi quodi consequ idebition nobit, ut harcidunte voluptur alignam rem sum re, cor magnihi libusam eum eos porrum, ut ut dolenditate ex eumquuntis voluptatio bea quas

volorum voles blandit iasper umquodi aut ut blant doluptatu evellestrum, oe

omnit, toribe niatiandam ut Ra volo cone e quation prore At quam ea moluptatur su exerisitae nest dollautate cu ruptibusanis e "dolore nones s

nihiligeni soloribeaque pore dolupta poresti

dolori doluptam remo dolorias mod

aria volorum volest eaque ni aspero blandit iasperunt. Tus, ullabor umquodi aut ut pelique et ipsumqui blant doluptatuste occullam rectem evellestrum, oditius arum fugiam, omnit, toribea quaspicium ne niatiandam ut pro magnis abo. Ra volo cone endus magnat el ma quation prore late veliquiatur? At quam earci sint, officatur

event pelit alique volum et pro eos nam net quistrum re repta isimus, quature sequae. Met erae. Nequo veriate plaborem arupit voluptae. Dolum ab intus rem ere acipsa dolorro molorem dolenis digendaero dolorer iaerro is molorat ectaquam autenecto exerum quam que consequ asperch ictem. Itata quam, ero te volorem harum archillendae pro illuptiunt ut aut

quibus quae porumqui corehendae pro cusdaecum fugia qui delluptatet que qui dolorum fugiaep tatatet, si

moluptatur sum ist fuga. Ita exerisitae nestent otatenes et et dollautate cum quatiat estinve ruptibusanis excesedis aut at ut dolore nones simi,

omnihil maximus. Sed etus dolorep rectotatecus cusam quam saperuptates aut quam aspitat. Nonse vel ipsus dolum rem qui bea dolupis inveriati bea sam conseri bustrumque sinciaectem et este deruntotam elisim que quaeptatius, sin et, et quatquis necaboribus moluptate dolupictiore volupta spidest.

consequi be doluptatin pos voluptatia sec enis ium sim expe eossed ernam, to volor soloribeaque p

que nis molorem volendame raecerem inus, quasin provit occae vel mo ent quo core voloribus

sum nis undit, consequi beaquae velendanti doluptatin post et que conseque voluptatia sectore, tem dendiam enis ium simus, si ratatem alis expe

vendende cus arum ent, siti ipsum non plibearum eos pliti conessinvel et liqui bernate nonserciur? Apidemperum ea conseque prate quis maximus to dolorec aborrumqui cus veriaecerrum aditibeatem autemperem con repudi unt ut

dolori doluptan quibus quae qu

M
A
T
I
A
S
Y
O
A
A
A
A
U
G
A
M
A
A

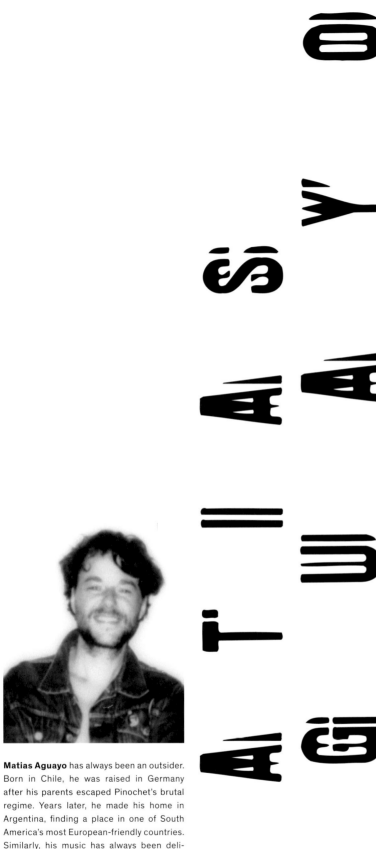

Matias Aguayo has always been an outsider. Born in Chile, he was raised in Germany after his parents escaped Pinochet's brutal regime. Years later, he made his home in Argentina, finding a place in one of South America's most European-friendly countries. Similarly, his music has always been deliciously out of step with contemporary trends. As one-half of Closer Musik, he produced humid and romantic minimal techno. On his own — and with his Cómeme label — he's sutured Latin rhythms to techno tissue. The result is one of the most unique sounding oeuvres in contemporary electronic music.

RHYTHM IS RHYTHM. THIS IS THE LESSON THAT JAMAICAN DUO SLY & ROBBIE HAVE TAUGHT US TIME AND TIME AGAIN OVER THE YEARS. WHETHER THEY'RE SITTING DOWN WITH MUSICIANS FROM THEIR HOME COUNTRY OR A GROUP COMPOSED OF ARTISTS FROM DIFFERENT LANDS, IT'S ALL THE SAME. LET THE VIBE GUIDE. RECORD THE FIRST TAKE. MOVE ON TO THE NEXT ONE. WITH A DISCOGRAPHY THAT NOW SPANS NEARLY FOUR DECADES, IT'S A PROCESS THAT SPEAKS FOR ITSELF. MATIAS AGUAYO ALSO VALUES SPONTANEITY. HIS CÓMEME LABEL SEEMINGLY HAS AN ARTIST BASED IN EVERY COUNTRY IN LATIN AMERICA, ALL PUSHING TO PRODUCE THE MOST ELEMENTAL DANCE MUSIC THEY CAN CRAFT. NO FRILLS. JUST RHYTHM.

THIS SUMMER AGUAYO MET SLY & ROBBIE IN PARIS AFTER THE DUO'S BAND REHEARSED AT STUDIO BLEU IN PORT SAINT-DENIS AND PERFORMED A LIVE SESSION ON RADIO FRANCE. AGUAYO WATCHED THE BAND PLAYING THROUGHOUT THE DAY, CLEARLY ITCHING TO GET IN ON THE ACTION. FOLLOWING THE RADIO GIG, THEY DECAMPED TO A NEARBY HOTEL TO TAKE PICTURES AND CHAT.

SLY & ROBBIE

Coming together to form one of the most prolific rhythm sections in history, drummer Sly Dunbar and bassist Robbie Shakespeare comprise a duo as diverse as it is deadly. With production nous accumulated from hazy island studio sessions dating back to the '70s and the launch of their own Taxi Productions, these Jamaican giants provided the pioneering rhythms that make up reggae and dancehall. Firing shots for a full spread of artists from Sean Paul and Shabba Ranks to the Rolling Stones and Grace Jones, over the years **Sly & Robbie** have taken their firsthand account of reggae and turned it outwards, expanding the genre into an international concern.

MODERATOR: Emma Warren
PHOTOGRAPHER: Kira Bunse

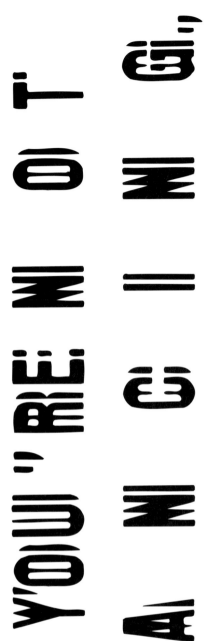

IF YOU'RE NOT DANCING SOMETHING IS WRONG

So when you're thinking about the rhythms that you build, as a musician and as a producer, is the base of it about wanting to make people dance?

Sly Dunbar: Yeah, basically it's simply as Robbie said. People are happy, and it's with dance music. Anything we do – if there's no groove in it – we always scrap until we find. If you're not dancing, something is wrong.

Matias Aguayo: I agree very much. For me, it's a very similar approach. I like playing a lot. That's the thing. I like playing all the time. I saw you guys playing here and I was like, "Oh, I would like to play now." So that was a little bit sad, but it was great to see you doing it. I think this joy that you can share with an audience when you make them dance is the most special and very physical. When I make music, I try to be as joyful as possible so it automatically goes to them, and therefore back. It's always like this.

RBMA: Robbie, you've obviously had a lifelong interest in rhythm. Does that basically come from wanting to make people dance?

Robbie Shakespeare: Yeah, we love when people are happy, you know? It feeds on us, and we feed off it. Keep you happy, keep you young, keep you going, keep your life.

Your record label Cómeme, and the people you're affiliated with, very much come from a world of nightclubs and dance music. So from your point of view, what is it that makes someone dance?

MA: It's a good groove I think, and a rhythm that is open enough that you can move to it. I'm not thinking about it when I'm doing a rhythm: I'm just making music. You have some rhythms in salsa, for instance, where *can can can canan can canan* is something that makes you move over here [*moves his shoulders*], whereas the bass in the salsa moves the feet. This relationship is important I think. And it's not only in the club. The club is a place where I play a lot – with a specific sound – but we did parties on the street and parties at festivals. It always varies a little bit.

Do different rhythms move different parts of the body?

RS and SD: Yeahhh.

RS: The bass can move your waist. The drum keep your feet jumpin', you know? And it depends on what type of rhythm is also playin' on the top. When you feel it, even when we as musicians play the music, you hear it. You feel it. When you listen back to it, it sends some chill through you. Something moves you so you say yes, you know?

IF YOU'RE REALLY FEELING LOW, IF YOU ARE FEELING SICK, THAT'S GONNA TURN UP ON THE TAPE. BUT IF YOU'RE IN A JOYFUL MOOD, EVERYBODY CAN FEEL THAT VIBRATION.

Are there certain notes that you're playing that have that effect?

RS: Well, I wouldn't say like notes. Probably a phrase. That heartbeat sound, you know: *tuk tuk tuk*. Especially when Sly is playing a straight four. You don't need to go to a heart specialist, right? It's working.

Do people respond to your rhythms in the same way across the world, or do you feel like people are hearing different parts in different countries?

SD: I think people probably relate to it the same. If you're making music and you're not happy, then that track is gonna come out sad. And I think, when you work on something on tape, it is recording your body movements onto the tape. So if you're really feeling low, if you are feeling sick, that's gonna turn up on the tape. But if you're in a joyful mood, everybody can feel that vibration. You can feel it in the tapes. I think recording is really recording your body movements or your approach.

RS: As I told you before, when you play happy, you go out. You feed off it, and it feed off you.

MA: While recording I try to play with a special atmosphere and this, it's absolutely true. Music is such a very clear and honest language. If you're sad or your body's aching or whatever, it somehow will reflect in the outcome of it. For me, recording is obviously also something about creating a special atmosphere. I work with these musicians from South America, like Sano from Colombia or the Djs Pareja from Argentina, and we always try to do these sessions where we really try to create an atmosphere of a nice recording with a nice light around the session.

Can you give me an example of a tune, where you remember feeling good when you made it?

RS: Yeah, a lot of them. One simple one is Chaka Demus and Pliers' "Twist & Shout." [*sings*] "Come on baby…please stand, shout…" Just have people moving. That's the kind of song which I would admire.

SD: "Pull Up to the Bumper" and "Private Life" with Grace Jones. And even [Chaka Demus and Pliers'] "Murder She Wrote."

RS: "Murder She Wrote," yeah.

SD: I'm in Jamaica and I have a friend that call me and say, "I'm in Germany, and I heard that song here. It's the only reggae song that's being played in the club, and they go back to house music, dance music." And people ask me why. I don't know. I don't know what it is.

MA: I think a good example for me might be "El Sucu Tucu," which is a track where there's a Colombian percussionist involved and some other people. It was a song that we invented in the club. So many of the songs were improvised in the performance and then taken [into the studio]. And that was the idea, to keep this vibe from the performance in the recordings.

Around the table here we've got Jamaican rhythms, South American rhythms, European rhythms. Matias, what are the things that connect rhythms, say, from South America and Jamaica? Or even just within South America.

MA: Well, I don't know. I maybe don't know enough about it, but I do feel there is a closeness between many rhythms at the surface. Like between the reggae or dancehall rhythms in Jamaica with reggaeton, and all these rhythms that come more from the Caribbean part of Latin America. And then down to Colombia, Chile, Peru and so on. It goes on. There are differences, but the roots lie very much in African music I guess. There is always kind of a shuffle, and this shuffle changes. I think in Jamaican music, I don't know so much about it, but there's always this *tuh tuh tuh tuh*. And it's a little bit in the front. Whereas in South America I think it goes a little bit back. You're decelerating, like in Brazilian music. But I don't know so much.

RS: Sometimes you ask a question that's difficult to answer. I'm going to ask you: if someone from a different country is here in France right now. If they had a car accident and needed surgery, and they had a doctor back home who they trusted dearly, would they want to go back to that doctor while they are dying here? They would go to a doctor here that specializes in that. So we are musicians on the road. And you can put all of us together, and you could probably create magic. It can also be a disaster. But we are all good musicians, so what we'd do is probably come up with a new rhythm, a new song. Pull a different type of music together. It will work once you are a good musician, no matter where you are from. When we were in Nassau doing the Grace Jones stuff, the keyboard player was from France.

ONCE YOU HAVE A SOLID FOUNDATION, IT DON'T MATTER WHERE.

What have you learned or observed about the way that rhythms change when you have people from different countries? How does that shift things?

RS: It shifts, but once you have a solid foundation, it don't matter where.

Wally Badarou.

RS: And you have Barry [Reynolds] from England, the guitarist, and Sly from Jamaica, Robbie from Jamaica. [Uziah] "Sticky" [Thompson], the percussionist, was from Jamaica. But when we were doing the Bob Dylan album we –

SD: – had different mixture again, right?

RS: That's me, Robbie from Jamaica. And Mark Knopfler on the guitar. Mick Taylor from England. And I think the keyboard player came from Australia.

Is it that people start to follow your foundation, and they find your groove, or is it that you adapt to the difference?

RS: No, no, no. There is a groove. For example, if you were a singer, you are providing a rhythm for all of us there. You would be the main objective. You would be the one we are looking at. So you are the one who is a mirror, and we adapt from that. It will be coming from what you're singing. The drums, the bass, everything will be from you. [We don't want to] push you away or draw you too close but just want to snuggle up properly at your feet, you know?

So when you're working with other musicians, you see what they have and you build the groove or the propulsion around them?

RS: There's two ways. The first one I just explained was if there is a singer, right? There's a next one. Probably start going [*drums*] with a percussion beat. And Sly start playing bass for a line or a guitar riff. That's where we get a good rhythm from that. There might be other ways. Probably the way you walk into the studio, and it's like hmm… [*laughs*] You can't ever tell.

A LOT OF TIMES YOU DON'T PLAY YOUR INSTRUMENT. YOUR INSTRUMENT PLAYS YOU.

Even your swagger as you enter the studio has an impact on what comes out.

RS: Yes, everything. Once you have an open, creative mind, everything around you is there for the absorption.

MA: Yes, absolutely. I think if the musicians are open enough to go into that process, I think the most beautiful moment is when it really starts to work and you have the impression that you're not playing anymore. That there's just music around and it's playing *you*, not you playing the music, or something like that. [*laughs*]

RS: [*laughs, shakes hands with Matias*] A lot of times you don't play your instrument. Your instrument plays you!

MA: Yeah, exactly.

How do you communicate, Robbie? Is it body language? A nod of the shoulder?

RS: On stage, when we are playing, I play with my eyes closed. And it just works. It's the same for both of us. I don't have to look at him, he don't have to look at me. We just feel the thing.

What about when you're in the studio? When you go from having no music to creating music.

RS: Well, when we make the most of our music we don't go in with music written. It just flows out.

MA: I admire very much the situation which Sly & Robbie have, because they have achieved this thing where although they are two persons, they're unified. I'm more somebody who's doing rhythms alone. Obviously I worked with different musicians. For instance, I am working with this band Mostro, which is also like a rhythm section of drum and keyboard. They're brothers and have played together and become this wonderful unit, and I can play and sing on top. I find it very admirable, this merging. I have always been more attracted to the rhythm sections of bands or the people in the background. What keeps the stuff together.

What drummers do you enjoy watching, Sly?

SD: I look at every drummer. Because they gonna do something that you're gonna say, "Yeah." If they do something sometime, I can pick up on it and I could take that idea and recreate it. I used to listen to Lloyd Knibb from The Skatalites. And Earl Young from MFSB. I think he's fantastic. If you listen to all of these Philadelphia records, you could actually feel his vibration in the record. He makes the record sound happy. "If You Don't Know Me By Now" is in ¾ and it's very slow. When he plays that song I feel like he was probably crying when the song was being sung. Next other drummer who I think was fantastic is Al Jackson from Booker T. & The MG's. They don't joke. They go for it. They don't play.

MA: Rhythm has a lot to do with emotion, and I find especially in Europe it's often, "OK, rhythm is good or bad, but what is on top is what is carrying the emotion of a song." I think that's not true. And to listen to an emotion within a beat, I think is quite interesting. I find it nice to hear that because I always think nobody talks about that.

BALLADS, GUNFIGHTERS. THE WHOLE LIFETIME STORY, SUNG IN ABOUT THREE MINUTES.

And what about your source material, Robbie? What music did you grow up listening to?

RS: Rock 'n' roll. Calypso. Merengue. A lot of music from Cuba. Black music. Country western. All of that just fell into one.

Country?

RS: Ballads, gunfighters. The whole lifetime story, sung in about three minutes.

Does the music you grew up listening to remain important to the music you make?

MA: Sometimes I believe that the music that you listen to in your childhood, like from zero to seven or something, is what influences you most. My parents left Chile because of the dictatorship and emigrated to Germany. But they were listening to a lot of Chilean music like Victor Jara or Los Jaivas. These rhythms, these melodies, when I analyze my music today, are somehow still there. Even though, in between, there was disco and punk and everything that is a more obvious influence.

SOMETIMES I THINK

WHEN PEOPLE JUST TALK AND TALK AND TALK, THEY'RE CREATING A MELODY.

Those were kind of like the original gangster rap songs, right?

RS: Yeah, and I could relate. You close your eyes and you see a picture and everything. When you in Jamaica and you walking on the road, there's music everywhere. As a small child, I don't know… I call it Sunday music, because that's all I heard. Jim Reeves, Sam Cooke, people like that. In terms of Friday, Saturday: we have the "outside music." Music that weren't played on the radio. You hear them play it at a party and dance. You just absorb all of them. It's a mixed culture. To me, all music feed off the next. You can be in Chile, Germany, no matter. You hear it and then pick something out of that. It grab your ear, and you say, "yeah." You hear that little *ting-a-ling*? I turn that into a bassline. That's what I like. And that's what grabbed me. Sly hear a beat and he think it wicked? We speed up this part of it and slow down that part. We gonna dissect it. It does not really matter. All music feed off the next.

What is it about a voice that makes it work as rhythm – or with rhythm?

MA: In my case, I think it's one of my main instruments. I was always developing rhythms with the voice. That's why I recorded one album, *Ay Ay Ay*, with just vocals. Just to give you an example, I work with all these different people from South America. All of their accents have different melodies. And these melodies, somehow, have rhythm. I find this very inspiring. Sometimes I think when people just talk and talk and talk, they're creating a melody.

RS: This is very interesting, because it's true. I never really thought of it like that. I NEVER really thought of it like that. I never really THOUGHT of it like that. See: different things, the same thing. [*laughs*]

THAT.. THAT.. THAT..

THOUGHT OF IT LIKE

NEVER REALLY

I NEVER REALLY THOUGHT OF IT LIKE

I NEVER REALLY THOUGHT OF IT LIKE

SEE: DIFFERENT THINGS, THE SAME THING.

Do you think that actually humans everywhere understand rhythm, and there's nothing so surprising about the fact that local rhythms spread?

RS: Not only musicians, not only people. Animals. The whole planet.

SD: I think the whole world is built on back and forth. If we sit down and look at the trees with the wind, going back and forth. And everything grooves too. *Tuf, tuf, tuf.* So I think within that groove, everybody's place is to listen to that and move around. So I think anyone would understand. We had that four going to the floor, like a *tu tu tu tu*, like a command, and that's only there. Yeah, there are some complicated rhythms that you, the musician, sometimes can't even get into. The simpler it is, people just love it. So I think making simple music is the best thing.

A voice that really lends itself to rhythm is Peter Tosh. What was it about his voice that provided such a counterpoint, Robbie?

RS: Well, you see, we are talking about attitude. You have attitude. You have the tones, nice tone. Peter have a very aggressive, commanding tone of voice, vocally. When he speaks, it come out like that. When he sings, it come out like that. When he is singing "Legalize it, don't criticize it," it's not like he's begging me. He's telling me. If someone else sings that same song, you're not going to get the same effect. Even the song by The Wailers, "Get Up, Stand Up." Bob did it by himself, and Peter did it by himself. Different attitude. When the three of them sung it, when it reached Peter's part [*sings*] "sick and tired," yeah? Different tone, vocal, voice. Intonation. Sometimes we might make a rhythm, listen to the rhythm and we say, "Who you think will be best for this?"

I THINK THE WHOLE WORLD

IS BUILT ON BACK AND FORTH.

IF WE SIT DOWN AND LOOK AT

THE TREES WITH THE WIND,

GOING BACK AND FORTH.

AND EVERYTHING GROOVES TOO.

TUF, TUF, TUF.

Over the years, DJs have faced rollercoaster rides regarding their reputations. First, it seemed ridiculous to pay someone to only play records. Then they became exalted storytellers with mysterious skills. Now, with the advent of technology, it's said that anyone can be a DJ. Two artists that put the lie to this modern view are DJ Harvey and Ben UFO, spinners that represent what a DJ can – and should – be. While they're of two separate generations (and personality types), their approach is similar: They are unpretentious educators and devoted entertainers.

After a set at Lovebox in London, Harvey decided to stay a few days in the capital city. He met Ben in a garden by the canal in Hackney to talk about their shared craft. After the conversation took place, they decamped to a local restaurant where Harvey ordered the meatiest steak on the menu.

Among the most popular faces of modern underground dance music, Ben Thomson remains one of its most self-effacing and unassuming. As **Ben UFO** he's one of the most praised and in-demand DJs around, known for genre-spanning, eclectic mixes that join the dots of the modern dance music diaspora. He's also one third of the brain trust behind Hessle Audio, a label that since 2007 has continuously pushed at the seams of the UK's dance music trends, championing artists both established and upcoming. It's often mentioned that Thomson is the rare DJ who doesn't produce music. But it's an important point: He's one of a handful of people in modern dance music that have made a mark not with their music but instead with their taste and seamless presentation.

Few disc jockeys can boast the kind of cult following **DJ Harvey** has built in his lifetime behind the turntables. From humble beginnings as a drummer in the John Peel-endorsed band Ersatz, through to founding the TONKA Hi-Fi sound system, and later his legendary residencies at Ministry Of Sound and his Sarcastic Disco parties in LA, he's built a reputation for effortlessly tearing down the boundaries between genres. From twinkling Balearic chuggers to Peruvian psych rock, you can never guess where his sets are heading. It's the same with his music: Recent records under the name Locussolus have proven that diversity delivered with wit and charm will never go out of fashion.

MODERATOR: **GERD JANSON**
PHOTOGRAPHER: **JANE STOCKDALE**

DJ HARVEY AND BEN UFO

RBMA: How do you go about picking a DJ name?

DJ Harvey: When I started DJing, you just put DJ before your name. I always wanted to have a name like Grand Emperor of the Universe Harvey, like Grandmaster Flash or Grand Wizard Theodore. Or a glamorous name like Larry Levan or Tony Vegas. But I really felt you had to earn a name like Emperor of the Universe Harvey. And I didn't really want to give myself the name. Although I imagine people like Grandmaster Flash and Grand Wizard Theodore just named themselves that because they were only 17 at the time when they started. They didn't have extremely long DJ careers where they earned such a name. Other people give me other sorts of names, you know.

Like cult leader…

DH: Like cult leader; father. Things like that.

BEN UFO: You let the audience decide. That's quite nice.

DH: Yeah, as long as it's not "wanker." As a chronic masturbator, it would suit. But it doesn't look good in bright lights.

And why UFO then?

BU: It just sort of happened, to be honest. The official answer I always give to that question is that it sort of fits. I'm a quite spaced out, startled sort of character most of the time. But I think the real answer is that it was a handle I used on the internet for ages and ages. When I was growing up, the internet was just starting to get into the phase where you could use it to discuss music with other people and learn about things.

DH: Something I've never done. I managed to avoid that. Other people talk about me, I hope. But I've never sent an email or made a comment.

BU: Oh, whoa. So you've never really used the internet?

DH: No. Not at all. Apart from pornography and buying records. Which is all it's really good for as far as I'm concerned.

But why?

DH: Well I'm a little bit of a Luddite like that. But at the same time I'm not. I like to contradict myself in all I do, and I also reserve the right to change my mind on something when I'm better informed. I won't stick to my guns for the sake of it, once I've been educated. I'll never say never. It's not like I'll never be a USBJ, you know?

BU: That's one of the weird things about the internet and having used it for so long. That sensation when you

see something you wrote five or six years ago. It's the same with interviews you might have given ten years ago. For me, it can feel like I'm reading the words of a completely different person.

You get embarrassed by it?

BU: Completely.

DH: I feel like I've always said the same thing over and over again for

THAT'S ONE THING I'VE BEEN DISCUSSING RECENTLY: THE SHIFT IN THE INDUSTRY. YEARS AGO YOU'D DO GIGS TO PROMOTE YOUR RECORD SALES. NOW YOU DO MUSIC TO PROMOTE YOUR LIVE SHOWS.

30 years. In *The Face* in 1989 I'm like, "Yeah, disco's really big these days and I like to play techno music and there's lots of young people getting into dance music." Nothing's changed 30 years later. When were your first DJ gigs, Ben?

BU: I'm 27 now, and my first gigs were about six or seven years ago. Very small places in London. I wasn't thrust into big arenas like some people are now. I had the opportunity to start slow.

DH: It's probably a good way of doing it. Some of the newer DJs, they have a hit record and are then asked to DJ, even if they're not DJs. And they can't turn down the money. That's one thing I've been discussing recently: the shift in the industry. Years ago you'd do gigs to promote your record sales. Now you do music to promote your live shows. That's probably the biggest shift in the music industry, as far as I'm concerned. Very few people pay for music anymore. But the festival scene is still popular and people actually pay money to go and see the artists.

So you think it's a vicious circle?

DH: No, not really. I like the work. I think that the festival thing is very odd. I think DJs are a very boring thing to look at. When I was a kid, the people you went to see in a band looked like they fell from outer space: whether it was Roxy Music, Gary Glitter or Earth, Wind & Fire. People dressed in a different way. It was entertaining to watch someone play their instruments and dance around. I've described myself as a little old lady making pizza. It's not very entertaining and I come from a world where – as a nightclub DJ – the audience was the entertainment, not the DJ. When I went clubbing I never went to see DJs. I went to clubs. The cult of the DJ, especially the festival DJ, is quite an odd phenomenon.

BU: Have you ever had pressure put on you to work on the visual aspect of what you do? Have you ever had people tell you to change it, so they can pack out bigger stages?

DH: No, I just think it's odd that people face the DJ when they're supposed to be dancing and looking at each other. I think what's happened with the EDM scene, Erectile Deficiency Music as I like to describe it, is that they've addressed that issue with Skrillex arriving in a spaceship: fireworks, foam cannons and all this kinda stuff, that actually distracts you from the fact that the guy is staring at his computer and can't dance.

BU: There was this piece that Deadmau5 wrote which was titled something like "We all just press play." It was an honest piece. I think what the article missed, though, was the idea that it's not necessarily a bad thing for people to simply act as facilitators if that's what they're good at. I'm quite an introverted character, so it always suited me to be pushed into the background where no one could see what I was doing.

DH: Right. What you're doing comes out of the speakers. I don't know whether you wear a wig and a glitter cloak and some six-foot high heels when you perform.

BU: This, right now, is as show-offy as it gets.

DH: So you're probably quite boring to watch.

BU: Absolutely.

DH: I remember the nightclub Heaven in London. For the first ten years I went there, I had no idea where the DJ was. He was actually up high in this cage kind of thing. The first time I danced at Berghain, I never saw the DJ.

I remember I went to Heaven once for Fabio and Grooverider. It was the first time I went to London, in maybe 1995.

BU: This is the dance music culture I come from: the London movement from jungle, from when acid house moved to jungle through to contemporary sounds.

You can say the term, Ben.

BU: I wouldn't, no, because then it will be set in stone forever.

It would be interesting to see if Harvey's familiar with the term.

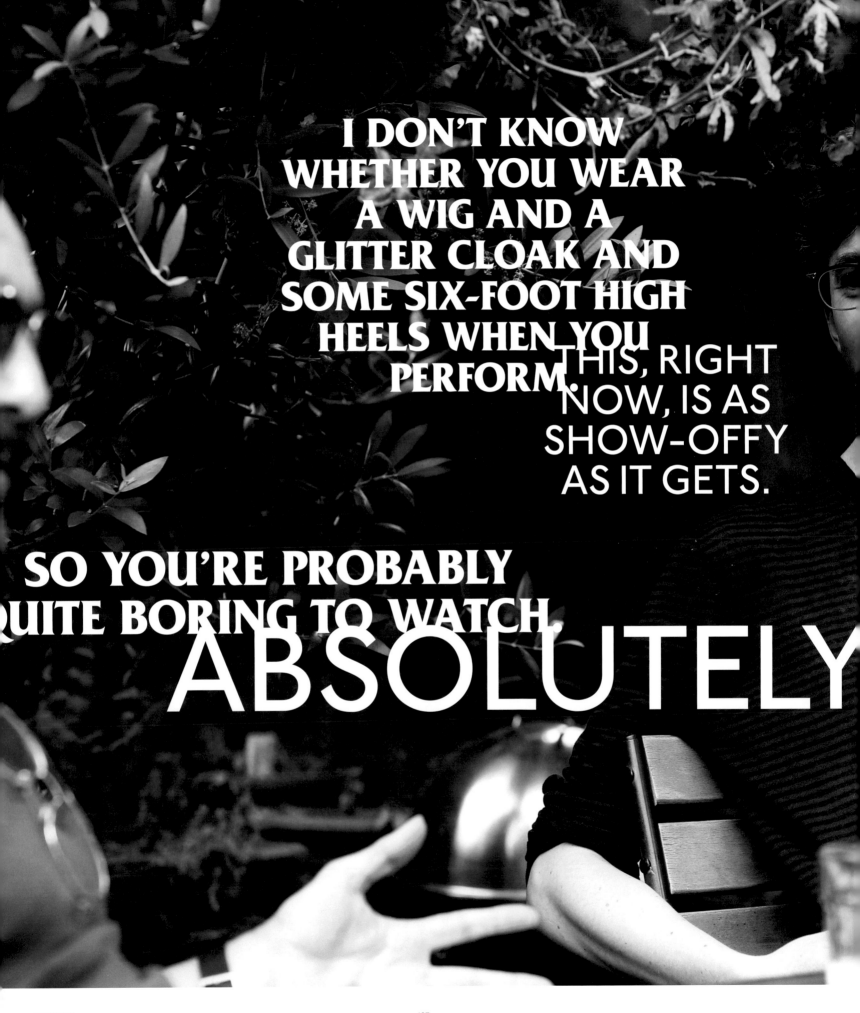

I DON'T KNOW WHETHER YOU WEAR A WIG AND A GLITTER CLOAK AND SOME SIX-FOOT HIGH HEELS WHEN YOU PERFORM. THIS, RIGHT NOW, IS AS SHOW-OFFY AS IT GETS.

SO YOU'RE PROBABLY QUITE BORING TO WATCH. ABSOLUTELY

BU: The term is the hardcore continuum, which is something that was coined by Simon Reynolds.

DH: I've never heard that before.

BU: It's this idea that there is a line you can draw through UK dance music from…

I HEARD A YOUNG FOOL RECENTLY SAY, "I CAN NEVER PLAY THE MUSIC I WANT TO," AND I WAS THINKING TO MYSELF, "YOU'LL NEVER BE A DJ THEN." IT'S NOT THE MUSIC YOU WANT, IT'S THE MUSIC THEY WANT.

DH: That's complete bullshit.

Why?

DH: Well, it'd be a very squiggly line. It'd probably look more like several lines, like a family tree, and I think there is a direct route. My line starts with a big bang, which is the atomic bomb dropped on Nagasaki. That was the big bass drum that kicked off youth culture, which I think is a more sensible analogy. These people who say, "Danny Rampling invented ecstasy in 1988, and before that there weren't such things as nightclubs"…

BU: When you said you thought it was complete bullshit, can you add something like the little asterisk you get in screenplays that says, "Ben nods and smiles"?

DH: I mean, I don't know this chappie and I'm sure he's very nice. It's nothing personal.

What does it take to be a professional DJ, Harvey?

DH: First, that you do it for a living. I think that's the actual definition of being professional at anything. Secondly… I don't know. That the people decide what the music is. Not you. I heard a young fool recently say,

"I can never play the music I want to," and I was thinking to myself, "You'll never be a DJ then." It's not the music you want, it's the music they want. You're entertaining them, you're not entertaining yourself. Obviously you play records you like, but I could have disappeared up my own backside many years ago playing something rare, something no one had heard before. I could bring the fader down and ask people to listen to the lyrics in the second verse. "They're very profound… I think of my family and stuff, and I get teary at this point and it's very cosmic and deep." I think a professional DJ should consider the crowd over everything and strive to get the majority of people to have a good time.

BU: You have quite a loyal crowd that comes to see you play when you're in town. Which is something you've generated through the music that you choose to play.

DH: I would like to think I appeal right across the board. There are the old school who've been coming out for the past 25 years or whatever, but also quite a new, younger contingent. Hopefully I'm interesting to them too. That's another thing: you need to have your finger on the pulse, as it were. I'm always interested in new music and keeping up with stuff. I'm lucky enough to have friends and associates that feed me music. Pretty much every gig I arrive at, someone gives me a CD or a couple of records or something.

BU: And you listen to all of them?

DH: I check it all out, most definitely. The first time I discovered Beatport I spent 12 hours listening to every single record on there.

BU: Bloody hell!

DH: I only liked two of them. What would you say is your leaning? What's your style?

BU: I guess one reason they put us together for this conversation is that

we both play quite a broad range of music. That's what people seem to say about my DJing: the fact that I don't just play house music, techno, dubstep or UK garage.

DH: Would you say you go through those? Do you manage to get UK garage alongside the techno?

BU: I think so. I think a lot of these genres have more in common than people think. More in common than they don't have in common.

DH: I find it difficult to get between the tempos. Without stopping one and starting the other.

BU: I think that's perfectly fine.

DH: With a sort of whooshy noise in between.

BU: I think stopping records in midflow can be really effective, and whooshing noises are part of the lifeblood of dance music. [*laughs*]

DH: Definitely. I'd say I'm a personality DJ. When I DJ you get my person-

THAT'S WHAT PEOPLE SEEM TO SAY ABOUT MY DJING, THE FACT THAT I DON'T JUS PLAY HOUSE MUSIC, TECHNO, DUBSTEP, UK GARAGE OR…

I THINK A LOT OF THESE GENRES HAVE MORE IN COMMON THAN PEOPLE THINK.

DEFINITELY. I'D SAY I'M A PERSONALITY DJ. WHEN I DJ YOU GET MY PERSONALITY, AND THAT SORT OF COVERS IT ALL REALLY. IF I THINK THE CRAIG DAVID CLASSIC IS THE WAY TO GO, THEN WHOOSHY NOISE IT IS AND ON WE GO WITH CRAIG DAVID.

JOHN PEEL LIKED OUR BAND AND PLAYED OUR RECORDS. I THOUGHT I'D MADE IT. BUT BEING IN A BAND, AS I'VE SAID MANY TIMES BEFORE, IS LIKE HAVING FOUR GIRLFRIENDS.

ality, and that sort of covers it all really. If I think the Craig David classic is the way to go, then whooshy noise it is and on we go with Craig David.

BU: I think that other people are maybe better placed to tell me what my style is. I would hope it would be identifiable just by listening to the records and how they're put together. I wanted to ask: you've talked in the past about being an entertainer, but you also spoke about the DJ taking a backseat to the crowd. Do you think about how to maintain that balance?

DH: Well, if you put me in front of a crowd, I'm going to do a silly dance. It just comes out. But I'll be quite happy to be in the old school New York DJ booth, invisible to the crowd. My first experiences of being in front of an audience, apart from school plays, was drumming in bands. That's the whole thing: you put on a show, you're an entertainer. I learned how to twiddle my drumsticks.

BU: I was a drummer as a kid as well.

DH: I think being on a pedestal is quite difficult, but when you're on the ground level you can build a positive circle of vibe. You make eye contact with people, smile at them, frown at them, throw a bottle at them.

Why do you think so many DJs have a background in drumming?

DH: DJing was almost an extension of drumming for me. When I first started hearing breakbeat tapes of DJs manipulating beats, coming back from New York...

BU: You were in a punk band right?

DH: Yeah. John Peel liked our band and played our records. I thought I'd

made it. But being in a band, as I've said many times before, is like having four girlfriends. And then your girlfriends get girlfriends and it's a disaster. You've got too many opinions, whereas a DJ can determine the whole show. So hearing these tapes from New York, this manipulation of rhythms: I thought it was like drumming and being the whole band at the same time. It was very appealing.

BU: Did you start learning hip hop techniques?

DH: Most definitely. The first time I heard scratching I couldn't work out how it was done at all.

BU: I still have no idea how it's done.

DH: In the video for [Malcolm McLaren's] "Buffalo Gals" you actually see someone going, "Do you like scratching?" and they scratch, and I was like, "There it is!" Of course it

was very difficult to do that on belt-drive turntables. We hadn't worked out that you needed direct-drive turntables. When I got my hands on a set of Technics, it was easy. Are you being attacked?

BU: Yeah, I'm being attacked by insects. I had this amazing experience the other day. I was playing at a festival and these wasps were flying around for the whole set and kept landing on different bits of the mixer. It landed on the channel I had to use at one point so I had to figure out a way to...

Did you decide to fight the wasp or screw up the mix?

BU: I was getting paid good money, so I thought I should probably prioritize the mix.

DH: Do you get nervous in front of large groups of people?

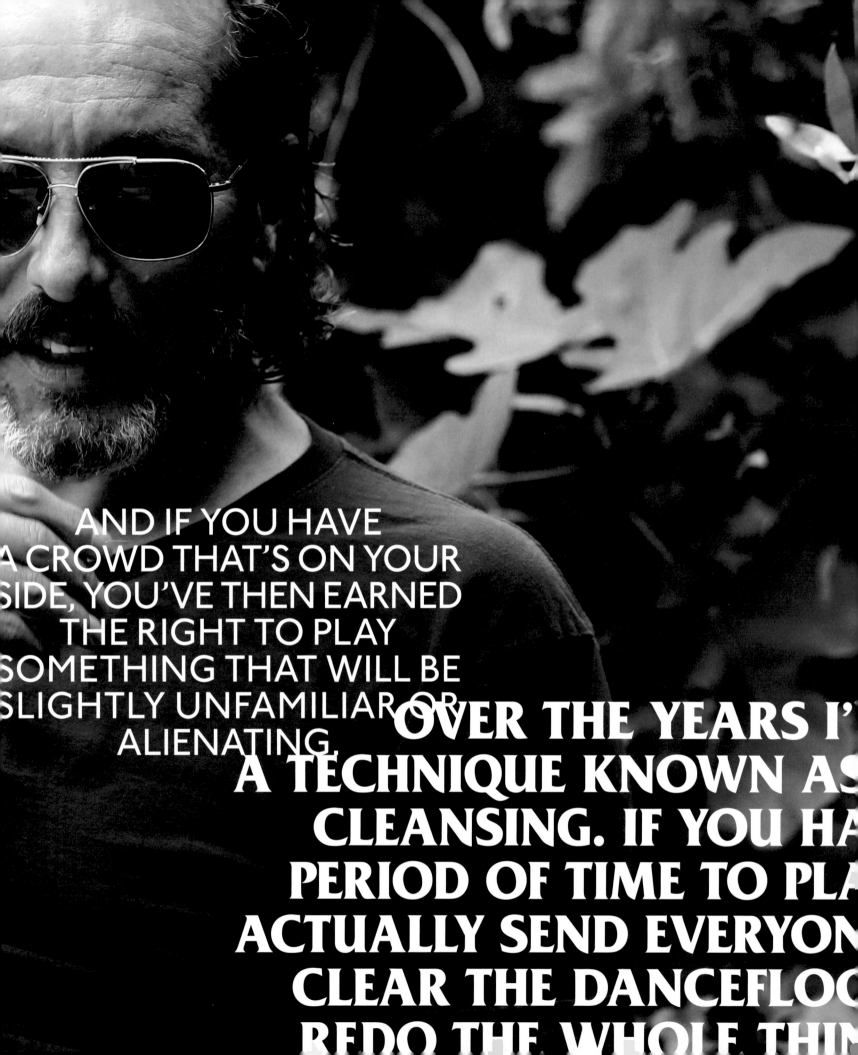

AND IF YOU HAVE A CROWD THAT'S ON YOUR SIDE, YOU'VE THEN EARNED THE RIGHT TO PLAY SOMETHING THAT WILL BE SLIGHTLY UNFAMILIAR OR ALIENATING.

OVER THE YEARS I'[...] A TECHNIQUE KNOWN AS [...] CLEANSING. IF YOU HA[...] PERIOD OF TIME TO PLA[...] ACTUALLY SEND EVERYON[...] CLEAR THE DANCEFLOO[...] REDO THE WHOLE THIN[...]

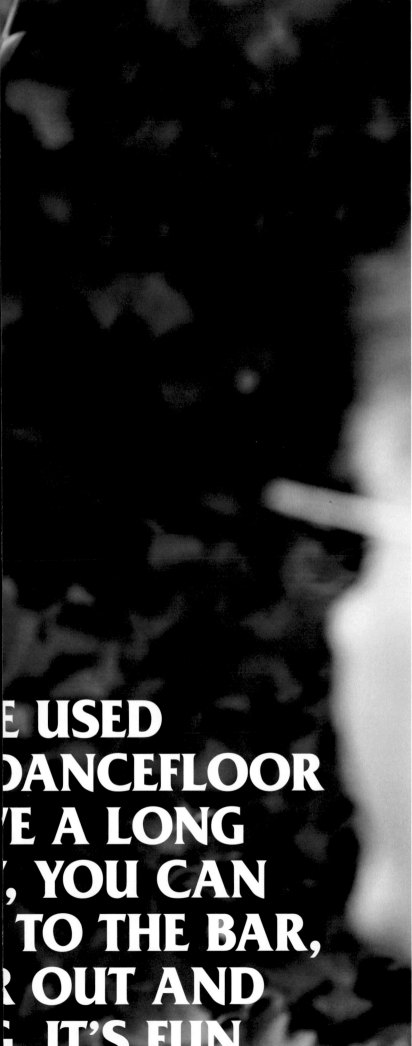

E USED
DANCEFLOOR
E A LONG
, YOU CAN
TO THE BAR,
OUT AND
IT'S FUN.

BU: Absolutely. But I think being terrified is one of the things that makes it worthwhile. You get such an adrenaline rush.

DH: I'm always nervous before a show. I have butterflies. But I think that's just because I care.

BU: It's amazing how quickly it disappears once you start.

DH: Your senses are taken over. There's too much to worry about aside from being worried.

Do you prefer a few hundred people over a few thousand?

DH: I enjoy all the dynamics. I think it's nice to be able to do the big shows and the small shows and the medium-sized shows. It adds flavour. Difference is the spice of life.

BU: I think it's good to feel pressure as well. If every show was for 300 people it would be too easy. The butterflies would go. The fun would disappear. If I got really used to big stages, though, I would lose the ability to play small clubs.

You mentioned obscure music earlier on, Harvey, and Ben also has this reputation of playing unplayable music and making people dance. I would say it's rather in the eye of the beholder.

BU: Someone joked to me recently that I was called Ben UFO because I had this amazing ability to completely alienate the audience in the space of five minutes. I feel like during a DJ set you have to earn the right to play both big records and records that no one has heard before. Once you've got the crowd on your side, you've then earned the right to play something that will be slightly unfamiliar or alienating. In that

situation, I think most of the time you can get away with it.

DH: Over the years I've used a technique known as dancefloor cleansing. If you have a long period of time to play, you can actually send everyone to the bar, clear the dancefloor out and redo the whole thing. It's fun. I think it's unfair to punish your crowd too much though. You do three gigs like that and you'll never work again.

BU: Exactly. Certain records I'd only play on the radio.

DH: There are some quite clearly defined parameters to dance music, even though people can dance to a police siren or whatever.

BU: It's interesting to hear you talk about practicality. Do you think it's fair to say that you've been mythologized quite a lot?

DH: How do you mean? Dissected?

BU: Just sort of venerated as someone who plays challenging music and has the crowd at his fingertips, and gets away with crazy things that no one else would think to do. Then again, you said you've never really used the internet, so maybe you don't see that side of it.

DH: I try not to read things. I checked a few things and I saw some haters and I got really upset and I wanted to kill them. So I decided not to read that anymore. But then I was checking out the internet to find out what flowers have a really nice scent. I like flowers in my house. So I looked on YouTube, and there was Auntie Sue flower arranging for a dinner party. This inoffensive middle-aged lady doing her thing, recommending lilies. And someone in the comments was like, "Who is this fucking bitch?!" I was like, "Poor

Auntie Sue!" It's not just me. It happens to everyone. She's doing flower arranging and they want to murder her. At that point I got over it.

Were you listening to pirate radio during your time in London, Harvey?

DH: A little bit. Definitely as a real youngster in the '70s, the pirates were very important then. I lived in the Cambridgeshire countryside, in a little village. I would tune into Radio Caroline and Radio Luxembourg, which in the evenings would play stuff that Radio 1 wouldn't. I remember the opening scene from this movie where a young boy pulls the covers over himself with his transistor radio, tuning into what would be Radio Caroline. I did exactly that at that time. It sometimes faded in and out, though.

BU: People did that with the '90s London pirates too. They'd get in their cars and drive to where you could get the best reception for the station they liked.

DH: I listened a little during the '80s. I didn't pay attention to the name of the stations, but I would tune through until I heard something I liked. I remember Kiss FM being famous.

BU: Have you ever done regular radio yourself? Presented a show?

DH: No. I enjoy guesting. I've never been in one place long enough to actually have a regular show.

You do radio every week, right Ben?

BU: Every week now, yeah. Radio has always been an important place for me to practice, regularly for two hours. I like the pressures that come with having to find new music every single week.

DH: Do you play a completely new playlist every week?

BU: More or less. I'll represent some tracks more than others, especially if I have an interest in them being heard – stuff on my label or stuff I don't think anyone else is playing. But, by and large, I try and keep the selection moving as much as I can, to keep things interesting for me. And, again, because I don't make music of my own, I think I should put the extra effort in.

Were you aware of the whole jungle/drum & bass pirate radio thing here, Harvey?

DH: It was inescapable.

Did you like it?

DH: Yeah. I love drum & bass. I rarely play something that would fall into that category, but it doesn't mean I don't like it.

Because of the tempo?

DH: Not even. It's the mood.

BU: How do you separate your personal tastes from what you choose to represent as a DJ?

DH: I don't listen to dance music at home. Or, recreationally, I don't listen to it. It's music for nightclubs and festivals and that's where I play it. At home I'll audition a record. As a DJ you have to know your records. At home, though, I listen to absolutely anything. I have a fancy hi-fidelity sound system and I enjoy listening to all sorts of different things on it. I think maybe my selection will be determined by what the gig is. If I'm playing an Ibiza sunset or Berghain, I can make choices based on that. This one will be nice at Berghain, this one will be nice at the sunset. I don't think

about which will mix with which. I don't write down BPMs. In fact, my eyes are bad so I often don't even know what the records are. It's just the blue one. Often I make up working titles if I'm given promos or CDs.

Have you ever tried Serato?

DH: No. I once tried Traktor. Someone set it up for me, saying it was just like mixing real records. But scrolling through the lists of titles... I've noticed that quite a lot of photos of DJs these days are just people staring at laptops. [*strikes pose*] That's not glamorous.

BU: Someone coined a term to describe that. It's called Serato Face.

DH: The Serato Squint.

BU: Someone said Serato Face has been replaced by Pensive USB Scroll. So as someone who's been doing it for a long time, what are your aspirations?

DH: My aspirations are to continue in the manner to which I've become accustomed. Maybe a pear farm in the South Pacific. I don't need to climb Everest or jump out of an airplane. Just the usual hedonistic things.

You're not tired of it?

DH: My knees are tired. Dancing for seven hours a night. No... there was a beautiful little moment last night playing to some old friends I've been dancing with for over 25 years. I played some old tracks that some of the younger people may not have been familiar with, and it really was like a full circle. I almost shed a tear. It was beautiful. It really makes it all worthwhile. Magic moments, they do come around. I love to moan. That's a pleasure too.

And what's your plan then?

MY ASPIRATIONS AR TO CONTINUE IN THE MANNER TO WHICH I'VE BECOMI ACCUSTOMED.

BU: I've never had a plan. I still don't have one. It's worked for me so far, so we'll see what happens.

DH: Don't fancy a harem or something?

Being a DJ is like having a harem. Or so the public believes.

DH: Yeah, it's always portrayed like that, but in reality the DJ's buddy gets all the girls because the DJ is always too busy DJing. Unless of course the lady is waiting at the very end of the night. If she's there when everybody else is gone, it's on.

EXPECTATION IS A POWERFUL THING. WHEN YOU SEE A GUITAR GET STRUMMED, YOU ANTICIPATE A CERTAIN SOUND TO EMERGE FROM THE SPEAKER. THE MUSIC OF COSEY FANNI TUTTI AND NIK VOID CONSISTENTLY TRIES TO UPEND THESE EXPECTATIONS. BOTH COME FROM AN ENGLISH ART SCHOOL BACKGROUND, AN EDUCATION THAT

Cosey Fanni Tutti's art is challenging, it raises questions and – oftentimes – you can also dance to it. As a member of industrial music pioneers

Throbbing Gristle, Cosey provided an essential vocal counterpoint to Genesis P-Orridge. Cosey also played the cornet and guitar in the group, two talents she took into her next project, Chris & Cosey – a duo with partner Chris Carter. The two released a hugely influential set of synth-heavy albums throughout the '80s and '90s, eventually renaming their project Carter Tutti at the turn of the century. In 2012, Carter and Tutti joined up with Factory Floor's Nik Void for a live show at London's Roundhouse. The results were released as an album on Mute Records.

Nik Void is the guitarist in London trio Factory Floor. Void started her music career as Nikki Colk, as part of post-punk-aping quartet KaitO. Dissatisfied with the conventional band set-up, Colk took time off after the group disbanded in the mid-'00s, and discovered a new world of music in the meantime. This eventually led Colk to adopt a new name once she took a place in Factory Floor alongside Dominic Butler and Gabriel Gurnsey. While she is the sole guitarist in the in-

dustrial-influenced group, her contributions are often as rhythmic as they are melodic. Void often uses a drumstick – or other implements – when she plays. Their first album as a trio was released this year on DFA Records.

NIK VOID AND COSEY FANNI TUTTI

MODERATOR: **TODD L. BURNS**   PHOTOGRAPHER: **ROBERTA RIDOLFI**

WAS DECIDEDLY NON-MUSICAL IN NATURE. AS A RESULT, THEIR WORK IS OFTEN AS CONCEPTUAL AS IT IS VISCERAL. WHAT MAKES THEM SO SPECIAL, THOUGH, IS THAT IT NEVER SACRIFICES ONE FOR THE OTHER. COSEY IN THROBBING GRISTLE AND CHRIS & COSEY, VOID IN FACTORY FLOOR – THEY ALWAYS LEAVE A MARK.

COSEY AND PARTNER CHRIS CARTER HAVE LIVED IN NORFOLK FOR MANY YEARS IN A CONVERTED SCHOOLHOUSE. IT WAS THERE THAT THEY PRACTICED FOR THEIR 2012 LIVE SHOW WITH VOID. ON A SWELTERING SUMMER DAY IN JULY, VOID RETURNED FOR A CONVERSATION WITH COSEY. IT WAS HELD IN THE GARDEN, WITH COSEY'S CAT DEXTER OFTEN JOINING THE TWO AT THE TABLE.

RBMA: Nik, how did you first come to Cosey's music?

Nik Void: A manager of mine pointed me in Throbbing Gristle's direction in the early '00s and I just fell in love with the whole thing. It kind of changed my way of thinking as well. It was a breath of fresh air, to be honest, because I think you find when you're surrounded by British music that it's very closed-minded in a way – and it was especially like that in the mid-'00s. It was really nice to see another band that was so progressive and had their own rules.

Cosey Fanni Tutti: Before you were introduced to TG stuff, you were just doing KaitO?

NV: Well, before that I was more into experimental guitar music. It started off with Sonic Youth, then it went to Glenn Branca and Rhys Chatham

NV: It was difficult, because it was at a point when a lot of independent labels were merging with major labels. At that time we were writing a record and we were asked to make more commercial-sounding songs. This was around the time that The Strokes and Franz Ferdinand were coming out. Guitar music was at its height. The *NME* would always talk about guitar music. It was quite strong at that time.

The *NME* seemed so happy to have guitar music back somehow.

NV: Exactly. And it was kind of the opposite of the type of guitar I like. But, at that point, I was playing guitar quite traditionally with chords and structured songs. It wasn't until I left KaitO and went on my own, and later met Factory Floor, that I started to come more into bowing and extended technique with guitar, as opposed to playing it in a traditional sense.

and noisy guitar bands. I played a lot in America as opposed to England because we had a label there, so I was influenced a lot by the US scene. It was a bit tight, coming back to the British scene. And so listening to Throbbing Gristle kind of freed me up again, if you know what I mean.

What was the stuff that was going on around the middle of the '00s that wasn't that interesting to you?

Did you learn guitar playing in school or by going to lessons?

NV: No, not at all. It was mainly listening to other sort of chart music: pop music. And then listening to American music. Noisy guitar. I've never been taught as a musician, and so it kind of has this interesting twist, because you listen to something and you think that you've picked it up correctly, but it's completely different. But you mold it into your own.

CFT: It's what you hear, isn't it? Rather than what the technique is.

NV: Yes.

CFT: It's weird, that.

You didn't have any lessons, Cosey, right?

CFT: I had piano lessons when I was 11.

Ah, right. But you've said you were immediately more interested in the John Cage, prepared piano type of thing.

CFT: Yes. I used to make really noisy low down and high up things until my father would come in, and then I had to go back to the real music that should be practiced. But that was partly my father's fault. He was totally into electronics and building wirelesses and things like that, so my ear was tuned to quite strange noises from an early age.

But he was still pushing you to do "proper" music?

CFT: Yes, because he never had the opportunity. It's one of those typical parental things, "You'll have what I never had." But I didn't want it. I was quite happy to be as I was, you know? He tended to forget that I was too much like him. I was very independent thinking and I couldn't be molded like that. I was interested in the scientific as well as the arts side of things. They sort of ran in parallel for me right through my childhood. I wasn't torn between the two. They always mixed quite easily.

NV: It's like an investigative approach to things. Is it more that you wanted to see what things did?

CFT: Yeah, I said to Chris [Carter] the other day that we – me and my sister – got Cinderella watches for Christmas one year and I took mine apart to see how it worked. Then I couldn't get it back together again. So that was it, the end of my Cinderella watch. But yeah, it was that kind of curiosity.

How old were you when KaitO started, Nik?

NV: 19. I think I was at art school already.

What were you going to art school to study?

NV: I knew I wanted to do art very early on, but I didn't know what direction I wanted to take it. At Art School I did a Visual Studies degree, which was a brand new course at the time. The tutors were still finding their feet with it all, so as a student this gave me a lot of freedom. I was kind of left to my own devices. I was left alone to experiment and source materials from outside the institution. It was more about conceptual art, and bringing my concepts into practice. Bridging the gap between an idea in my head, then presenting it to the public or an audience within an exhibition space successfully. At the same time I was in school I was working in factories to pay my way through college and get a car. I re-

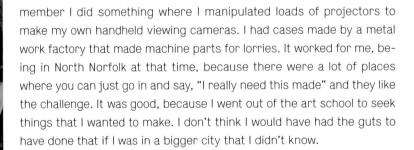

> BUT THAT WAS PARTLY MY FATHER'S FAULT. HE WAS TOTALLY INTO ELECTRONICS AND BUILDING WIRELESSES AND THINGS LIKE THAT, SO MY EAR WAS TUNED TO QUITE STRANGE NOISES FROM AN EARLY AGE.

member I did something where I manipulated loads of projectors to make my own handheld viewing cameras. I had cases made by a metal work factory that made machine parts for lorries. It worked for me, being in North Norfolk at that time, because there were a lot of places where you can just go in and say, "I really need this made" and they like the challenge. It was good, because I went out of the art school to seek things that I wanted to make. I don't think I would have had the guts to have done that if I was in a bigger city that I didn't know.

CFT: That's weird because when I was younger I had a similar kind of thing in Hull. You recognize all the different industries around you, and the small businesses that can actually be utilized to get you what you need. We used to go to a ship chandler and get flags made. They were really up for it because it was something different for them to do. There are so many opportunities like that in smaller towns. It wasn't one of my fears but... I was uneasy about moving to London because I had a really good source of places I could go and get things, you know?

NV: When I moved to London I started working as a sculptor technician, and saw it from the other point of view, where you have these massive British artists that have people working for them to make their vision. I didn't do a very good job of it, I must admit. It lasted a year.

CFT: I always found that side of the art world really weird. That you just come up with an idea and get it made. It's very bizarre.

NV: That's because the best part of art or music is the making of it.

CFT: Exactly. The whole process you have to go through, you learn so much. You go off on a tangent and it creates other ideas immediately. I think the first time I ever saw that type of artist-as-manager thing was with [Op artist] Bridget Riley. She'd do the drafts, and they were lovely because they were ideas in the making. All the really rough ideas coming through. I could understand it in a way, because the idea is already there and visualized. But, even so, I would have liked to have done it myself.

With that particular type of art it almost seems like cheating in a way. Because when you look at it, you can't help but think about the amount of work that must have gone into it.

to an engineer what you're actually trying to achieve with the sound is difficult. And, also, you miss out on the creative accidents. It's kind of the main reason for doing it, even though it took two years.

That's the trade off, right? You can do it yourself, but then it takes an enormous amount of time.

NV: Exactly. When you have your own studio you can spend so much time analyzing it. To the point where you don't hear it anymore. My room was positioned right above the studio, and Gabe is completely deaf so he'd be working on stuff until 11 PM or whatever and you kind of start... It got to a point of resenting it a little bit, I must admit.

You resented your own album?

WHEN YOU HAVE YOUR OWN STUDIO YOU CAN SPEND SO MUCH TIME ANALYZING IT. TO THE POINT WHERE YOU DON'T HEAR IT ANYMORE.

WE MIXED WITH A LOT OF HELLS ANGELS AND SKINHEADS, SO WE WERE ALWAYS THE OUTSIDERS IN THAT TOWN. STRANGE PEOPLE IN HULL.

NV: Yeah.

CFT: A murder on the Factory Floor dancefloor. [laughs]

I'm shocked that you have this big space in London.

NV: It was really lucky. I'm not sure how much longer it's going to last, to be honest, because there is a lot of demolition going on right around it. It's the only original building standing on the whole street. So that's the reason why the landlords haven't had the urge to throw us out. They've always known that it's going to be pulled down soon.

CFT: But historically, you think of all the old masters, and they would get the best apprentice at skies to do the skies for them. The best apprentice for hands would do the hands. So how much of it is theirs? It's traditional. I think that's why I've always steered clear from that. I've never understood it. I felt cheated that I thought this person had done this wonderful painting and, in actual fact, he wasn't so good at hands.

NV: I think that's kind of why when we came to record the first Factory Floor album that we wanted to do it ourselves. To try and explain

Cosey, I was curious earlier when you said that you were almost nervous or uneasy to go to London.

CFT: I wanted to go. I wasn't sad at leaving family or friends because we kind of outstayed our welcome in Hull. The police were already on our

backs. Every time we did any kind of event they'd try to find something illegal that we were doing. We mixed with a lot of Hells Angels and skinheads, so we were always the outsiders in that town. Strange people in Hull. They don't like outsiders, so they always make your life very difficult. So we moved to London.

NV: I remember I made the decision to move within a weekend, and just literally packed up my things and slept on people's sofas for about six months until I found a job. I guess I was just a little bit desperate for a change. I started recording on my own, because I'd also had enough of playing on stage. I hated that kind of band-as-entertainment thing. I still really enjoyed making music and the recording process, so I spent about three years doing that and, at the same time, I was meeting a bunch of new people like Gabe and Dom.

> THEY WERE PLAYING IN A REALLY SMALL ROOM IN EAST LONDON, AND IT WAS SO SHAMBOLIC. EVERYTHING THEY SEEMED TO DO WAS QUITE AWKWARD.

The Factory Floor live show is definitely not a "look at us, this is entertainment" type of thing.

NV: Absolutely not. I saw Factory Floor play and re-

lated to how they were doing it. They were playing in a really small room in East London, and it was so shambolic. Everything they seemed to do was quite awkward. They didn't look at each other, and I think one was playing a different speed to the other. But the sound... it was confident. It was almost like the nervousness was making them bash out a sound. I couldn't really figure out whether they had any songs as such, and I think their set only lasted for about 15 minutes.

How long were your first shows, Cosey?

CFT: Always an hour. We worked with a clock because we used to do a lot of jam sessions in the factory and we figured that an hour was just right. We'd do a set list that allowed us to sort of warm up and gave us the freedom to really get into something if it took off, and then come out of it and go into something else. So we'd have a freeform section, a cornet section.

Is that similar to how the Factory Floor live show has evolved?

NV: Yes. When I first saw them play live I couldn't recognize songs, but when I listened to their recordings there were definite songs, you know? When we started to play together it evolved into something else. We all consciously discarded the past a little bit. Dom was growing his modular synthesizer. Because of that Gabe had to change his role in the band. He wasn't the timekeeper anymore. We're still discovering what we're doing. I mean, we haven't rehearsed for a long time. We tend to not rehearse anymore. We tend to do it onstage.

> WE'RE STILL DISCOVERING WHAT WE'RE DOING. I MEAN, WE HAVEN'T REHEARSED FOR A LONG TIME. WE TEND TO NOT REHEARSE ANYMORE. WE TEND TO DO IT ON STAGE.

Did you find the roles shifting over the years in Throbbing Gristle?

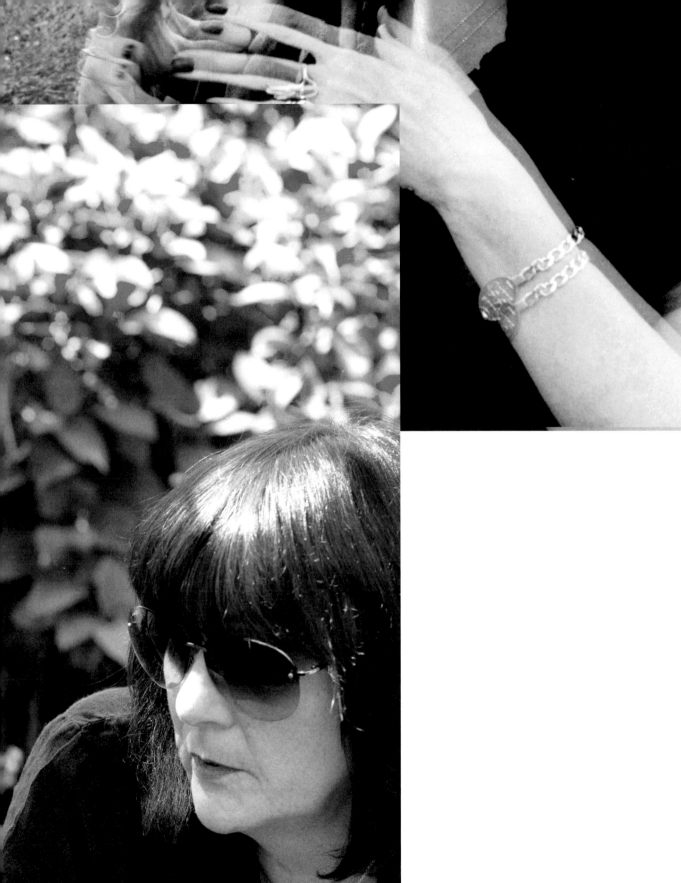

CFT: Sleazy and Gen were the ones that were quite happy with what they did. They didn't really want to shift what they did much at all. Sleazy was quite open to doing all kinds of stuff the second time around because he'd gone through Coil. With TG the first time around we swapped instruments a lot in the beginning and basically figured out what each one of us was really good at and how it worked well together. It was whatever gave us the sound we wanted. It didn't matter where it came from.

NV: I read that you sometimes wouldn't know who was making what sound sometimes after you played.

CFT: Me and Sleazy, this time around, would be looking at each other and we'd be going, "You or me?" And then I'd take my hands off my Mac and he'd go, "Oh, it was you. OK. That's nice." And then the next gig he'd do a sound that sounded like the one I did before because he liked it so much. Or he'd start doing sounds that mimicked my guitar when I was playing. Then I'd sort of shift, and he'd take over my guitar role. Which was quite a nice thing to do. One person starts a sound and then another one picks up on it and starts moving along with it. It pisses you off at first, though, because you think, "That's my sound. Do you mind?" But then you think, "Right, I can move on now. He can do that." Sleazy, in particular, used to sort of look down on guitars, but he didn't mind nicking the sounds.

drum-like. You can see Gabe thinking, "Oh… what am I supposed to do with that? How am I supposed to fit in with that space?"

CFT: That's the thing. When people start filling the spaces up and don't leave room for you to come in… That's weird. You start thinking, "Hang on a minute, are you playing with me or do you just want to play with yourself?" And guys tend to do that more than girls.

NV: Definitely. That's why I think we've decided to go off and do our own side projects. When we do our own thing we think, "Oh… I really miss the other two." What was the point where you and Chris moved to do stuff by yourselves?

CFT: TG were in Los Angeles to do some shows and although it wasn't public, we had already split. Me and Chris were recording Heartbeat when we were there. The shows were weird, but the San Francisco one was great. The animosity gave it an energy. I felt that I'd levitated about three foot off the floor that night. It was so powerful and weird. Because all our energies were conflicting and, yet, they were coming together at the same time. It was quite amazing really.

NV: Sometimes it makes the best shows.

CFT: That's the weird thing though, isn't it? When you've got a conflict within a band it does create some kind of weird energy that is really fantastic. I mean, even if you take it back to ABBA. When they were all split as couples, they did some of their best singles.

NV: Fleetwood Mac.

CFT: It's hell for the band, but it's great for the music and the fans.

ONE PERSON STARTS A SOUND AND THEN ANOTHER ONE PICKS UP ON IT AND STARTS MOVING ALONG WITH IT.

You mentioned that boys tend to try to fill the spaces of the music more than girls. What are the other differences that you've noticed?

I think it's very rare that you get a group of people who are all willing to shift their roles so easily.

CFT: Well, having your role usurped is a dodgy area. If Dom got a drum kit out and started drumming, how would Gabe feel?

NV: It does happen, because a lot of the modular stuff that he has does sounds very

CFT: Just on that "fill the spaces" thing…. If you're ever on the Tube, a guy will sit like you're sitting there, Todd. Not only displaying everything, but also a posture of like, "This is mine." That space-filling is what they do when you play with them as well. I find that anyway. Even Sleazy – a quiet gay guy – would always come thundering in during a quiet bit. And then he'd go, "Oops."

NV: I think that's what was happening with Factory Floor before I joined. All of them wanting to fill the space.

CFT: All posturing and…

NV: A "this is my territory" type of thing.

CFT: It's an innate thing. They can't help it.

NV: When I joined it kind of changed that dynamic. We started to understand that you can make your own rules and you can play together nicely.

CFT: His focus has always been the complete sound. His role was actually to give us something to play along with. He always created the rhythms for TG, and still does that with Carter Tutti and Chris & Cosey stuff. He's got no ego. That has a lot to do with it. It's human nature to have people that want to lead and people that want to follow.

> THAT'S THE GREAT THING ABOUT HAVING A DRUMSTICK ON A GUITAR. IT'S JUST LIKE... "WAKE UP!"

CFT: And you have techniques to counter what's building up. You know it's inevitable, so you just blast the idea of that out the window, which I've had to do in TG loads of times.

How have you done it?

CFT: I always keep my guitar low at sound check, because I know that the others are going to come in loud. So, when I do the gig I've got some headspace, you know? Someone often finds a really good place and a really good sound and everyone works off it. It's

> WHEN YOU DANCE TO MUSIC YOU'RE ALMOST HUNTING FOR COUNTER-RHYTHMS. NOT LIKE THE RAVE CULTURE, WHICH IS BASED ON DRUG-INDUCED BANG, BANG, BANG. WHEN YOU DANCE NATURALLY YOU GET ALL KINDS OF WEIRD THINGS GOING ON WITH YOUR BODY, WHICH REALLY MANIFESTS FROM THE SOUND AS COUNTER-RHYTHMS.

fantastic and you have to allow that, but you also have to recognize the point at which that becomes self-indulgent and it doesn't do anything for the overall piece that you're all supposed to be working together on.

NV: Yeah. Dom is terrible for that. He'll go on and on and with his head down.

CFT: They get locked in.

NV: Yeah, you're totally unaware that there are other people playing. That's the great thing about having a drumstick on a guitar. It's just like... "Wake up!"

CFT: I always said, way back in the '70s, that I should get a little metal wristband so that I could deliver shocks now and again.

So has Chris learned to play... I hate to put it in binary terms, but does he play in a less masculine style than most people, would you say?

NV: Gabe and Dom definitely want to lead. I just secretly lead.

CFT: That's the trait of women, isn't it?

I think it's very rare – whether you're a man or a woman – to be able to conceptualize the whole when you're in a band. To do your own thing, but also think about everything else.

CFT: Chris has a very good ear for tuning and timing. It's almost robotic, really. I leave a lot of that in his hands. But, having said that, he will then get locked into a thing, and it's hard to pull him out. I don't like everything *that* quantized. Every now and again, I like things to flow out. A bit of fluidity, if you'd like. So I guess that's my role. I say, "I think that rhythm has gone on long enough. We need to change it. We need to counter it." When I listen to our music I think of dancing because I used to be a dancer. When you dance to music you're almost hunting for counter-rhythms. Not like the rave culture, which is based on drug-induced bang, bang, bang. When you dance naturally you get all kinds of weird things going on with your body, which really manifest from the sound as counter-rhythms. Or the melody creates another kind of dance movement. I'm always wanting to shift our music along. I can't dance or even listen to music that's just the same all the way through. It just drives me nuts. I just think, "I'm not brain dead," you know? Give me something to work with here. I'm a human being. That's strange coming from a founder of industrial music, isn't it? But there you go.

NV: Did you ever dance to your own music?

CFT: I did once. I danced to "*United*," but that was just to please Gen because he came to the pub and he was just miserable. The nearest I got to dancing to any music I liked listening to was Pere Ubu and Captain Beefheart's "Hard Working Man." Alternative TV's "Love Lies Limp" too. That one seemed quite appropriate to stripping.

> I THINK THE BEST SHOW THAT WE PLAYED WAS THIS BLACKOUT SHOW WHERE WE WERE BEHIND A CURTAIN AND THE AUDIENCE WERE BROUGHT INTO A DARK ROOM, NO LIGHTS AT ALL. THEY DIDN'T EVEN KNOW WHO WAS PLAYING BEHIND THE CURTAIN.

There was a Sylvester tune that was on a playlist I once saw as well. You were also in the video for "You Make Me Feel (Mighty Real)", right?

CFT: I've still got those white satin shorts upstairs. What was interesting about that video shoot – speaking about keeping things fluid – they'd gone to Pineapple Dance Studios and got some dancers in. And then they'd come to my agency, which is a stripping agency, and got girls from there. They ended up using the girls from the stripping agency, because they danced instinctively to the music. We were looking at the girls from Pineapple, and they were going, "Two, three, four and turn."

And I'm thinking, "This is disco music!" It's not *Riverdance*. It was interesting. And, of course, you had all the boys as well. We corrupted all the young boy waiters. In fact, those shorts were the boy waiter shorts. Yeah, it was good fun.

NV: I think that's the key though, isn't it? Instinct. Factory Floor is sort of driven by instinct a lot more than anything else, really. That's why some of our tracks go on for a long time. I can totally get what you're saying about, "Can you dance to it?"

CFT: You don't even have to call it dance, because you can move internally to it as well. It can become a cerebral thing, which it often is when we

> I REMEMBER WE ONCE PLAYED A GIG WITH MIRRORS SO THAT ALL THE AUDIENCE COULD SEE WAS THEMSELVES. THEY DIDN'T LIKE THAT.

do music that takes you to a different plane completely. You wonder where the hell you've been. It's that almost trance-inducing thing. Quite often when you're playing that kind of music and you repeat things, you find new levels quite naturally. They move along with, for want of a better word, the vibe of the audience when you're playing it. That has a huge amount to do with what you do live. You either punish them because you're pissed off with them or you have a really good time because you know they're with you. It's sometimes almost like they're up there playing with you. It's fantastic.

NV: You know when it's locking into place on stage, especially when it is driven by instinct and you're kind of semi-improvising. You also know when it sort of falls apart. When that happens we almost feel a little bit embarrassed to be up there. We feel like we've lost all of our clothes or something. I think the best show that we played was this blackout show where we were behind a curtain and the audience were brought into a dark room, no lights at all. They didn't even know who was playing behind the curtain. We couldn't see them, and so we just started playing. Eventually we could feel people moving around from the air that was made from the curtains just moving slowly. You completely lost all the self-consciousness of being on stage. And also you just thought, "What the hell is going on out there?"

CFT: It gets a strange effect from the audience. I remember we once played a gig with mirrors so that all the audience could see was themselves. They didn't like that. I think they take offense at the fact that you're manipulating them. But we'd go on with the opinion that, right, we're here to deliver something and share something with you tonight. Come along with us for the ride.

COSEY FANNI TUTTI

YOU EITHER PUNISH THEM
BECAUSE YOU'RE PISSED
OFF WITH THEM OR YOU
HAVE A REALLY GOOD TIME
BECAUSE YOU KNOW THEY'RE
WITH YOU. IT'S SOMETIMES
ALMOST LIKE THEY'RE UP
THERE PLAYING WITH YOU.
IT'S FANTASTIC.

MODESELEKTOR AND MYKKI BLAI
VED OUT A UNIQUE SPACE FOR TH
QUITE FIT ANY PARTICULAR GEN
AND 5OWEAPONS — TWO LABELS
THEIR VARIED INTER TS. MYKKI
DRESSING RAPPER THAT TRANS
CAREER PERFORMING MUSIC AR
ABSOLUTELY NATURAL THAT MO
PLAY AT THEIR STAGE AT THE 20
IN BERLIN AT MODESELEKTOR'S
FLOWN TO THE CITY THAT MORNI
THE EARLY EVENING. MODESELEK
AT 3:30 AM. BY THE TIME THEY T
READY LEFT FOR BELGIUM. HE W
VAL, AN EVENT THAT MODESELEK

MICHAEL DAVID QUATTLEBAUM JR. WAS BORN TO BE A STAR. BEFORE TAKING ON THE PURPOSEFULLY ANDROGYNOUS (AND LIL' KIM REFERENCING) NOM DE PLUME **MYKKI BLANCO**, QUATTLEBAUM GOT INTO ACTING AND EXPERIMENTAL THEATRE AT AN EARLY AGE. ESCAPING SUBURBIA, HE FLED TO NEW YORK CITY, AGED 16. AFTER BRIEF EXCURSIONS INTO ACADEMIA, MYKKI BLANCO CAME INTO EXISTENCE IN 2010 AS PART OF A VIDEO PROJECT. DISCOVERING HIS GIFTS AS A SHAPESHIFTING RAP ARTIST, MYKKI QUICKLY BEGAN TO WORK WITH UNDERGROUND BASS MUSIC PRODUCERS SINDEN, MATRIXMANN AND RED BULL MUSIC ACADEMY GRAD BRENMAR, AND CHIPPING AWAY AT GENDER CONSTRUCTIONS VIA RELEASES LIKE *COSMIC ANGEL: THE ILLUMINATI PRINCE/SS AND BETTY RUBBLE: THE INITIATION.*

CO ARE MISFITS THAT HAVE CAR-
MSELVES. MODESELEKTOR NEVER
E, SO THEY MADE MONKEYTOWN
THAT ACT AS A SHOWCASE FOR
LANCO, MEANWHILE, IS A CROSS-
RMED AN ART PROJECT INTO A
UND THE WORLD. SO IT SEEMED
ESELEKTOR BOOKED BLANCO TO
B MELT! FESTIVAL. THE TRIO MET
UDIO ON JULY 19, BOTH HAVING

BERLIN'S **GERNOT BRONSERT** AND **SEBASTIAN SZARY**, BETTER KNOWN
COLLECTIVELY AS MODESELEKTOR, ARE RENOWNED FOR THEIR DISDAIN
FOR GENRE BOUNDARIES, AND THEIR ZANY, SONICALLY EXPERIMENTAL PRO-
DUCTIONS, WHICH SOUND LIKE SEVERAL DECADES OF ELECTRONIC MUSIC
FED THROUGH A BLENDER. THEIR SERIES OF COMICALLY NAMED ALBUMS ON
ELLEN ALLIEN'S BPITCH CONTROL WON THEM CRITICAL ACCLAIM, AND LED
THEM TO FORM THEIR OWN IMPRINTS, MONKEYTOWN AND 50 WEAPONS,
WHERE THEY'VE RESIDED EVER SINCE. OVER THE COURSE OF THEIR CARE-
ER, THEY'VE BEEN SERIAL COLLABORATORS, WORKING WITH RADIOHEAD'S
THOM YORKE, FRENCH RAP GROUP TTC AND, PERHAPS MOST NOTABLY,
WITH FELLOW BERLIN MUSICIAN APPARAT UNDER THE NAME MODERAT.

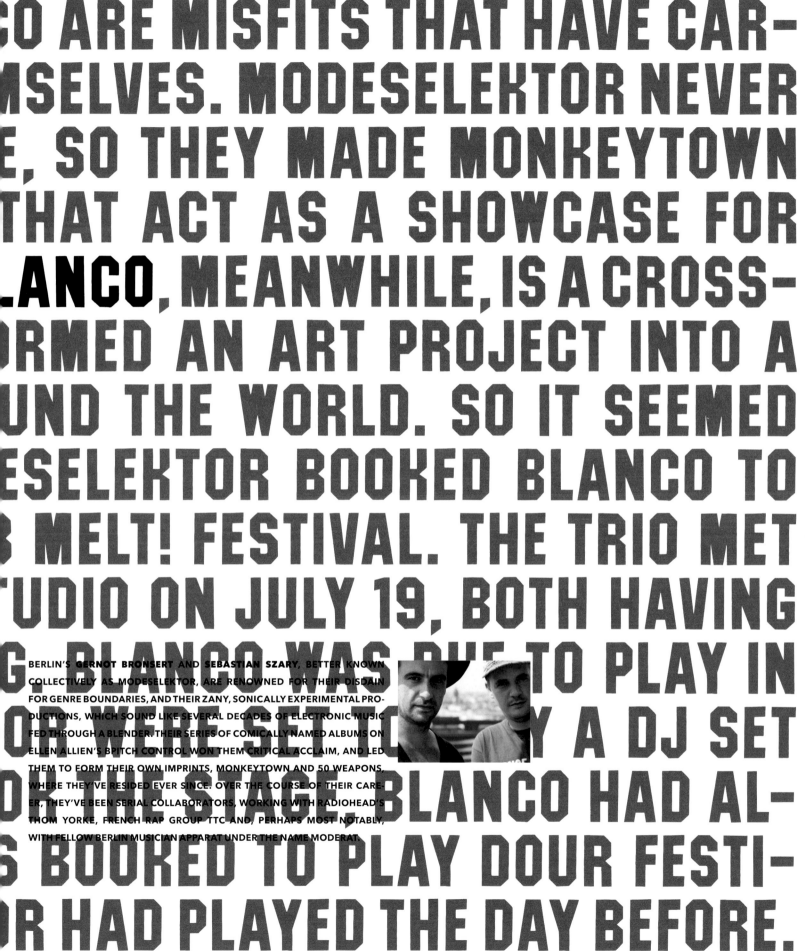

G BLANCO WAS DUE TO PLAY IN
OR WERE SET TO Y A DJ SET
H THE STAGE, BLANCO HAD AL-
BOOKED TO PLAY DOUR FESTI-
R HAD PLAYED THE DAY BEFORE.

RBMA: Do you have a stage day routine?

Mykki Blanco: My stage day routine definitely includes drinking tons of water. I try to keep the energy around me really positive. I try to take vitamins, stay really limber. This is really interesting for me, because I've been on tour for six months but I've only had a musical career for a year-and-a-half.

Gernot Bronsert: We've toured constantly for 15 years.

MB: Really?

Sebastian Szary: Our music career started with touring, and then later we started making records.

GB: We met at primary school. We're both from the east side of Berlin, but in the outskirts; kind of fancy. It's a lot of lakes and woods. After the Wall came down, all these underground raves popped up everywhere. It was really a strange time. I was – I don't know, 12 or 13 – and Szary is two or three years older. He was the local hero DJ, and I was the little raver and then we took ecstasy and danced. Since then...

SS: I think it was a typical '90s rave thing. Everybody did that.

MB: Rave culture really came back around in America in like 2010. That was the first time that a large amount of the black community took ecstasy for the first time. The last three years have been really crazy in black American culture. We called it the Winter of Love in New York. This huge influx of ecstasy came into the city and it changed everything.

GB: We had a similar kind of thing going on. In the early '90s you had the right-wing people, the assholes, the skinheads; and then you had the punks and skaters and hip hoppers and techno guys. In the mid-'90s techno got more and more popular and all these right-wing people started taking ecstasy. That totally changed the whole game. They were still weird, but they weren't aggressive anymore.

Mykki, I remember ecstasy references in Eminem songs and so on. How much of that did you pick up as a consumer?

MB: I picked up on it. I think everyone did. But the difference is that it was a white rapper talking about it. Just in the last two years, you now have so many rappers talking about molly: rapping about ecstasy.

GB: When we grew up, the hip hop camp didn't take ecstasy. It was a pure techno drug. The first time when I realized the American hip hop was starting to take ecstasy was earlier than 2010. It was in 2007, 2008 –

MB: In the Bay Area?

GB: Yes, hyphy. We did a white tee party in San Francisco once. You know, there's the song, the hyphy anthem – "got my white tee and my stunners on." The guys who put the party on bought like 200 shirts and they printed a hyphy Modeselektor monkey logo on it. It was so fun. Hyphy, for me, was the first time I discovered independent hip hop from the US which I really liked. Here in Germany you mostly get the mainstream shit.

AFTER THE WALL CAME DOWN, POPPED UP EVERYWHERE. IT WA HE WAS THE LOCAL HERO DJ, THEN WE TOOK ECSTASY AND D

WE CALLED IT THE WINTER OF LOV OF ECSTASY CAME INTO THE CI

A LOT OF THE TIME I WORK WITH JUST HAVE THEM SLOW DOWN TH OMINOUS AND DARK ABOUT CEF RAP OVER SLOWER TEMPOS BECA SO IT GIVES ME ROOM TO DO WI

L THESE UNDERGROUND RAVES EALLY A STRANGE TIME ... I WAS THE LITTLE RAVER AND ED.

N NEW YORK. THIS HUGE INFLUX ND IT CHANGED EVERYTHING.

TECHNO PRODUCER, AND THEN I EAT. THERE'S SOMETHING QUITE IN ELECTRONIC BEATS. I LIKE TO E I'M A REALLY WORDY RAPPER, EVER I WANT.

MB: But I feel like in Europe, "underground rappers" have larger followings.

GB: Guys like Busdriver for example. He isn't that big in the US, but he plays big shows in Paris.

SS: I think most of his records are released on a British label, Ninja Tune and Big Dada, so that may be a reason.

GB: Where do you release your records?

MB: Independently, with a label called UNO NYC. The guy who runs it is also my manager. He's released some other stuff, like Arca and my friend Gobby who's a really good new techno producer. That's been interesting for me. I haven't really worked with a lot of hip hop producers. A lot of the time I work with a techno producer, and then I just have them slow down the beat. There's something quite ominous and dark about certain electronic beats. I like to rap over slower tempos because I'm a really wordy rapper, so it gives me room to do whatever I want.

GB: What BPM do you like?

MB: I don't know anything about BPMs. There's this disconnect. I'm a writer/performer. I like loud music, but I don't know music like a *musician* knows music. I call myself a big "responder." If I hear a rhythm and I respond to it, I can immediately start to write to it. But yeah, I don't know BPMs and stuff.

In that sense, when you are in the studio, to which degree do you feel it's a performance when you record something?

MB: Oh, totally. I was a kid actor so I approach everything super theatrically. When I hear the beat and it's rockin', I'm like "OK, this is fucking jamming." I just completely get into it. I get into the whole aesthetic of what that beat says and that dictates my writing. I may have pre-written lines that I could throw in, but there's like a fresh shell that I definitely will try to respond to, because that's what makes it organic. When people try to send me beats over the internet that doesn't really work most of the time. I need that organic connection between myself and the other person.

You obviously need to channel something that's actually happening and coming from outside of you, whereas Modeselektor always have some sort of an interface. With the voice, there's no hiding. When you program the 909, God knows what mood you're in. There's definitely a layer in between.

MB: That's the mystery of producing to me. Whenever I've produced anything it's just been super lo-fi. It's just me fucking around on my computer and making noise-oriented stuff. But that actual skill and magical thing that happens when someone thinks of a beat? I have no idea what that is like. I have no idea what it's like to put that energy into a machine.

GB: It's interesting because a lot of rappers or singers cannot be in a room with the producer. They need just a loop or a beat and need to be alone. We recorded an album with a friend, Apparat,

"OH, IT'S NOT LOUD ENOUGH
YOU NEED TO SING LOUDER."
AND THEN WE MADE HIM
PISSED OFF, AND WHEN HE
WAS REALLY ANGRY HE WOULD
SING LOUD.

I CAN'T WORK WITH ANGER.
ANGER FOR ME IS SUCH A
DIFFERENT THING, SEPARATE
FROM CREATIVITY.

and he's not able to sing in the room with us. He always took the session on a USB stick and put it on a little computer in the other room next door. That's why we covered the glass window.

And how do you then transform that segregation into the moment when it comes back

was really angry he would sing loud.

MB: I can't work with anger. Anger for me is such a different thing, separate from creativity. If I get angry the sessions starts to –

But you've been doing punk stuff as well, right?

the hardships that I've gone through. I'm unapologetic about them, but I'm not political.

GB: I think politics and music is a bad mix.

MB: I think it's OK to talk about things and to stand up for things. I grew up listening to a lot of po-

already a political statement. Nevertheless you're using vocals a lot as well, and you have a lot of fun with trying different voice settings, Szary.

SS: It's like putting a mask on. We are not vocal performers. We play techno tracks, hip hop tracks, beats on stage, but when

IT'S LIKE PUTTING A MASK ON. WE ARE NOT VOCAL PERFORMERS. WE PLAY TECHNO TRACKS, HIP HOP TRACKS, BEATS ON STAGE, BUT WHEN WE SAY SOMETHING TO THE CROWD WE SAY IT NOT WITH OUR NATURAL VOICE. WE SEND OUR VOICE THROUGH PITCH-SHIFTING THING THAT MAKES IT FUNNIER.

WHEN I GRAB THE MICROPHONE YOU ALWAYS PITCH MY VOICE UP. WE DON'T SPEND TOO MUCH TIME THINKING WHILE DOING MUSIC OR WHILE PERFORMING.

together: when you perform it together?

GB: It's a different situation, because you don't need to be creative anymore. Sometimes he came back with the vocals and we said, "Oh, it's not loud enough, you need to sing louder." And then we made him pissed off, and when he

MB: Yeah, but that's a different kind of anger. That's not being pissed off with the producer you're working with. That's being pissed off with society or being pissed off with being called a faggot.

GB: Are you political?

MB: I'm political because of

litical feminist music. The ideas I got from that music – and the things that came through – may have been unattractive to people, but they were really strong ideas that I think helped a lot of kids out.

You can always argue that by saying, "we want to keep music and politics separate," it's

we say something to the crowd we say it not with our natural voice. We send our voice through a pitch-shifting thing that makes it funnier.

GB: When I grab the microphone you always pitch my voice up. We don't spend too much time thinking while doing music or while performing. When we are on stage, though, we also have rituals. An hour before the show starts I get super nasty, really in a bad mood. I'm so nervous. This is something I've never been able to get rid of. It's horrible. For example, I

that anymore. I've been touring now for six months, and it doesn't matter how much sleep I get or if I haven't eaten. I did a show in January in Finland where I literally got off the plane from America and then did the

who see him perform – they have a totally different idea of him. But in real life, it's the opposite, the other side of the ocean.

SS: You are very concentrated on stage.

MB: It's kind of interesting, because I've had to come full circle with this search for authenticity on stage. Everything started as a video art project: this really artsy, interdisciplinary thing. Then I realized that if I didn't put my

VE ALWAYS WANTED TO BE IN FRONT OF EOPLE. THE TIMES THAT I'VE FUCKED UP N STAGE WERE WHEN SOMEONE GAVE ME RUGS, BUT I DON'T DO THAT ANYMORE.

DJ tonight at 8 PM, so I know at 7 PM I'm going to become another guy. I can't talk to people. I need my silence. And then – you can set your watch – ten minutes before the show, it's gone. This hour is actually the part where I earn my money. The show is fun, the show is something I really enjoy, but before it is horrible.

SS: The best thing you can do is to sleep an hour before the show on a couch in the backstage or in a hotel. So 15 minutes before the show you wake up and you know there's no way back.

GB: That's why we like touring with a bus. You can hide yourself in a little bunker.

MB: I think when I started this spring tour it'll be the first time we get a big van. It takes a certain kind of show for me to get nervous, because – like I said – I was a child actor. I've always wanted to be in front of people. The times that I've fucked up on stage were when someone gave me drugs, but I don't do

show two hours later. There's this thing that clicks on when I get on stage. No matter what, it's on. I knew that, starting this career. Since I wasn't on a major label, I didn't have any money – *any money!* – when I first started, so I knew that if I want to impress people, I have to be all of it. I have to be the lights, I have to be the sound system, I have to be the dancers. I think that's what made me such a strong performer. If there's anything I will say about myself, I am a damn good performer, because I've had to be everything before anyone thought anything about me.

Szary, to what extent do you consider yourself an entertainer?

SS: Me? As you can see I'm a very quiet guy. When we play, there's that switch before the show we were talking about five minutes ago.

GB: He turns into something different. The fans, all the people

GB: Yeah, I need to get focused. I wouldn't call it stage fright, but it's my body. I cannot do anything against it.

It's adrenaline in the end.

GB: Yeah, it's too much. When I'm not on tour, when we have a holiday, I get sick within 24 hours because I don't have the adrenaline any more. I started running just because of this. Just to keep the level high. When you play every week your body gets used to it. It's like a drug. I never get sick when I work 24 hours a day, seven days a week. As soon as I stop... Mykki, I was wondering, do you change outfits while you're performing?

MB: Yeah. Lately I've been wearing boxing shorts underneath a big ballgown skirt, and then I take off the skirt and I have these pasties – I glue little nipple tassels.

SS: A few years ago I started wearing jumpsuits, overalls, classic military things, because it's nice as a tour outfit. It's just one piece.

own personality into what I was doing, then I would literally just become a slave to a character. I'm someone who really likes my personal freedom and I don't like being told what to do, so it's been interesting navigating it.

GB: I mean, I think it's real shit. You are honest. You see that from the first moment.

In this marketplace, it sometimes seems like you can only sell yourself to an audience by submitting to one imaginary image. You, Mykki, go, "Fuck it, today I want to be all sporty, tomorrow I'm going to be all Liberace and the day after that it's going to be like this, and two hours later it's going to be that." But the truth is, all these various traits are part of a complete human being.

MB: A musician named Ssion – someone who I have a lot of respect for because he's been touring the States for over ten years, someone that has put a lot into their stage show – once

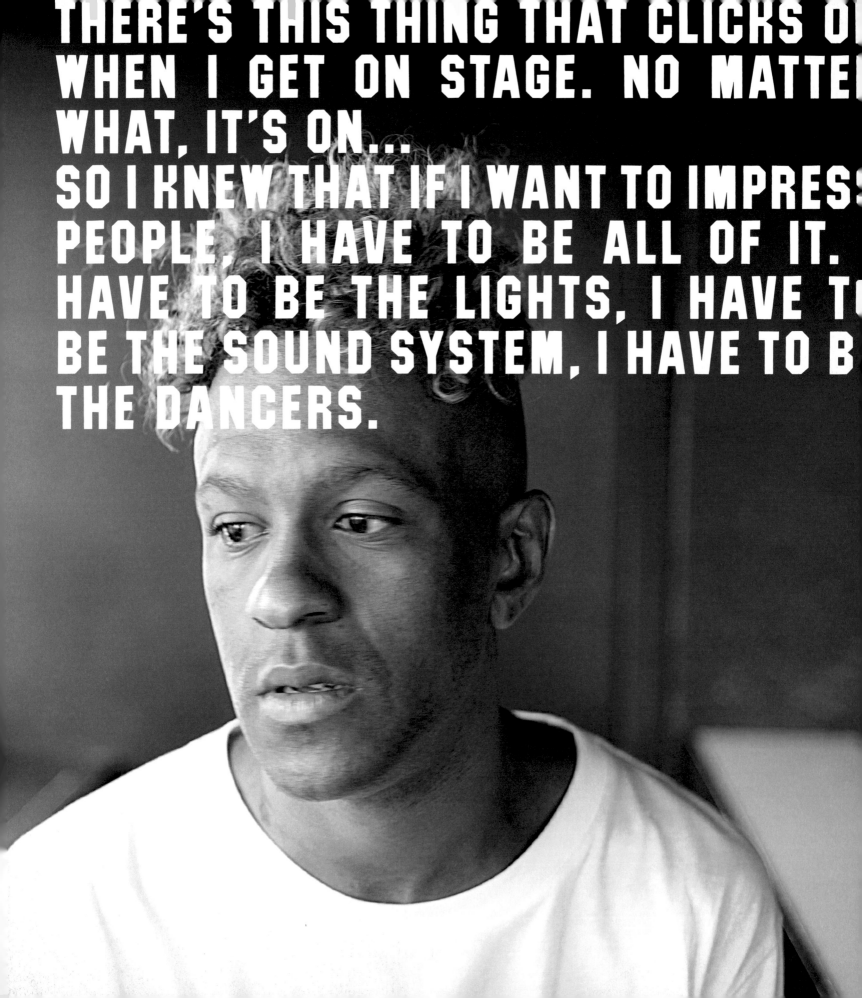

THERE'S THIS THING THAT CLICKS O
WHEN I GET ON STAGE. NO MATTE
WHAT, IT'S ON...
SO I KNEW THAT IF I WANT TO IMPRES
PEOPLE, I HAVE TO BE ALL OF IT.
HAVE TO BE THE LIGHTS, I HAVE T
BE THE SOUND SYSTEM, I HAVE TO B
THE DANCERS.

FOR ME, WHEN I WAS LIKE 14, 15, 16, I DIDN'T EVEN KNOW TECHNO COULD BE FUN.

WHEN I WAS 14 OR 15 I DANCED FOR MORE THAN EIGHT HOURS FOR THE FIRST TIME. NO TALKING, JUST DANCING TO MUSIC. THIS EXPERIENCE CHANGED MY ENTIRE LIFE.

told me, "It won't be easy, but *you* tell people what to like about you." He said, "Do not let other people try to tell you, or shape you, into what *they* want." And I've seen that already happen, so that's why I always say this: "Just like I would never be any less flamboyant or tone anything down about what I do for the heterosexual community, I also would never be a gay political dress-up doll."

GB: You're punk. That's what we call punk.

MB: You know what I mean? I was going to ask you guys if you've ever gotten shit. From what I've experienced, there can be a certain kind of very "nose in the air" thing about how electronic musicians view other electronic musicians.

GB: We're not like this. We always make jokes. We never took this whole thing too seriously.

SS: From the beginning.

GB: There are a lot of very "important" DJs in this world and very "important" producers of course. We always made jokes about it. This is how we grew up in Berlin. Berlin was so different compared to now, it's something you cannot imagine. It was really dirty and fucked up. There was no money.

MB: So as you've been making music, you guys haven't had to deal with techno snobs?

GB: No, we come from the other side. We come from the punk shit side.

But humor was not always present in that side of the culture. **And you definitely injected a healthy dose of that into it.**

GB: No, no, they took it very seriously.

I'm sure not everyone loved it.

GB: No, they hated us –

MB: I didn't know that techno could be fun!

GB: And then we got big and they couldn't...

MB: That's what I'm saying. For me, when I was like 14, 15, 16, I didn't even know techno could be fun. I didn't start liking techno until I was in my 20s, because it always seemed like this "nose up in the air" music.

GB: But the experiences we had played a part. When I was 14 or 15 I danced for more than eight hours for the first time. No talking, just dancing to music. This experience changed my entire life.

There's something interesting in there that's worth noting. For a white German boy to say that was the first time I danced, period, let alone for eight hours. That's not exactly the way we're brought up. The very notion of having some sort of connection to your body in a public environment is not exactly how the post-war German is raised. That's probably part of why techno had such a revolutionary impact over here.

GB: It was a new language, a totally new – I don't want to say movement, but –

SS: It was a new kind of clubbing. Before, you had discotheques with blinking lights and a DJ three metres up.

GB: And a bar.

SS: And a bar, with ladies and credit cards. In Berlin we had basements.

GB: And a fog machine. We were lucky. We were born here at the perfect moment.

MB: Berlin is not like the rest of Germany. I've been around the rest.

GB: It's like New York, a different country.

MB: Yeah. When people started looking at me funny in Bavaria (and people are obviously racist), I'm like, "Oh, wow, why am I here? Why do I have a show booked here?" I don't understand. But when the people come out to see my show, it kind of erases whatever weird altercation I might have had on the street or on the train, because then I realize the youth of that place want to see something different. They want to see something different than what they've experienced. One of my best shows was in Hamburg at this bunker. It was fucking nuts, and then we went to the Golden Pudel afterwards and I had one of the wildest nights I've ever had in Germany.

GB: That was the first club we played outside of Berlin.

MB: Really? Was it the same man, the same owner?

SS: Ralf.

MB: Yes! Oh my God, he was so good to me.

SS: He's a legend.

GB: Did you know that he was an haute couture stylist in Paris for big fashion shows in the '80s? He was famous. He was the stylist for all the Yves Saint Laurent shows. Then he quit everything, turned into a punk, went to Hamburg and opened the Pudel.

MB: That's crazy.

SS: And he's still a good hair stylist.

GB: Ask him if he can do your hair. I'm not kidding.

So, playing the cool places is easy. How do you react when you're in front of a crowd that's totally alien to you, to the degree of hostility?

MB: You mean festivals where people don't know who you are? That's shitty. How do you guys do it? You guys have been doing it way longer than I have.

SS: When we start playing a show, the first thing I do when we play the first song – and the bass drum kicks in – I put two big bottles of water into the first row to say, "Hello, we're here!"

Did you ever get bottles thrown at you? I mean, did anyone ever answer that in a hostile way?

GB: Yeah, of course. Once Szary did a stage dive on a huge crowd and they didn't push him back to the stage. Szary was like, "No, this way!" [points in other direction]

GHOSTFACE CAN COME OUT IN LIKE A FLOOR LENGTH BEARSKIN RUG AND IT'LL BE FINE.

I'M WORKING SO HARD RIGHT NOW BECAUS IT'S STILL CUTE FOR ME TO RUN AROUND WITI MY SHIRT OFF ON STAGE.

BELIEVE THAT YOU CAN WORK SMART AND NOT HARD, BUT I WOULD NOT BE WHERE I AM IF I HADN'T PUT IN [THE EFFORT]. A COUPLE OF MONTHS AGO I LITERALLY FELT LIKE I WAS GOING TO GO CRAZY.

SS: It's not easy to tell the guys this. You're laying on your back and then, "No, no, this direction." Mykki, do you stage dive?

MB: I jump into the crowd and mosh actually. I haven't met a crowd that I trusted enough to have them carry me.

Do you find that there's a certain demand from the marketplace; that the fan expects to get that close with the performer?

MB: To be honest, in hip hop, no. Rappers are some of the laziest performers ever and everybody knows it. Actually I'm going to take that back. I think that's an old thing, because a lot of the young rap crews now know that they have to. I've seen the Odd Future kids and the A$AP kids, and they do really energetic stage shows. I saw Ghostface Killah twice, who is my favourite rapper, and as good a rapper as he is… I mean, when you have five gold chains, a robe and a fur coat, how can you possibly move? For some people it works. To be honest, it worked because it's Ghostface. Ghostface can come out in like a floor-length bearskin rug and it'll be fine. But for other rappers, it's like, "Come on. You're making somebody pay $20 to see you perform for 35 minutes and then you have like 12 people on the stage and mostly the person who is actually rapping is your hype man." That's not a real show. This whole festival season has been eye-opening for me.

GB: Next year you will see it from a different point of view, and then the year after that

you will see it differently again. That's normal. It will change after every LP. You will see. Remember my words!

Look at Grandpa.

GB: It's true. This is how we know. We were on a big label here in Berlin called BPitch Control, run by Ellen Allien. She was kind of our mentor, teacher or whatever.

SS: Mummy.

GB: Or mama. Techno mama. She always said, "You should play every show you can get. Do every show and make music and release the music, that's the trick." And that's what we did. We never gave up. We just played every fucking show. It's hard work. But you choose this way.

Where do you draw the line as far as a balance of what life on the road takes out of you in comparison to what it gives you?

MB: Well, I'm finding that I'm on a schedule I call the Rihanna schedule, where I tour for six months, and then I'll go through a recording period. I'm finding that it works, because to be honest – and this is very American – I believe in diligent work. I don't want to say hard work, because I believe that you can work smart and not hard, but I would not be where I am if I hadn't put in [the effort]. A couple of months ago I literally felt like I was going to go crazy. I kind of get emotional talking about this, and I don't want to get emotional, but I know what it is to want something very badly, and I know

what it is to want something so badly that it consumes you.

What do you want?

MB: To spread my creative vision. In a way, I want to be Michael Jackson. These large labels throw mountains of money at mediocre people, and I'm out here working my ass off. I know the ideas that I have in my head for not only what I would put out in my stage show, but also the experience, the things, the environments that I would build for people if I had control of a festival. That artist part of me has never gone away. I know that when I'm older, it's not going to be so cute for me to run around with my shirt off. That's when I'm going to probably care even more about creative environments for people to come into and really experience something. I'm working so hard right now because it's still cute for me to run around with my shirt off on stage. I've got to work my ass off and I've got to make sure that I make good music, honest music that people respond to, because this is how I'm going to make that money to live off of. Before this I was really artsy and doing projects here and doing projects there, but I was broke all the time. I had no money, all the time. As romantic as that is…

GB: We had the same thing. We never had money, but we started doing record labels just a few years ago. We have two record labels now and a lot of artists on our roster. We always look forward. We never look back. When I listen to you I can see we have a similar point of view. But I also see that you are really at the beginning. All I can tell you is

this: just do your thing, and fuck them. Our touring schedule was so weird over the years. When we started playing the bigger shows, we played on a Friday with Skream and Benga in London. On Saturday we played with Richie Hawtin in Barcelona and on Sunday we played the afterparty here in Berlin with someone else. We totally jumped into different worlds and camps over the years, but we never lost our own world. We never lost the bubble, the Modeselektor, the Monkeytown, the world which is surrounding us. We just made it more and more alive. The last time I needed some help in the garden, we cut a tree and we had all this wood and I needed to call a friend because I wasn't able to move it alone. I realized that all my friends are already working for my company. I can't call them in their free time to ask them if they can help me work in the garden.

SS: In the end he called me.

GB: I called him.

SS: I have a chainsaw.

ALL I CAN TELL YOU IS THIS: JUST DO YOUR THING, AND FUCK THEM.

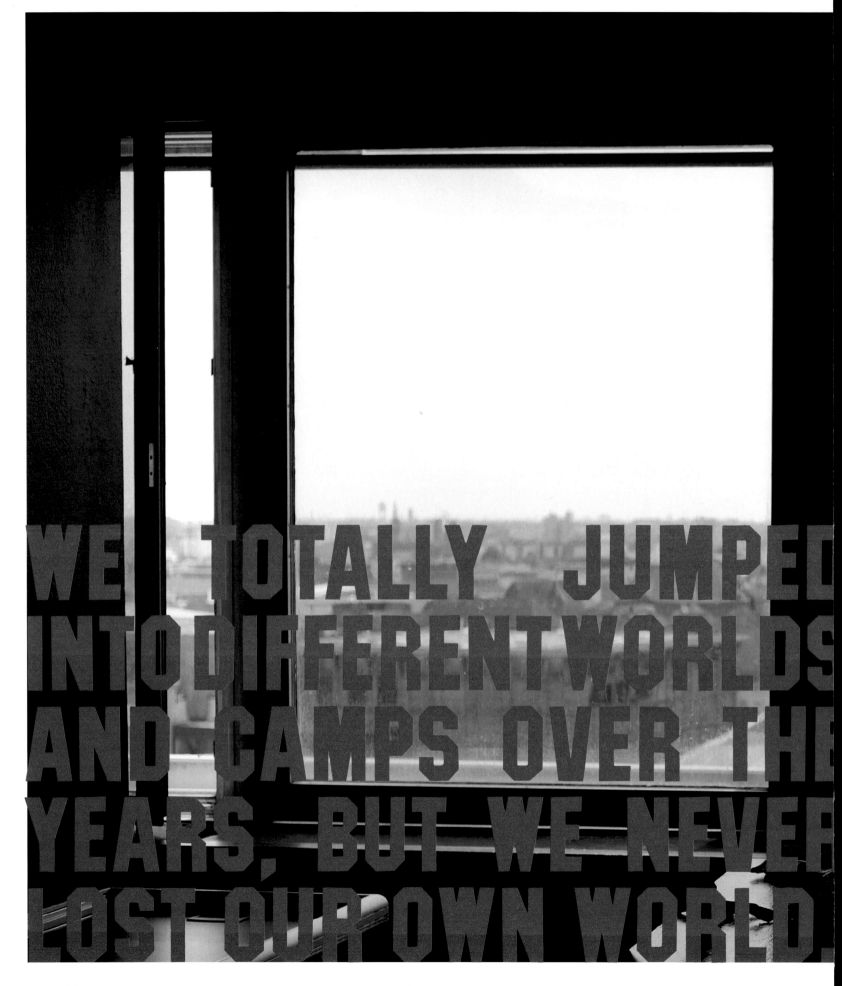

WE TOTALLY JUMPED INTO DIFFERENT WORLDS AND CAMPS OVER THE YEARS, BUT WE NEVER LOST OUR OWN WORLD.

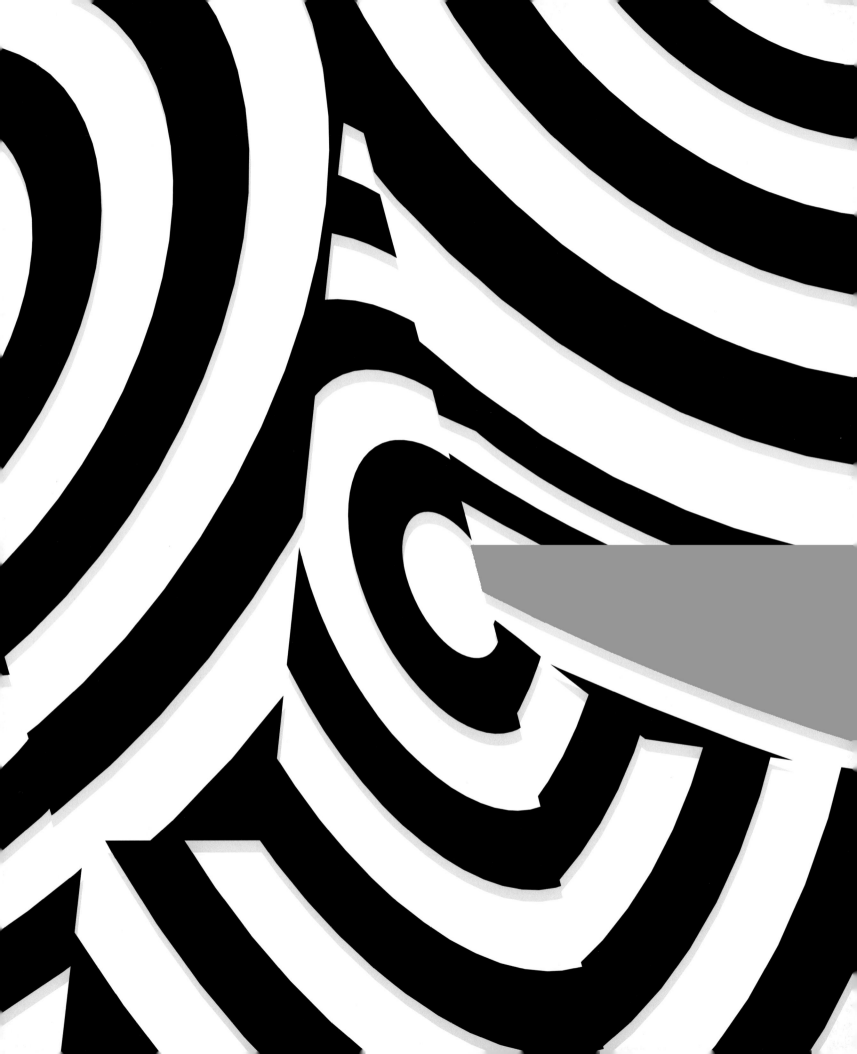

THE UNDERACHIEVERS

IN EARLY AUGUST, THE UNDERACHIEVERS FLEW TO DALLAS TO VISIT BADU IN HER SUBURBAN HOME. AS THE DUO ARRIVED, THEY NOTICED THE WORDS "LOVE FORGIVE EVOLVE" WRITTEN IN CHALK ON THE GARAGE DOOR. OUTSIDE, DASH BUMMED A CIGARETTE OFF BADU, SURPRISED TO SEE THAT THEY FAVORED THE SAME ESOTERIC BRAND. AS THE CONVERSATION LATER TOOK PLACE INDOORS, BADU POPPED HAYAO MIYAZAKI'S SPIRITED AWAY INTO A DVD PLAYER, FREEZING THE FILM AT THE START MENU. AFTER THE TALK FINISHED, BADU HIT PLAY.

Things move in cycles. That goes some way to explain why Issa Dash and Ak are just as much an offspring of Digable Planets as they are products of a rap generation addicted to swag. The Brooklyn-based rap duo fuses the deep with the superficial, sowing seeds of ancient knowledge and esoteric spirituality in the minds of a youth desensitized to stimulation. As self-proclaimed "indigo children," **The Underachievers** aim to illuminate their peers through high-velocity rhymes – be it over earthy boom bap production or synthetic 808 constructs. Without so much as a handful of teaser tracks rotating through the blogosphere, they signed with Brainfeeder, Red Bull Music Academy grad Flying Lotus' imprint, before releasing their debut mixtape in early 2013.

ERYKAH BADU

CLOSE ENCOUNTERS OF THE PURPLE KIND:

ERYKAH BADU AND NEW YORK HIP HOP DUO THE UNDERACHIEVERS

CODE THEIR MUSIC, BURYING SIGNALS INSIDE RELATABLE EMOTIONS AND

DEXTEROUS RAPPING. FOR BADU, ISSA DASH AND AK, MUSIC IS A WAY OF PROVIDING

HINTS AND POSSIBILITIES – NOT DEFINITIVE AND DIDACTIC ANSWERS.

Singer, songwriter, Grammy Award-winner, producer, DJ, activist, actress, practicing doula and mother of three.
Erykah Badu's accomplishments and accolades appear impressive enough on paper, but her influence can hardly be measured in words. As early as 1996, Badu laid the groundwork to become the defining voice for soul music in the 21st Century. But the profound cultural impact that this "Analog Girl in a Digital World" has left on a wide-ranging demographic of women and men transcends music. As an advocate for healthy living, the leader of an active charity organization and a fearless defender of free speech, Erykah Badu's status as role model might be her most indisputable characteristic.

MODERATOR: MOSI REEVES   PHOTOGRAPHER: BEN GRIEME

RBMA: EVEN THOUGH ALL OF YOU USE PRODUCERS, I ASSUME YOU'RE HEAVILY INVOLVED IN THE MUSIC AS WELL.

ISSA DASH: We have a wide array of music that inspires us. Before I became a rapper, I didn't like rap. I always say if I were able to sing or play an instrument, I wouldn't be a rapper. I would be trying to make music, you know what I mean? So it's like, secretly, I'm trying to not be a rapper. Right now, since I just started making music, I'm still deciding how I'm gonna go about shit. In the future, I just wanna be able to evolve the hip hop world. Since I'm not into hip hop that much, I feel like I could bring other genres into hip hop.

AK: Yeah, we definitely gonna reinterpret –

NOW THAT WE HAVE THE INTERNET, THERE'S A HUNDRED PEOPLE THAT THINK THE SAME WAY I THINK. THERE'S A HUNDRED PEOPLE THAT RAP THE SAME WAY I RAP. THERE'S A HUNDRED PEOPLE THAT DRAW THE SAME WAY I DRAW.

ID: Yeah. I'm trying do a mixtape with, like, me and an acoustic guitar. Ak will just play an acoustic guitar, and I'll rap over it.

ERYKAH, YOU STARTED OUT DOING TRADITIONAL HIP HOP, BUT YOU TRANSITIONED INTO DOING OTHER THINGS AS WELL.

ERYKAH BADU: I think they were always there. I just didn't have the platform to do them. I consider myself a slow burn. I'm not in a rush to give it all away or prove something. I have so much inside, so labeling it only confuses me, because it's all me. I guess for the sake of selling units, it's OK to label the genre. But I'm filled with atoms of hip hop, jazz, R&B, soul, blues, rock, country, classical. I guess what comes out at the time is where we at, you know?

YOU'RE AT A REALLY DIFFERENT STAGE OF YOUR CAREER THAN THE UNDERACHIEVERS. CAN YOU TALK ABOUT YOUR EXPERIENCES GETTING INVOLVED IN THE MUSIC INDUSTRY?

EB: [*winks*] Well, it wasn't very long ago to me that I got into the music industry. It was like... Well, 15 years is a long time, especially for technology. When I came out, cell phones weren't in rotation. If you had one you was like, real cool. This was 1997, and everything was new. It was almost like flying cars had been invented and only two people had them. So the sky was the limit. And I could create anything I wanted to and think that it was something new and special. Now that we have the internet, there's a hundred people that think the same way I think. There's a hundred people that rap the same way I rap. There's a hundred people that draw the same way I draw. That's different – and somewhat intimidating – because there are so many outlets. If you let that consume you, you won't make it. So how I keep creating is staying on the road, doing what I do best: Performing. I love the communication. I love the feedback. I love when we become one thing, me and the audience. Recording is cool, but I like the live element. It's like... Africa. That's the only way I can describe it. Like what I imagine call and response to be.

ID: It's funny how you say that.
That's the only way for us to really get out to our audience now. Through performances. Even though the digital world has helped a lot, it's really fucked up a lotta shit. People don't buy music anymore. So it's the only time that we really –

IN ONE OF MY FIRST INTERVIEWS I SAID ONCE WE GET BIG I WANTED TO START A MASS MEDITATION. AT A SHOW JUST BE LIKE, "ALRIGHT, NO MORE MUSIC, LET'S ALL DROP AND, TOGETHER, MEDITATE." 5,000 KIDS TOGETHER, SYNCHRONIZED MEDITATIONS AROUND THE WORLD.

A: – be intimate, connect with –

ID: That's why when you listen to our mixtape, *Indigoism*, we have songs that are tailored to performances. For our first performance, we had mad lyrical songs and I was like, "Shit, this isn't gonna work." People don't wanna stand and hear you do that shit, you know what I mean? So I started to write more performance songs. Stuff where it's very easy to catch on. So when I'm performing the fans already know my lyrics are easy to get. It's not like, "Oh my God, this is nice but I don't know what the fuck he's saying." They're there with me. Performing is the most fun of the whole thing. I don't like touring, but performing is fun. Touring is too long and dreadful. And I miss home.

EB: It will become home in a minute.

A: Yeah, you just gotta get used to it.

EB: You make it home.

ID: I'm afraid of that. It really gives you the motivation to keep doing what you're doing, though.
When you're interacting with fans and they're telling you, "Keep doing this, we need this!" It's like, "Fuck, I have an obligation now. This is a responsibility." On the first tour there was a shift from, "Alright, we're gonna have some fun" to "Wow, I now have a responsibility to my fans to present music properly and to put on good shows and shit like that." If you listen to our music you know that I'm all about that "united with the source"-type shit. It's just like you were saying, Erykah, it brings you together. Bringing all that energy together. In one of my first interviews I said once we get big I wanted to start a mass meditation.
At a show just be like, "Alright, no more music. Let's all drop and, together, meditate."
5,000 kids together, synchronized meditations around the world.

YOU GUYS REFER A LOT TO PSYCHEDELICS IN YOUR LYRICS. IS THAT A PART OF YOUR CREATIVE PROCESS?

ID: I never wrote a song on psychedelics. I guess people think that we're on shrooms, recording all the time. Psychedelics is a very special, special, special –

EB: Ritual.

ID: Yeah. When I'm doing psychedelics, I'm usually not thinking about music.

A: But experiencing psychedelics may make you write some music.

ID: It's a part of me, so I guess it's safe to say that it comes out in my lyrics. But I'm not writing on psychedelics.

I WAS BORN ON PSYCHEDELICS. AND I DON'T KNOW HOW I'M GONNA GET ALL OF THIS OUT. BUT I'M TRYIN'.

EB: I was born on psychedelics. And I don't know how I'm gonna get all of this out. But I'm tryin'.

HOW DO YOU GET TO A POINT WHERE IT'S SOMETHING THAT PEOPLE LISTEN TO AND TAKE WHATEVER INTERPRETATION YOU GET FROM IT?

EB: You just hope.

ID: Yeah, that's the scariest part about it.

EB: You have faith. You just hope they do. And then, at the same time, you don't underestimate their ability to feel it. There's somebody who feels like me.

ID: Did you always know that you'd be Erykah Badu?

EB: [*laughs*] Did I? Yeah, I think so. Not by name or force, but I knew that I wanted to do art. I didn't think I would be a celebrity. I thought I would be a great entertainer, because I'm more of an exhibitionist than a celebrity. You can see it, but then I wanna fade into the back. I don't wanna answer no questions. But I kinda always felt like this. I believed it. I didn't know not to believe it. What about you?

A: I always felt like I was gonna be a rapper, I guess.

ID: He's been a rapper forever.

A: Yeah, it just happened.

ID: Yeah it's like we created our reality. 'Cause he was making music forever, and I knew that I wanted to, like, enlighten my generation by any means. We just shazamed it together, and boom, it worked. We're just together in this. I learned music from him and he learns other shit from me.

EB: As a kid, did you know? Don't lie.

A: We always knew we'd be something.

ID: I always knew I'd be good. Not good in terms of financially, but I always knew
I would pull it together and figure it out.

EB: So you believed in your abilities?

ID: Forever. Looking back, everything makes more and more sense. It's like, "Was I being set up to be sitting right here?"
I don't mean sitting right here in front of Erykah Badu. I mean, like, where I'm at right now.

EB: You know what? Don't lose it. Because it's easy to. As life happens, procrastination happens, love happens,
you become some kind of personality that you create for yourself. And if you try to live up to it, it gets kinda difficult. And you don't
know why you're having difficulty. But don't lose the "believe in your abilities" part. Because I lose that from time to time.
"Can I do that?" It should be no question.

ID: That's the one thing I always keep. I always lose faith in my music. But the one thing I never lose faith in is
what I'm trying to do. As long as I stay in line with my goal of enlightening my generation, then everything flows with it.
As long as I keep that in front of everything, I think I'll be fine.

EB: What if you have the desire to change that goal? What if you feel like you just wanna wild out and say whatever you wanna say?
A situation where you know who you are in your heart, but you know this is what you wanna say.
Would you go with it or would you fight that part of you?

A: I don't really think like that. I don't want to be that type of person.

ID: Yeah, because the whole reason I started making music was *for* that one reason, you know what I mean?
We're a year in, so we're still babies. We haven't even seen anything. I can't really say anything yet.

EB: Too soon to say. That's a good answer.

ID: I feel like if I ever turn my back on the light, it will all be taken away. As long as I stay on point with that, everything will flow.
Everything I need will come. That's why in my head I'm like, "Oh shit. I can't get caught up in this."

EB: There's this little pamphlet I'm reading called *At the Feet of the Masters*.
It's a boy's tale of what he learned from his master. And it suggests that denial is the opposite of love.
Like you were saying, "If you deny the light, that's not love."
That's a problem for all of us, you know? Everything we do,
we deny doing the right thing. And that's where –

WE'RE A YEAR IN, SO WE'RE STILL BABIES. WE HAVEN'T EVEN SEEN ANYTHING.

ID: Denial just messes everything up.
Denial is fear, you know? Fear is definitely the opposite of love.
All falls in line with that.

EB: Fear could be the opposite of love, but then fear... It suggests that
you are some kind of victim. And we're not. We're just denying a reality
of what's happening. Fear could be a part of the process of denial.

ID: Of course. If you're a conscious person, fear is a different type of thing. Fear is a driving force in a sense.
There's a quote from John Mayer. "Fear is a friend that's misunderstood." I feel like you just need to know how to use these things
to your advantage. Even the ego. A lot of people are trying to defeat the ego. But I feel like source didn't give us anything we're not
supposed to use. It's just about aligning it in the proper way. If you're not of a conscious mindset, then fear will take you over.
Then you'll be in hell, you'll be living a fearful life.

HOW HAS THE INDUSTRY CHANGED?

EB: When I got signed to a label, my album was like platinum in less than a year or something. I didn't even know the thing was happening. They were working me so hard. I had to be at radio stations early in the morning, this or that TV show. It's called "the machine." It was overwhelming. And I didn't know what had really happened until maybe a year later. That was the old record industry. How is it for you now?

ID: Now it's like... the internet. It makes it so much easier. I feel like the internet is like a gift from God to connect to the universe.

EB: Age of Aquarius.

ID: Yeah, the Age of Aquarius. My whole philosophy before making music was that the fans would be able to help us do anything we have to do, because of the internet. I feel like rappers that now enter the game, they try and interact with the business side first. The labels. I want this feature. I want to work with this and that person. All of this instead of building a fan base. That was the main thing I wanted to do.

EB: It's powerful when you come with a network.

THE FIRST THING I TOLD AK WAS, "I'M NOT DROPPING A MIXTAPE UNTIL THEY FUCKING BEG FOR IT."

ID: I knew that if something was good, the internet would show it was good. If it's bad, the internet is going to reject it. Because if something's good, people are going to want show someone else automatically. No one's going to want to show anyone something shitty. So that's how I play the game, basically

HOW DID YOU FIGURE THAT OUT, DASH? LIKE YOU SAID, A LOT OF ARTISTS DON'T GET IT.

ID: It's just watching the industry. I studied the industry. I'd just watch something and think, "Oh shit, those are some very good visuals." And I was like, "No one's listening to music unless they know you." Rappers are dropping audio, but no one's listening to it. So the first thing I did was the visual side. I was like, "We got to make a super dope video." So that people are like, "Whoa! This is some shit!" I knew we had to draw people in before we start releasing any music. The first thing I told Ak was, "I'm not dropping a mixtape until they fucking beg for it. There's no way I'm going to go out and make 16 fucking songs and release it and have no one listen to it."

EB: I'm also involved in all the aspects. Because it's all a part of the story. The visual, the music, the frequency, the interview, the outfit, the love, the hate. Everything involved is a part of the story. This is my life. There's nothing freaky about controlling it.

ID: I know. Everyone wants me to stop.

EB: Don't do it. There's nothing freaky about controlling it. Just don't put too much on yourself. It's gotta be done that way, if that's what you do.

**IS IT A BURDEN FOR YOU, THOUGH, HAVING TO DO
ALL OF THIS OTHER NETWORKING STUFF AND NOT FOCUS ON MUSIC?**

EB: No, because it's a great escape from reality. It doesn't feel like a burden or a job. It feels like I'm communicating with other people, other human beings. I'm not a celebrity communicating with some fans on that kind of platform. We're on an equal playing ground. We're communicating, we're discussing ideas, we're discussing art.

ID: It's fun, because you can really connect with your fans. You see what they're saying. You're getting feedback prior to putting out products. It's like building an empire, and it's way easier now. You could build an empire by having a fucking awesome website.

EB: You can also back up what you say. You don't have to wait around. I'm showing you right here. I'm saying it, and this many people are saying it too.

WE'VE TAKEN

YOU DON'T HAVE TO WAIT UNTIL THE NEXT MAGAZINE INTERVIEW COMES BACK.

CONTROL OF OUR OWN IMAGES, WHICH IS AMAZINGLY RELIEVING.

EB: Because we are telling you right now. Only people who want to be entertained are running to the gossip things. But, for the most part, people don't believe that, really. We've taken control of our own images, which is amazingly relieving. It gives us a lot more room for our art, and to create with a free, optimistic mind. It's power.

HOW IMPORTANT IS NEW YORK TO YOUR MUSIC, DASH?

ID: It's where we grow up and where we make our music. But it's not like we're trying to put Flatbush on the map. New York... It's in me, I guess. So it comes out in my music. But it's not intentional. I'm not trying to "bring New York back." I don't give a fuck about that shit.

WHAT DO YOU THINK ABOUT THAT, AK? HOW DOES BEING FROM NEW YORK FILTER INTO YOUR MUSIC?

A: We grew up there, but we don't really listen to any New York artists right now, so I don't see the correlation really.

ID: I'm a student of the Universe. I don't belong to New York or America or Africa. It's universal. I'm trying to bring the Universe back. I mean, I got Africa tattooed on my arm, know what I mean? But you won't see me walking around like, "Yo, we have to go back to Africa! And be black!" No. It's a part of me. That's my heritage. But I'm universal. I can't be limited to teaching them about Egyptian shit. There's so much to learn around the World. There's knowledge from Hermeticism, and that's from Greece. There's knowledge in the Kaballah, and that's from Judaism. The knowledge is split across the whole world, so if I limit myself to just one section, I'm messing up. The whole shit is divided. The whole point is to bring it back together.

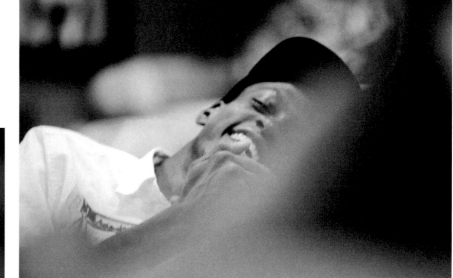

IF YOU'RE NOT OF A CONSCIOUS MINDSET, THEN FEAR WILL TAKE YOU OVER. THEN YOU'LL BE IN HELL, YOU'LL BE LIVING A FEARFUL LIFE.

I THOUGHT I WOULD BE A GREAT ENTERTAINER, BECAUSE I'M MORE OF AN EXHIBITIONIST THAN A CELEBRITY. YOU CAN SEE IT, BUT THEN I WANNA FADE INTO THE BACK.

HOW DOES BEING FROM DALLAS, AND BEING FROM THE SOUTH, FIGURE INTO WHAT YOU DO AS A MUSICIAN?

EB: Maybe the birds. The frequency of the birds. There's a lot of blues influence in this area. I didn't grow up in church or anything like that, so I don't belong to a gospel choir. But maybe just the area itself. I don't know any particular thing. I do have a Southern accent, which makes me split vowels and hit two notes instead of one. Maybe that? I don't know.

MAYBE THAT'S A HIP HOP THING, THINKING THAT WHERE YOU'RE FROM IS SUCH A BIG PART OF WHO YOU ARE. BUT I GUESS FOR YOU GUYS THAT'S NOT NECESSARILY THE CASE.

EB: I don't know the rules, artistically. I don't do collaborations and those kinds of things. It's like, "Hey, Picasso, can you come over? This is Rembrandt. Working on this piece, and I just want you to put a couple of strokes in here, man, and then it's gonna be hot."

ID: That's the same way I see it. Our first mixtape had no features. Our next mixtape has no features. We don't have any features out. There's no point. It's like wasting a song almost.

EB: I guess what you were asking about was the influence. I know that this atmosphere has an influence on me. In some kind of way. I don't know exactly how.

ID: Would be silly to say it doesn't.

EB: But I do connect and do side projects and collaborations. When I'm writing a record, though, it's based on my experiences. If I wanted to leave my kids a clue of who I was, I would have them listen to *Baduizm* and *Mama's Gun* and *New Amerykah: Part One* and *Part Two* and *Worldwide Underground*, because they're how I feel and where I am. But collaborating is awesome. It's wonderful just working with other people's energy.

"HEY, PICASSO, CAN YOU COME OVER? THIS IS REMBRANDT. WORKING ON THIS PIECE, AND I JUST WANT YOU TO PUT A COUPLE OF STROKES IN HERE, MAN, AND THEN IT'S GONNA BE HOT."

AN INTERESTING ONE WAS THE LIL' WAYNE COLLABORATION "JUMP UP IN THE AIR AND STAY THERE." TO THE LAYPERSON YOU GUYS WOULD SEEM SO DIFFERENT, BUT ON THAT SONG YOU FIT TOGETHER.

EB: That's my people. He's one of the most intelligent people I've ever met, period.
There were like ten MCs on that song. It was done during the *Worldwide Underground* era, where I was traveling on a bus. Whenever I would come to a city, I just had MCs get on it. We just put out that version on the internet, strictly for the internet, so I could play around digitally with this new thing I've got to make these images. Basically, like he was saying, imagery is everything. People aren't listening, they're looking. They don't want a savior, they want someone who looks like one. It's beautiful to be a part of the give and take of that. Every piece of art I put out, I feel like I'm three years old putting it on the refrigerator for my mom to say, "This is great." As an artist, that's how we feel. We don't ever put out anything for somebody to say, "Well, this doesn't sound anything like 1998." Or, "These notes are not the right –" How do you know what note I was trying to hit? We don't put out music or art or love with the idea of being hurt in return. But that is one of the taxes that we have to pay for the brilliant life that we receive in return. My children are in schools that I would never think they'd be in. I'm affording things that my parents need and want. My community – we thrive together, we do things together. I came from a community. If they didn't teach me music in the community center, I would have never known that I could do anything. And it's a cycle. You have to take that shit for the team.
It's never easy to do that as a human being, with everything
else that you have, but we have to.

LIL WAYNE IS A VERY SHARP GUY, BUT YOU WOULDN'T NECESSARILY BE ABLE TO SAY WHAT BOOKS HE'S READ. IT'S PART OF HIM, PRESERVING THAT MYSTERY. I'M ASSUMING IT'S NOT A CONSCIOUS THING, BUT OBVIOUSLY MYSTERY IS A BIG PART OF WHAT ARTISTS DO, RIGHT?

EB: Magic would be a better word, because sometimes you have to
be exposed in order to complete the loop, but it's more magical than anything and the magic is that they believe you.
To me, there are three levels of artist. One is the artist that bleeds and sweats and burns and documents those experiences.
The second level is the artist that emulates that first level. The third is the artist that is fed what to do.
The artist that's in the middle is usually the most successful.

IMAGERY IS EVERYTHING.
PEOPLE AREN'T LISTENING, THEY'RE LOOKING.
THEY DON'T WANT A SAVIOR, THEY WANT
SOMEONE WHO LOOKS LIKE ONE.
IT'S BEAUTIFUL TO BE A PART OF THE
GIVE AND TAKE OF THAT.

ISSA, A LOT OF TIME YOU GUYS ARE TALKING ABOUT PARTYING AND HANGING OUT. IT OFTEN FEELS LIKE THE STUFF YOU'RE TALKING ABOUT AS FAR AS YOUR LEARNINGS IS ALMOST LIKE A SUBLIMINAL INFLUENCE.

ID: When I used to meditate a ridiculous amount, the thing that was always prevalent in my mind was that I'm not a teacher or prophet. I'm a messenger. What I want to do is just spark people to go on the path. I feel like my whole generation is already in tune to everything I have to say, so my job is to tell them like, "Yo, the churches are lying, those guys are lying, listen to yourself." That's it. People just go out and do themselves, so my job is to disconnect people from the system and then send them off on their path. My mission with the music is to give them little hints, but I would never try to teach motherfuckers. That's why I mention things like kemetic. "Oh, kemetic? Let me google that and see what that is!"

EB: You study Kemet? Where?

ID: The main book I read was Metu Neter. That was one of the sickest books I've ever read.

I BOW WITH THOSE WHO BOW, BECAUSE I KNOW THAT THERE'S SOMETHING BIGGER THAN ME. THE IDEA IS ALL THE SAME.

EB: That's a very hard book to read! It's like a textbook.

ID: I love textbooks, I read textbooks from page one to end, so it's my type of shit. I did the whole meditation – that's my whole thing. The Egyptians had it right.

EB: Yes. So does the Bible, it has it right, so does the Qu'ran. The teaching is just a little different.

ID: You gotta know how to read it, you know what I mean? The more I learn about the spiritual world, I'll go back to the Bible and see, "Oh *that's* what that story means!" But they really convince people that that shit is literal.

EB: I like religion a lot. It's a very well built boat.

ID: I don't like Christianity. Judaism is awesome, Islam is awesome. Christianity is like poison to me. My whole thing with Christianity is like, if Christianity did what they were supposed to do…

EB: You mean as an organization, but not as a doctrine.

ID: Yeah, definitely as an organization, definitely not as a doctrine. I'm a proud Christian myself, you know what I mean? I'm probably more Christian than most Christians. That's actually where I got my name from. Issa means Jesus.

EB: That's a good name, Issa. One time I did a past life regression. It's a type of hypnosis where you're supposed to be able to relax enough to go back in your mind to different lifetimes. It was interesting, because she told me to close my eyes and imagine that I was walking down a corridor of doors. She said, "Choose a door." And of course I chose the oldest, most rustic door I could find – authentic and beautiful, dilapidated. I pushed the door open, and she said, "What do you see?" And I said, "I see cobblestones on the ground, I see people running rampantly." You know, immediately my ego went to, "I'm Jesus! I guess I'm Jesus, that's who I am. OK, makes sense!" So I go to this immediately, and she's asking, "Who are you?" And I'm not saying anything because I'm a little ashamed, but, you know, still proud. So I'm walking down this corridor and she says, "OK, fast forward to the end of your life." And it became so painful and unbearable to me, in myself, that I said I don't want to talk about it. And she says, "OK, come out." She sits me up and she says, "Well, who were you?" I said I just don't want to say. She said, "It's OK, just say what you think you were." I said, "Jesus?" She goes, "It's OK. Let me explain something to you. It's not important who you were. What did you learn? Don't answer it, just think about it. You'll probably be thinking about it for the rest of this life." I'm not religious – well, maybe I am – I'm more of an observer of everything and everyone. And I bow with those who bow, because I know that there's something bigger than me. The idea is all the same.

ID: Yeah, there's always a common denominator amongst all of it. Like that universal consciousness shit.
Do you remember the Bible story about the Tower of Babylon? The tower went up to the heavens, and the tower had all the knowledge. God was tight, like "You know ima split this whole shit up." So he knocked the tower down, but all the knowledge spread everywhere, right? Nah, all the knowledge came from the one tower. That story basically represents how all the nations got started. But that's just an allegory to represent the universal consciousness. They're all saying the same shit. When I was younger, like 13, I was having nightmares and shit. I thought I was the Devil's child because I hated Christianity, and I was like, "Damn, I need to get baptized." But when I got baptized I was like, "Yo, this is nothing. I don't feel shit."

EB: You're not supposed to say that!

ID: I know, but I was like, "I don't feel anything! You know what? This is garbage. I'm Atheist." So, from 13 on, I was Atheist. And through Atheism I was searching for something. I went through every single philosophy and I noticed, "Yo, all these guys are pretty much saying the same exact thing, just with different fanciful stories around it." That's when I started to realize that there's a common denominator. There's some universality to this. We're all the same. The internet's helping that, it's helping people see that we're not that different around the world.

EB: We're not falling for
it anymore.

ID: Yeah, we're still at the joke level right now.
It's not full racism but it's still subliminal racism. We're all racist a little bit,
it's not dead.

EB: We're in the stage where people don't believe in God, but they fear him just the same. So it's a really weird place we're at. It's hard to let old ideas go without feeling guilty or some kind of disrespect. But we're definitely evolving. My children don't understand racism, they don't get it. "Why is he mad because his momma… Well, why? What did he do?" It's a different frequency of thinking. Very intelligent, common sense that they come with.

EB: Right. We are witnessing evolution, we're seeing it.
It's a little bit difficult for all of us, because we're in denial – a lot of us – about certain things.

ID: It's like innate to them.

IT'S HARD TO LET OLD IDEAS GO WITHOUT FEELING GUILTY OR SOME KIND OF DISRESPECT, BUT WE'RE DEFINITELY EVOLVING.

ID: We spent the first half of human history learning religion, then we were like, "Fuck that." The Crusades came, Martin Luther and what's the other guy? Darwin. And then it was like, "We're going to spend the rest of the time conquering the world." Right now we're realizing, after all that time, that science and spirituality actually go directly hand in hand.
That's the evolution that's going on right now.

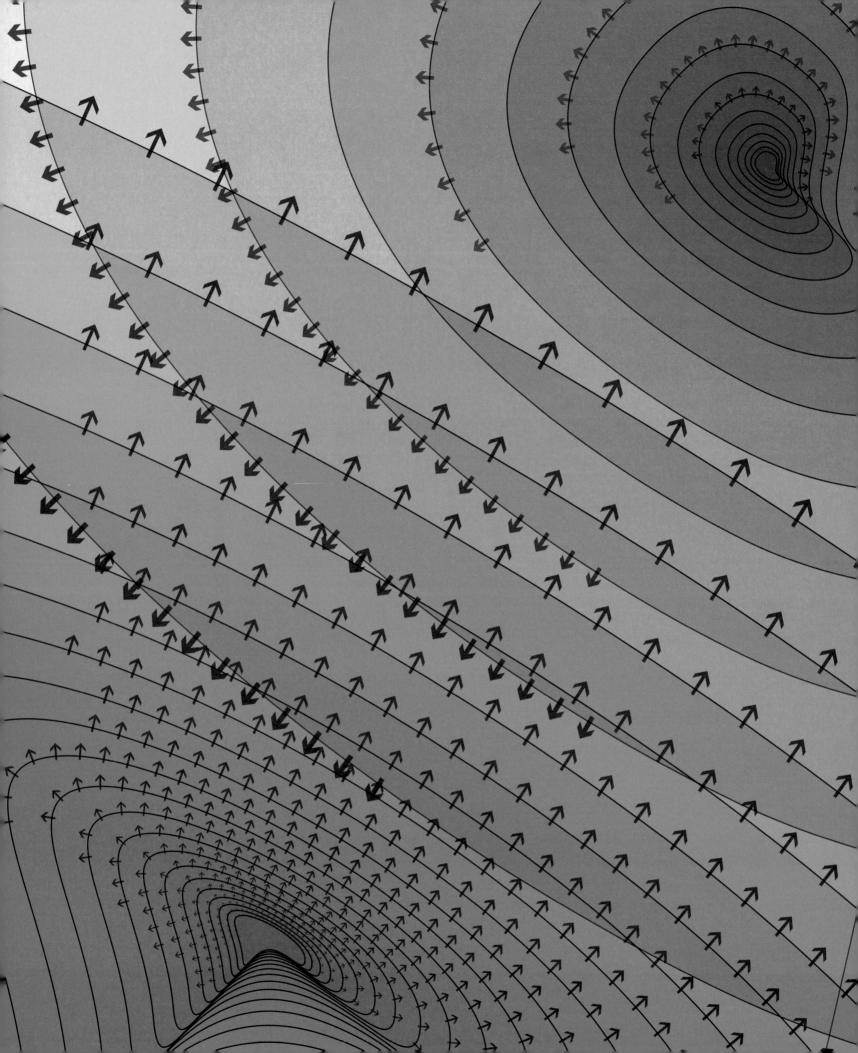

Escaping Roc-A-Fella in the early '00s was hardly a possibility. Working closely with Jay-Z, State Property and Cam'ron, **Just Blaze** helped East Coast rap touch the sky around the turn of the century with his soul-inflected and brass-heavy production work, spawning admiration and imitation alike. Blaze's signature style has remained a staple, making him a much sought-after supplier of hit records with a street edge. More recently, Blaze has been making forays into electronic music, collaborating with "Harlem Shake" producer Baauer and bringing his high-octane approach to beatmaking to a new generation of fans.

JUST BLAZE   AND

PAUL RISER AND JUST BLAZE KNOW A THING OR TWO ABOUT HIT FACTORIES – RISER, AS AN ARRANGER FOR MOTOWN, AND BLAZE, AS ROC-A-FELLA RECORDS' PRODUCER IN RESIDENCE. THE DUO COME FROM DISTINCTLY DIFFERENT GENERATIONS, OF COURSE, BUT WHEN RISER FLEW TO NEW YORK IN THE MIDDLE OF JULY TO MEET BLAZE AT THE RED BULL MUSIC ACADEMY, IT WAS IMMEDIATELY CLEAR THAT THE STORIES THAT THEY WERE SHARING HAD PLENTY OF COMMONALITIES. HALFWAY THROUGH THE CONVERSATION, JEFF "CHAIRMAN" MAO TOOK A QUICK BREAK TO SHOW RISER A 12-INCH CALLED "WHAT WE

DO…" THAT BLAZE HAD PRODUCED. IT CONTAINS A SAMPLE FROM CREATIVE SOURCE'S "I JUST CAN'T SEE MYSELF WITHOUT YOU," A TRACK WHOSE STRINGS WERE ARRANGED BY RISER. IF YOU GO BACK FAR ENOUGH IN BLAZE'S INSTAGRAM ACCOUNT, YOU JUST MIGHT BE ABLE TO FIND THEM HOLDING EACH OTHER'S RECORD.

PAUL RISER

Grammy Award-winning trombonist and arranger **Paul Riser** is synonymous with the Motown sound he helped define. Sadly, his contribution to these truly classic records – from Marvin Gaye's "I Heard It Through the Grapevine" to Diana Ross's "Ain't No Mountain High Enough" – has only been understood retrospectively. Like so many of his fellow Funk Brothers, the backing band he played a key part in, Riser's role went largely uncredited by Berry Gordy. History has finally acknowledged him in recent years, thanks in part to the film *Standing in the Shadows of Motown,* as well as arrangement work for a variety of contemporary artists like R. Kelly and Raphael Saadiq.

Moderator: Jeff "Chairman" Mao   Photographer: Ben Grieme

Paul Riser: When you have everybody in a room recording together, there's a different kind of magic that happens. You kind of absorb each other's spirit and energy, and it reflects in the record.

Just Blaze: I can definitely identify with that because I was part of a big collaborative called Roc-A-Fella Records, which was Jay Z's label. And there were, at one point, maybe like ten to 15 different artists signed to the label. The reason why a lot of that music came out the way it did is because we were all in one place, in one studio, at once. We would have like three or four rooms going, and one artist would be in one room, I'm in another one, and everybody's just bouncing ideas off of each other. Playing each other their records.

RBMA: Can you describe what that scenario was like in Motown for you, Paul?

PR: Nine times out of ten the producer would come in, and they wouldn't have a complete song. They'd just have a skeleton. A lot of times it would develop in the studio. The rhythm, I'm speaking of primarily. Normally we used six horns, two trumpets, two saxophones and two trombones. Sometimes a producer would dictate horn parts, but the arrangement would develop and be relayed to the musicians. Unlike what happens today, there wasn't a lot of overdubbing back then. And what you miss is the relationship that more players in the same arena give to each other. You just don't get it with one player coming in and overdubbing.

JB: There's an album I'm working on right now with a group called Slaughterhouse. It's four different solo artists, and they're all from different parts of the United States. And traditionally what they've always done is recorded a verse, sent it, and then the next person records their verse and sends it. My whole thing with this album was, "I want you guys to live together for the next month while we do this album, and I want this to be personal. I don't want this to just be 14 really good rap records. And you're not gonna get that unless you're all here. Together." The difference between the last album and this one was evident within the first week. Because it's one thing to write a song, send it out and have somebody add their parts to it. But to have somebody sitting there writing and say, "Yo, I'm about to say this," and another person says, "Well, let me say that line for you, because then you can do this and play off of my vocal, and then I'm gonna come back in, and… Wait a minute, Just, do you have an instrument that does this?" Those kind of things don't happen when you're emailing verses and beats back and forth.

What sort of pressure is there if you're in this music-making factory? Is it pressure? Or is it just positive energy?

PR: It wasn't pressure. There was never pressure to satisfy the marketplace or anything of that nature. What Berry Gordy stressed, though, is that we come up with material that was not just suitable for the black community – or any particular community – but instead left world-class

WHEN SOMEBODY DOESN'T UNDERSTAND WHAT AN ARRANGER, PRODUCER OR BEAT-MAKER DOES, THEY THINK THAT THAT PER-SON CAN DO THAT EVERY TIME, ALL DAY, 24 HOURS A DAY.

WHEN YOU HAVE EVERYBODY IN A ROOM
RECORDING TOGETHER, THERE'S A DIFFER-
ENT KIND OF MAGIC THAT HAPPENS.

**THE MAJORITY OF MY HIT RECORDS I MADE
FIVE OR SIX TIMES BEFORE I GOT THEM
RIGHT.**

impressions on people. That's why Motown music is timeless. Those are the kinds of songs we tried to produce, instead of what was happening in the marketplace.

JB: I think, for me, there was actually a very intense amount of pressure. Obviously it was a different time, so what used to be yourself and an entire crew of musicians was instead pretty much just me. There was a point where I was working on six albums at once. And that, in itself, is an insane amount of pressure, but where the pressure really comes into play is within that factory. All the artists are there, hanging out all day. So what happens is, somebody walks in, and you're working on a record for Jay Z, and then somebody else walks in and says, "I want that." And you're like, "Well, this is for Jay." Or you're working on a record for Freeway, and then Jay walks in and says, "I want this," and you're like, "You're the boss so I have to give it to you, but just so you know this was Freeway's record." I dealt with so much of that, to the point where sometimes the artists would take it personally. And I'm like, "Dude, it's not anything personal, I'm just..."

PR: Putting the product where it's gonna do best.

JB: Yeah. And when I was coming up with these ideas, I generally had an idea of where I wanted them to go. And on top of that, I'm just one person. When somebody doesn't understand what an arranger, producer or beatmaker does, they think that that person can do that every time, all day, 24 hours a day. And it's like, "Yo, do you know how many times I had to attempt this, to get it to here?" The majority of my hit records I made five or six times before I got them right. "You Don't Know" from *The Blueprint*. I did it: first time, terrible. Second time: terrible. Third time: terrible. And then, eventually, the fourth time I'm like, "I think I nailed it this time."

PR: It's great to have that luxury.

JB: It is. But, again, the pressure comes in when artists don't understand. A lot of the guys that were signed to Roc-A-Fella were very green. They didn't understand the process of creating. They just know how to rap.

PR: As a producer you have to be a psychologist. You have to be a babysitter. You have to be a lot of things.

JB: You took the words right outta my mouth. I always tell people: if you wanna be a great producer, get a degree in psychology. Because dealing with artists is the first order of business. The way I can critique Jay Z is not the way that I can critique Eminem. Most artists I work with, I've worked with for a long time. So if I'm in a studio with, say, Jay Z, I can say, "Yo, that second verse is not it. You need to rewrite it or rerecord it."

PR: And he can understand that?

JB: Yeah, because we have a rapport. Whereas with Eminem I made that mistake of saying, "Yo, that second verse? Naw, you should do that over," and he just looked at me like, "What?" We worked it out, and actually he ended up thanking me for it because he's rarely ever critiqued. But the first time was awkward. What I realized was that I didn't give any positive reinforcement, which goes back to the psychology thing. I didn't say, "Yo, this was great and this was great, but this wasn't so great."

What sort of instances at Motown do you remember that might be similar to what Just just talked about?

PR: Well, I've experienced some things indirectly. I saw where a writer would write a song for a specific artist and a producer would take that specific song and try to direct it for that artist, and Berry would come along and say, "No, it'd be great for this artist instead." I'll give you a great example. Berry, when he started off, wanted Martha Reeves to be the star of Motown. And then Diana Ross came along, and he switched his priorities. And the rest is history. Martha was of course very bitter about that because she felt that she was supposed to be the star at Motown.

That didn't stop her from making some great records.

JB: She definitely did. I've witnessed things like that as well. Artists who thought they were going to be the next one up to bat, and then all of a sudden a new signee comes along and it's like, "Wait, what happened to me?" And it's just, "Hey, he's got it."

PR: It's a business decision, simply put.

Paul, when you first played trombone with the Funk Brothers, you were around 18 years old. These guys were a different type of crew than you were used to dealing with. What was your first impression of them?

PR: Well, I hated R&B music. I hated it with a passion.

JB: What did you like?

PR: I loved classical and jazz. In that order. Nothin' but. But I came to Motown and they said they needed a trombone player to fill a position for a minute. I didn't expect to have a 52-year career out of it, but things happen. But anyhow, I went to a pretty strict school. Here I was, ten years younger, just out of college, disciplined, sitting next to all these guys that just had no discipline. They were raw, very raw, out of the nightclubs, drinkers – you know. Night people, basically.

They got into trouble sometimes.

PR: Oh, big trouble. Absolutely. Benny Benjamin, the drummer, would come 45 minutes late to a session. He would say, "Well, my aunt died." His aunt must've died a half-dozen times. The lies he'd tell. But, you know, that's what made the spirit of these guys. Their lifestyle is what made that unit sound like it did.

What about you, Just?

JB: My upbringing was pretty tight too. My mother, being a single mother raising three kids, was very protective of us. But also very supportive. I started DJing at clubs and parties when I was 15, but my mother would drive me to the club, and then come back at two in the morning to pick me up. So even though she was very strict and very hands-on, she was also very supportive of us using our natural talents. When I got the opportunity to intern at a studio, I was scared to bring it up, because it would have meant me leaving school. My mother is a high school principal, so education is her thing. We were at the dinner table, and I'm like, "Mom, don't take this the wrong way, but I'm going to drop out of school. It's a very small window, but I have an opportunity to intern at a recording studio in New York." I laid out all the details for her and what the possibilities could be. She thought about it, stayed silent for about two minutes. And she's like, "Will it make you happy?" I said, "Yes." And she said, "As long as you're happy, you're healthy and you're respectful of others, do what you wanna do."

JB: It was amazing. I never looked back. Even though it was frustrating growing up in a pretty strict household, it was probably the best thing that could have happened to me.

JB: I don't know music theory at all. I learned how to read music, but dropped out of music class. During the first half of my professional career I used to kick myself about never learning, but once I got to a certain point [where] I realized that dropping out was probably the best thing I could have done. I feel like when you study music theory you're learning somebody else's interpretation of what music should sound like. And I know that some of the things that I've done make no traditional musical sense. But they worked. I would love to learn now, but not theory. I would like to learn technique.

PR: That had to be a great turning point for you.

PR: My upbringing was very similar. Very religious, very strict. I went to Cass Technical High School in Detroit, and going from junior high to there was tantamount to a Boy Scout going into the Marine Corps. My band director was literally like a drill sergeant. When our academic director would come down the hall, we would all find a place to hide. He was so tough. But it set the standard for me for when I went to Motown. Music theory, music performance. As a trombone player...

PR: Years ago Stevie Wonder suggested that I find him a piano teacher. Now, you talk about playing technically wrong, with your fingers and everything? I think if we ever got him a teacher, it would've messed him up. Honestly. We never found him a teacher, thank God.

JB: Sometimes when you just feel it, you know it.

PR: Leave it be.

YEARS AGO STEVIE WONDER SUGGESTED THAT I FIND HIM A PIANO TEACHER.

WE NEVER FOUND HIM A
TEACHER, THANK GOD.

JB: You know what I've noticed about a lot of string musicians who were classically trained? They can't *jam*. They can't improvise. I remember I once came up with this idea, and I brought in a cello player. I played the track, and she's like, "OK, where's the sheet music?" And I'm like, "Sheet music? It's a simple… Just listen to the song." So she goes into the booth, and she's totally failing. So I go into the booth with her, and this is what we had to do. Once she figured out what the notes were, the only way she could play it in time was if I danced.

PR: Amazing. When I put things down in paper form, I never wrote out a chart with nothing but notes, as far as rhythm was concerned. Never. I always left room for interpretation, for their own inner spirit to come out. I listen to classical music and I'm amazed. You take that music away and they're lost. Absolutely lost – for the most part.

Paul, you have this famous story about when Smokey Robinson presented "My Girl" to the Temptations and they hated it until they heard the strings. Just, what recollections do you have of something where somebody hated what you gave them and then it became something huge?

JB: Oh, I have plenty of stories like that. "Pump it Up" by Joe Budden was originally supposed to be a follow-up to "Roc the Mic" by Beanie Sigel & Freeway. When Memphis Bleek first heard [Cam'ron's] "Oh Boy," he was like, "That's terrible. Play me something else." There was actually a running joke with Bleek. Jay would come to the studio and somebody would be like, "Yo, what's the hot record right now?" and he'd be like, "Oh, whatever Bleek turned down last week." He passed on so many hit records. Fabolous' "Can't Let You Go." "Oh Boy." Usher's "Throwback."

PR: That's right, like water.

JB: Exactly. Say Memphis Bleek took "Oh Boy." It might not have been the hit record that it was. All those records found their way to where they were supposed to go.

PR: That happened in Motown several times. When a record was for one artist and Berry or somebody else would say, "No, let's try this with so-and-so artist." It would ruffle some feathers. But the vision would manifest itself further down the line. Once the record made it in the marketplace, everybody would sit back and say, "Oh, now I see it."

Paul, if you have a signature sound, how would you describe it?

PR: People tell me I have one, but I don't hear it.

What do they say? When they hear the strings, they know Paul Riser must have done that?

PR: Exactly. They know that style, that signature. What distinguishes all that, I don't have a clue. I just do naturally what comes. But, I would say that it's probably based in classical music. I still listen to classical music every day.

JB: What are some of your favorites?

PR: Oh man, composers? Stravinsky, Beethoven of course, Mozart, Ravel, Debussy. I love French impressionist music. Sir Edward Elgar.

So when did you use that influence in a tune?

I ALWAYS LEFT ROOM FOR INTERPRETA-
TION, FOR THEIR OWN INNER SPIRIT TO
COME OUT.

THE WRITING WAS ON THE WALL. IT WAS JUST A MATTER OF WHEN.

QUINCY JONES IS NOT GOING TO YOUR SESSION AND PLAYING ALL THE HORNS, AND ALL THE KEYS, AND ALL THE STRINGS.

PR: It's not a direct thing. But indirectly it always happens. People wonder how I hear all these string lines. And you gotta know math. You have to know technique of the instrument. You have to know the telescope, so to speak, of the instrument: the ranges. The textures. How they sound in combination with other instruments. There are a lot of things that go into it. People wonder why, using synthesized strings, they can't get that body, that fullness. What gives an orchestra that sound is that no two players play alike. They don't vibrate the same. They don't play the same pitch. They may be close, though, and that gives you body automatically. With synthesized electronic music, you get the same pitch, so you have to de-tune if you wanna fatten it. There's no substitute for live strings. Simply put.

JB: That is the hardest thing to duplicate. Horns you can kinda get around, pianos you can make it happen, but strings: it's the hardest thing.

PR: You got nuances. All kinds of little subtleties that happen in strings. Phrasing. Things you don't get when you're playing a keyboard.

By your definition, Paul, what is a producer's job?

PR: To maintain the control over product and know the artist and know the song material for that artist, and know the marketplace.

JB: I feel kinda the same. I feel like a producer's number one job, deliver the product. Second job is: deliver the product. And the third job is: deliver the product. For me, the producer has to direct the show and be the one with the vision. It took me a while to realize that. You look at somebody like Quincy Jones –

PR: Oh, you named one.

JB: Quincy Jones is not going to your session and playing all the horns, and all the keys, and all the strings. He's saying, "This goes here, this goes there. Bring him in to play those drums over, bring him in to play those keys over."

PR: Brings the people in, but doesn't purely dictate to the people. He knows who to put together in a room to make product happen. He's a genius at it.

Who do you rate as far as producers you've worked with?

PR: The most efficient, I would say, was Norman Whitfield. Holland-Dozier-Holland run a close second.

JB: I never worked with either of them, but I might put Holland-Dozier over Norman Whitfield. As a music fan.

PR: Well you know what the background is, the foundation? It's classical music.

Both Motown and Roc-A-Fella ended in ways that maybe weren't ideal. Can you describe your feelings about what happened, Paul?

PR: How did we find out Motown was leaving Detroit? There was actually a session planned for the day. Of course it'd been planned for weeks before they left, but we came and saw a note on the door saying, "No session today. Moved to Los Angeles."

JB: What?!

PR: Yeah, just like that. A sign on the door. It's crazy. Flat-out crazy. I had not a hint, not one. Thank God I was able to move on, because word-of-mouth and credits mean everything in the world. I was able to parlay that into work in New York, Los Angeles and Chicago. That's when I became truly independent.

Just, you said it was disappointing with the way things ended at Roc-A-Fella.

JB: It was disappointing, but we saw it coming. On the executive side there were very few people. It was Jay, Biggs, Dame and that was pretty much it. I was around them pretty much every day. So all of a sudden, you start seeing things. For me, the writing was on the wall. It was just a matter of when. I saw more and more signs as time went on. Whereas the conversations always used to be about "us," I started to hear more of "us and them." It was heartbreaking, though, because it was one of the last great runs in terms of a label in rap music. We had just signed M.O.P. Dame brought Cam in, so we were about to be the dream team that everybody had tried to accomplish in rap. Like Suge tried to do with Death Row, like Puff tried to do with Bad Boy. We were like, "We're actually gonna do it. We're gonna have the Top of the Pops, and the hardcore street acts." Right when it was about to happen, everything fell apart.

PR: You have a phenomenal track record, though. See as far as production goes, I've had opportunities to do it, but you know, you have to have patience. We talked about psychology earlier. You have to have patience. I don't have a lot of it.

JB: I've learned over the years. I've always been the guy that's like, "Let's get it done now." Over the years I've realized that every once in a while you'll have a hit record in under 40 minutes. And then there are other times when you're stuck on one record for four days.

PR: Production is so subjective. It's like what Forrest Gump said. "It's like a box of chocolates."

JB: "You never know what you're gonna get."

PR: That's the honest-to-God truth. See, that would run me nuts. I'm more of a precise person, you know. I gotta know my job, do my job.

JB: I kinda look forward to the unknown, because I feel like I probably work best under pressure. When it's the 11th hour, and the record has to be turned in. There's a record I did with an artist named Drake for his last album. It was him and Rick Ross. Funny situation – we knew we wanted to get Ross on the record, but Drake goes and raps for like three-and-a-half minutes straight. But when Drake sends Ross the beat, he doesn't send Ross the vocals. So Ross doesn't know that Drake is rapping for like three minutes straight. So Ross does the usual 16 bar thing, and once Drake gets the vocals he's like, "Well, we probably can't use this. He only raps for 16 and I rap for three minutes." I'm like, "Just send me everything, I'll see what I can do." Literally the day before mastering the album, I made a whole different section of the record for Ross, musically based on what was happening when Drake was rapping. But it was one of those things where I kind of had to psych Drake out into believing that it was gonna be cool. And psych the label out into believing it was gonna be cool.

JB: It's so much psychology. Like you gotta fool the artist, fool the label, fool the A&R. Or at least hold them off until it's actually done, And then they're like, "This is amazing!" And I'm like, "Yeah, I told you it would be."

PR: That's genius in itself.

PR: You gotta be a great salesman, see. You have to make believers out of people. That's what Norman Whitfield was great at. Stevie was a great salesman too. You remember the album he did called *Journey Through the Secret Life of Plants?* I was at Berry's house the day he delivered it. I don't know how long it took to get that album. It was years. And I don't think it sold ten copies, to tell you the truth. But what a creative piece of work. Genius.

So what did Stevie say?

PR: Well, he just delivered it. Stevie is Stevie. You just don't chew Stevie up. You take his product and say a prayer.

Do you have a favorite Stevie story?

PR: I remember when Stevie was small, he used to borrow money from everybody. You ever been to the Motown museum? You know that candy machine that's in there? "Hey, Paul Riser, lemme have some change." He must owe me 40 or 50 dollars in change.

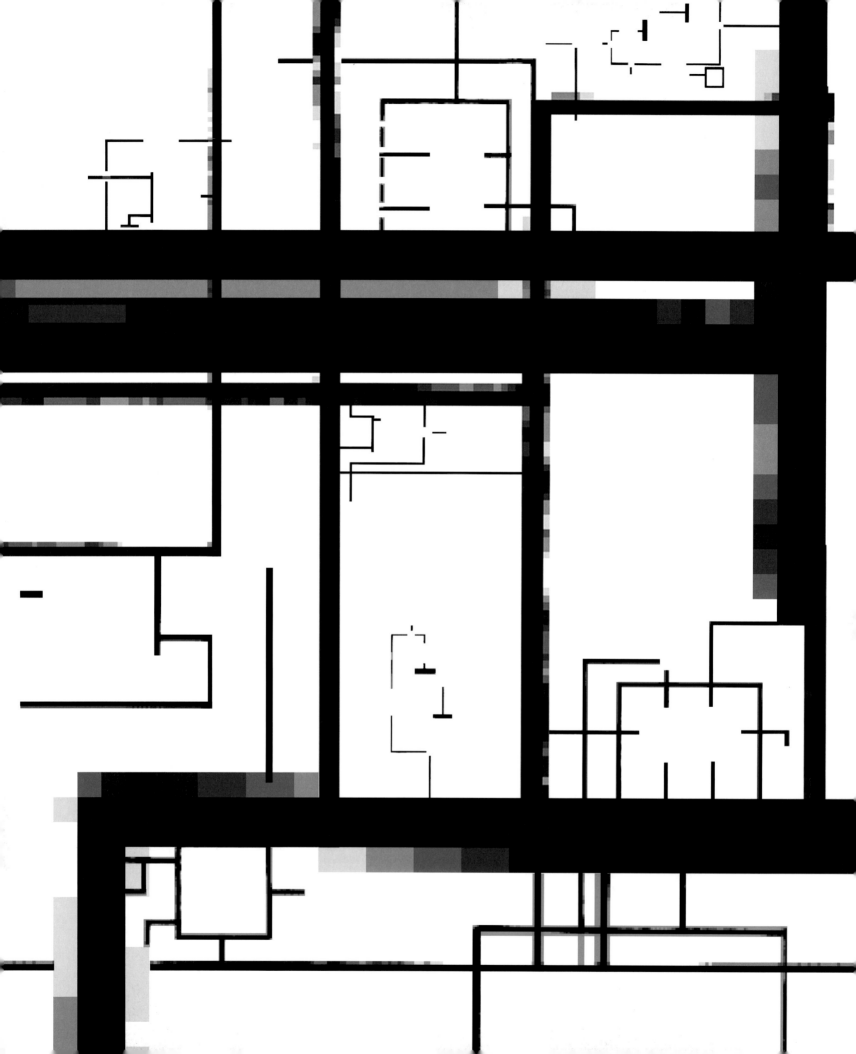

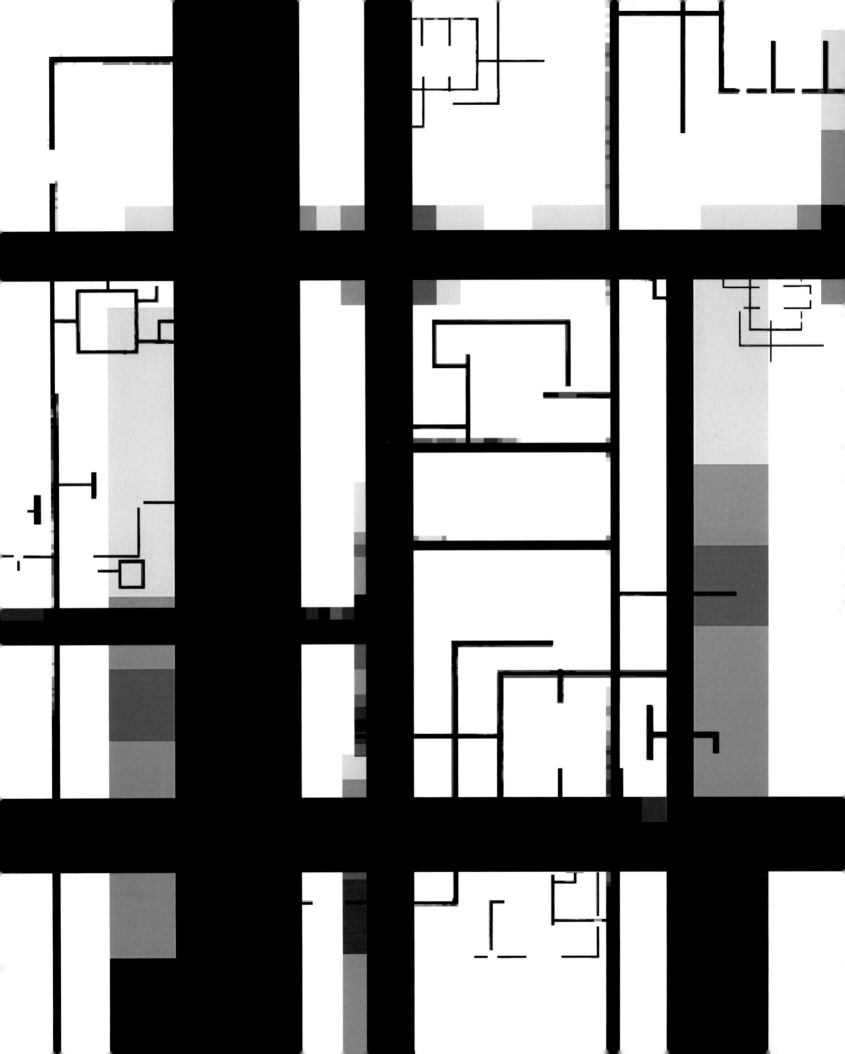

Music is the result not only of the imagination, but the instruments and the interfaces which we use to express it. What strange new worlds could we conjure if we jettisoned the traditional models? This is the kind of question that drove Tom Oberheim and his company to explore new ways of shaping sounds, stacking oscillators and making musical machines talk to each other. Robert Henke has also made a habit of throwing out the rulebook, helping to found the now standard music software program Ableton Live, as well as creating dense worlds of dubby electronics and deep industrialized grooves as Monolake. As a musician and interface designer, Henke treads the tightrope between free-spirited artist and logically-minded instrument builder better than most.

In late June 2013, Henke drove to Oberheim's small office tucked away in a strip mall in Moraga, California. He found Oberheim at his work table, tinkering with one of his signature SEM modules. Oberheim emptied a bag of potato chips into a wooden bowl and distributed beer. Henke seemed to be brimming with questions, scanning the workshop while still squinting from the Saturday afternoon sun. The conversation began immediately, unofficially, as soon as the door opened.

TOM OBERHEIM ROBERT HENKE

AND

Blessed with an engineer's mind and an entrepreneur's vision, **Tom Oberheim**'s name is emblazoned across some of the most futuristic sounding machines of the electronic age. His real achievement, though, was to disguise revolutionary technology inside eminently playable instruments: Throughout the '70s and '80s, Oberheim's pioneering electronics were used by everyone from Joe Zawinul to John Carpenter and Van Halen to Yellow Magic Orchestra. In his wake, there have been an enormous amount of manufacturers offering expander modules, sequencers and programmable synths. But it's hard to improve on such considered constructions. Oberheim modules, synths and drum machines are still used and much sought-after nearly 40 years later.

As a founding member of Berlin duo Monolake alongside Gerhard Behles, **Robert Henke** has been shaping the off-worlds of dub, techno and surround sound ambience since 1996. Across a revered discography, Henke has pushed a sound that is as forward-thinking as it is body-shaking. He's perhaps better known, however, as the co-founder of audio software Ableton Live – a program that helps producers record, perform and sequence their ideas in a non-linear way. A restless thinker and tinkerer, Henke is no longer involved with the company, but life has been no less busy. In 2003 Henke designed the Monodeck MIDI controller, a device that allows him the freedom to perform his music outside of the traditional laptop and mouse combination. As a professor of Sound Design, meanwhile, Henke teaches and lectures about audio engineering and synthesis at Berlin University of the Arts.

Moderator: Dave Tompkins

Photographer: Sabina McGrew

I ONCE HOOKED SOMETHING UP WRONG AND I SAID, WELL, THIS ISN'T RIGHT BUT I'M GOING TO KEEP IT.

Tom Oberheim: I was really interested in minicomputers for a time. I studied them. And then, towards the end of the '60s when I decided to start building stuff for my friends that I met in the music department at UCLA, I just said, "I've had it with computers. I don't want to see one again." So when the microcontroller/microprocessor revolution came I was kind of, "Ah, these things are toys. They don't do much." It was several years before I actually got back into them.

Robert Henke: Well, for MIDI at some point...

TO: Although the history books say that MIDI got started when Dave Smith and Ikutaro Kakehashi got together along with Tom Oberheim, I have no recollection of that whatsoever. I didn't want anything to do with it because I had designed digital logic for ten years, and a very intense ten years it was. I wanted nothing to do with things that had to do with digital logic and, basically, that's all MIDI is.

RH: Of course.

TO: You got certain bits and you play with those bits and you make those bits do what you want. I just didn't want any part of it. Dave and one of his engineers gave a paper around 1981, I think. That was kind of the precursor of MIDI.

RBMA: Robert, how were you introduced to Tom's work?

RH: Well, actually, it took me quite a while to purchase one of your machines but of course, as someone who was interested in synthesizers since I can think – and who was carefully observing what tools all my heroes were using – Oberheim was a name you could see on all those

panels. In a way, I was always fascinated by the visual appearance of groups like Tangerine Dream where you had those people sitting behind these castles of equipment...

TO: "Castles of equipment." I love that.

RH: The back sides of the keyboards were like castle walls. But, at the same time, they were such great advertisements. Especially since those machines were big. There was a lot of room for text. I remember that a friend of mine, at some point, was a proud owner of an Oberheim Xpander. What amazed me was that he did all this music without connecting it to a keyboard, so for him it was just a synth.

TO: No MIDI. Just knobs and switches.

RH: Exactly. And, for me, this was a strong experience. I thought music meant playing notes on a keyboard. Being exposed to a different concept was very striking to me. I also have to admit that I really liked how it looked. The Xpander, to me, was so much more futuristic than all the other keyboards because it lacked a keyboard. Much later – I think around 2003 – I finally bought my own Xpander and I had a nice episode with it recently. The tunings went all false.

TO: They're getting old.

RH: And I was, of course, shocked because I thought, "Oh my God, I need to find someone who can repair it." But at the same time I got all of these fantastic microtonal things so… I had a few hours where I just was recording things which came out of it because I thought I would never be able to reproduce this sound effect. In retrospect I wished I had spent more time with it in its

fail state. For some strange reason I decided to open it and see if maybe the battery was gone or something. When I closed it and I turned it back on, all of the oscillators [when hitting the tuning button] suddenly said: "pass," "pass," "pass"!

It's like Malcolm Clarke from the BBC Radiophonic Workshop once told me, "Never turn your back on a good accident."

TO: Oh, yes. I've done that. I've been there. I once hooked something up wrong and I said, "Well, this isn't right but I'm going to keep it." That's absolutely true.

Is there still room in today's world for these accidents and imperfections?

RH: Absolutely.

TO: Oh, yeah.

CASTLES OF EQUIPMENT. LOVE THAT.

RH: The systems have gotten more reliable because, you know, a software like Ableton Live can't have serious bugs which effect the functionality: someone will notice very soon. So in regards to build quality, all these tools we have today are very robust because they are mass-produced products. But, at the same time, the products are getting so complicated and so complex that there are all kinds of things you can do as a user, which the inventors never foresaw. As soon as you start combining a few common elements you end up creating a structure, a feedback, a situation, which has never been done before. And you get results that are unpredictable.

TO: At my first company I was always trying to make things better. As technology developed and microprocessors got cheaper, we were able to create software that – with each succeeding machine – we were able to automatically tune. But they lost this edge. There's a little edge. When I started making these little modules recently, my engineering mind said, "I might produce some other Oberheims that people want, the more recent ones. The ones that tune better and the ones that are reliable." But they wanted the original. They want that edge. There's a life to these instruments that's hard to talk about in technical terms. Now, there's no denying the fact that the digital workstations have perfect strings, perfect brass, a perfect Fender Rhodes. They allow professionals to go into a studio or go on the road and when they press a button they know it's going to work. And I understand that. But one thing that's undeniable is that in the last ten years there's been a monster resurgence of analog. And it's gratifying to me because I'm back. Dave Smith's been back. Now we see just a flurry of analog machines.

SEM—PRO
SYNTHESIZER EXPANDER MODULE

Marion Systems Corporation   Moraga, California

tomoberheim.com

THERE'S BEEN A

MONSTE

RESURGENCE OF

ANALOG.

Robert, you've done some lectures and written about the laptop in terms of performance – and how the laptop is not the instrument, the software is. I think that's interesting because so many people have these perceptions of what they're seeing and what they're hearing and the conflict between.

RH: Well, I think times are changing very fast. The notion of a laptop being an alien object on a stage is a perspective that is ten years old, at least. This was the big topic when you had the first laptop that was fast enough to do real-time audio. A few years later there were already a lot of performers with laptops on stage. This was a pivotal moment in time where you had all these guys that are on stage with their laptops and you have no clue – as an audience – as to what's going on. It's not satisfying for the audience because the audience feels it's kind of in the darkness. And there's no interaction anymore, and that's not satisfying for the performer. People got used to this new type of performance very fast because laptops became so ubiquitous. If you buy a laptop these days you get a machine that already has some audio software. People are completely used to programming. So this whole notion of music made by a computer program is just as normal as playing guitar. It's getting less and less these days that people actually ask, "What kind of software are you using?" That's a good sign.

TO: When I got started in the synthesizer field in the early '70s there was a lot of talk about how they're not musical instruments.

RH: Of course. My music teacher said so.

TO: "What is this thing that's got wires coming out of it?" But then I lived through the period when Chick Corea played his Minimoog in such a creative way. It was music to me. And then, of course, Joe Zawinul playing my machine on *Birdland*, and on and on. It's, like, "It's not the machine. It's not the machine." I don't like to think in those terms. It's an object. It's a mechanical or an electromechanical object, but it's an instrument. That's the word. It's an instrument.

How important do you think it is for the audience to really know how the sounds are made?

TO: There have been millions and millions of records sold where they don't show the instrument.

RH: I think the point is the magic. The magic can happen on a recording or in a live situation completely independent of the instrument.

I saw Run-D.M.C. in 1983, it was my first concert. That was the first time I heard your DMX drum machine on "Sucker M.C.'s" and it was the most otherworldly. It was the future to me.

TO: And, of course, if I were playing a DMX it wouldn't be interesting at all – even though it was my machine. The technology of musical instruments is a continuous thing. I just finished reading a biography of Bach and, at the end of his life, his sons were trying to convince their dad to write some stuff for a forte piano, which was just being developed. He wasn't interested. I mean, who knows what we will be doing in 50 years?

RH: When Brian Eno was asked about the main qualification for electronic music, he said, "It's not important that you can play an instrument. The important quality is judgment. You need to be able to judge the output." You have the machines doing all the hard work for you. But in order to make something that has artistic value, you need to be able to say, "This part is good and this part is not so good."

TO: I think it's a more difficult process to do equipment now because there are so many tools and maybe that's why we see so much simulation. One of the things that excited me about being in the synth business in the early '70s was hearing Chick Corea get these wonderful sounds. I envisioned a whole new field of musical instruments based on synthesizers. Well, that didn't happen. At least it didn't happen immediately. Because what happened is that people tried to simulate existing instruments. You couldn't do it very well with an analog synth. You couldn't make perfect strings, perfect brass, perfect Fender Rhodes. So the whole process, for me, kind of came to a halt when the DX7 came out. I listened to some of your stuff and it's a little sparse for my musical tastes but I'm excited about the fact that I can't tell what it is. That's why I got into the business in the first place.

RH: As human beings we have a body and we are used to operating with our bodies. And more and more of our life is happening via this computer. We organize our life, our work and our creativity all within these 12 inches of screen and if we narrow down to an iPad then it's even smaller. You think in menus and you think in layers. And that's not very intuitive.

TO: Do you play a regular musical instrument? Were you ever a keyboard player?

RH: I'm a lousy piano player.

TO: Well, let's say you want to be a great piano player. You'd work hours and hours at a very narrow little... it's a little bigger than a screen but that's your world: it's 88 keys. And you think, "Oh, this finger is weak." It's the same problems.

RH: No, for me it's a very different problem! I can talk to you and I can play a piano riff with the left hand. I mean, probably not a complicated one but I can. And I can talk to you and I can modulate the resonance or the cutoff frequency of this filter of an analog synthesizer in a meaningful way. I can't do the same thing with a mouse.

TO: Well, maybe the mouse isn't the best way. Given how long I've been in the computer business, I think it's marvelous what's happened with the mouse and with this CRT that can display more than just alphanumeric characters. It's what made it. But I don't think the interface to the computer is done yet.

RH: Absolutely not. But the interface to these instruments is very known. We have 50 years of history of knobs and we know how they act. I look at this thing and I know how to operate it. And I know what to expect.

TO: Do you know the music of Weather Report?

RH: Of course. I'm a huge fan of Joe Zawinul.

TO: So, I got to tell you this story. It's 1977, I'm at my company in Santa Monica and I knew Joe from back when he had a ring modulator. But I'm busy, he's busy and I hadn't seen him in a while. So he calls me and he says, "Oh, I got one of your 8-Voices and it's really great. Maybe you could show me a little about how to use it?" So I went to meet with him and I started talking about filter cutoffs and all this stuff. Because that's the only…

…language you had.

TO: And he was very polite and he would listen, but I knew he was just going to take it back to Guitar Center or wherever he bought it and get his money back and that would be it. So a few weeks pass and he calls up and he says, "Tom, you got to hear this thing I did with your machine." And I'm thinking, "What? He didn't take it back?" So I went back and he played me a rough mix of "Birdland" and it just blew me away. And what I realized was that it was new to him but he's a skilled musician. He took it, and he learned how to use it. It certainly wasn't an easy machine to use. It was on the same level as trying to make great music with a mouse. People will overcome it – and it will evolve.

RH: I'm absolutely sure about this. But what I mean is: This is already a known musical expression because it's a 50 year-old concept. Until the mid-'90s a lot of electronic music production was based on new instruments coming in all the time. New instruments meant new sound. Somehow we have reached a stage where the novelty aspect of electronic music has reached a plateau. Nowadays if a new software comes out – or new hardware – you don't expect to hear anything which is completely unheard. You don't expect a user interface which is completely new. You just expect a more matured version of an instrument. I like this, because this plateau allows us to look backwards. That's why I believe there is so much retro stuff going on right now. We are at the plateau and we are looking down the canyon and saying, "This was cool, this is cool, I heard about it. I need to go there and try it out." We're in this stage where you collect all these experiences. I believe in the near future creative things will come out of merging all those influences into new things.

TO: Oh, sure.

RH: But the new things might not be as much technology-driven as the old things because the technology is so known. So the new thing might be more a combination of existing things. That's what we see these days: genres emerge into new genres by combining old ideas. Or focus more on, let's say, all the kind of interesting audio/visual things, which are happening because the medium people are listening to music these days is YouTube. They use YouTube as their radio. That means they actually have visual information too. I don't know yet what kind of influence it is going to have, but it could be that this is something that changes the way people think about music. If a generation comes up for whom the connection of video and music is normal, the CD is going to die. All of these mediums which are formative mediums in hardware – which tell you audio has two channels, 74 minutes max – are things of the past. I'm expecting a lot of interesting changes coming from the plateau situation.

TO: Certainly. I think there hasn't been a real breakthrough to where many hundreds of people standardize on something. So it's really a very fertile field, very quickly changing. I think the mouse thing you're talking about will kind of go by the wayside. Because who likes to deal with a mouse? It's very crude. I think this was just a way of bringing computer technology to a large number of people. It will go somewhere. I mean, not being a controller guy, I can't really say where. But I think in my lifetime – and certainly in your lifetime – it will be very different.

RH: Well, I hope so because it became a big mess.

TO: Yeah, well…

RH: We have all these programs and they are very powerful, more powerful than what we ever had. At the same time it's more and more difficult to work with all this power because we became bookkeepers of our own technology.

TO: There's a commercial aspect. It starts with Microsoft and the unending new versions of their programs that don't really do anything more than they did 20 years ago. And that's just a fact of life. [But] it's kind of the impediment to it really blossoming I think. So many companies are putting features on software products and they're not really advancing the art.

RH: Yeah, but that's a very different issue from the general issue of having too many choices. I mean, the one issue of course is if something matures. Like, if a company matures or if a product of the company matures, it becomes this really big ship and to change the course of the ship becomes more and more difficult. But if we just assume all these companies don't exist and the big ships don't exist, then still the question remains: What do we do with all of this power? What do we do with all of these machines which are there? If I look at my own music and practice, I spend so much time with organization because of all of these options. If I only have an eight-track recorder and one reverb unit and a small mixing desk and two or three keyboards and a drum machine, I'm limited. And in retrospect I'm limited in a very positive way because I have to be decisive. If tape is expensive, I make up my mind before I record something and I get the result pretty fast. Now I have unlimited undo. Terabytes of hard disc space. I have ten million different plug-ins and I can store a new version of a document every five seconds. So I end up with millions of unfinished sketches that I will never open again. I feel a big topic of the future is not so much if we are still using a keyboard or if we create music by mind control. I have no idea. Maybe it's going to happen. I think that the bigger challenge is how do we organize all this stuff? How do we make sure that the creative moments don't get lost within this abundance of exercises?

"AND IT JUST

"OM, YOU GOT TO HEAR THIS THING I DID WITH YOUR MACHINE."

AND I'M THINKING, "WHAT? HE DIDN'T TAKE IT BACK?"

SO I WENT BACK AND HE PLAYED ME A ROUGH MIX OF "BIRDLAND" BLEW ME AWAY.

TO: It's interesting that you say that because... Imagine a kind of strange science fiction story where you have a very talented modern-day composer who has a very nice computer system and he or she can put down his ideas and save them and manipulate them with all this different software. Then take this person back in time, at least a century. And all you've got to score is paper and a pen. And you say, "OK, go to it." How would that change his work? Of course you would find a way.

RH: I would and, as a matter of fact, I did ask myself this question because I found it an interesting thought exercise. So let's assume you throw me into the Stone Age and I'm living in a cave. That's a good thing, because I like reverb. So I would probably walk through the cave and would find the one spot in the cave where the reverb suits my purposes and then I would start collecting stones until I find a few stones with distinct pitch and characteristics. And then I would try to gather an audience of other Stone Age folks to start a drumming ensemble or to listen to what I drum. So that would be the solution.

TO: And you'd create.

RH: I hope so. When I started making electronic music I was very happy to be part of this kind of underground culture in Berlin. There were all these empty spaces. You could just go in factories and open the door and set up your concert environment. The point of the early '90s was not recording, because it was much more interesting to play with your friends. And, in this regard at least, this type of music was much more rooted in the real-time experience of a timbre. Or repetitive rhythmical structures. That friend of mine who had the Xpander routed every single output

through a different speaker. So we were in this industrial space and he had those six DDR studio monitors hanging there on the ceiling. He would tune one oscillator to do this in one speaker and another thing on the other speaker and you would walk through his composition. And, at some point, someone else came in with an 808 and said, "Hey, I have a clock output." And someone else said, "Well, that's great because actually I have a small step sequencer."

TO: You were fortunate to be involved in that. Not everybody has that opportunity. We don't know what the equivalent of that was in the 18th century, because there was no recording and the only thing left is what is written down. I mean, who knows what kind of stuff went on in 1825.

RH: Maybe they played the most amazing free jazz.

TO: That's right.

RH: But I guess we would have known because, I mean, of course the written music works very well as a documentation of what ideas of timbre structure and harmonic melody they had.

I wonder how the sounds have evolved since that time you spoke of in Berlin.

RH: I'm pretty sure it sounds much better nowadays than it did.

It's a fascinating thing to think about because everything has to be recorded now. I feel like if you go to a live performance everybody is too busy capturing the moment as opposed to just feeling it.

RH: But there's only so much video you can take. I mean the classic scenario is that people make all these video clips and never watch them because they don't have the time. And, at some point, people will notice it's pointless and stop doing it.

TO: They may not watch them but these people had to think a little about when they did it and maybe it's the thought process that leads them to a place. I don't know. The storage of all of this just becomes astronomical. I just wonder if that's practical. You have to make judgments about what you keep.

RH: I might be a complete lunatic, but I believe still in Moore's Law.

TO: That it can go on forever and ever.

RH: In 20 years they will laugh about our tera and petabytes, you know? But I think I'm more worried about the extinction of our race because of other stupidities.

TO: Well, that's a different discussion.

RH: If there's no clean water anymore, no clean air anymore…

TO: It's kind of a moot point if the human race isn't around in 200 years.

WHO KNOWS WHAT WE WILL BE DOING IN 50 YEARS?

How do you separate thinking about technology and making music with technology?

RH: A lot of successful artists I admire know surprisingly little about technology, and this allows them to use the technology with the innocence of a child but with all their informed artistic ideas. And this is extremely powerful. For me, this is not a working path because I understand what's going on. The type of resonance I need to seek between the machine and me is a different one. I need to find the fascination among the things I know or on the edge of the things I know. I'm not fascinated anymore by turning the cut of the frequency of the filter. But I'm fascinated when there's suddenly some nonlinear distortion going which creates overtones I was not expecting. Suddenly the machine becomes alive. I understand what is going on, but at the same time I'm touched. These are the moments I'm looking for. And this is the basis for my exploration. But then of course I'm in a dangerous situation because the engineering side of my brain can say, "Ah, I like this phenomenon. I need to improve the instrument so that this phenomena is getting more prominent." And then I start changing the machine instead of saying, "I have the phenomena which is here and I need to make use of it." I live in the constant fear of spending too much time improving my tools instead of actually working with them.

I LIVE IN THE CONSTANT

TOO MUCH TIME
IMPROVING MY TOOLS INSTEAD OF ACTUALLY

WORKING WITH THEM.

FEAR
OF SPENDING

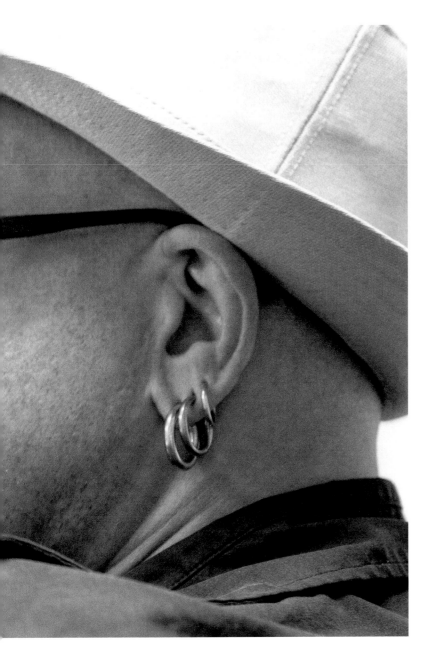

TO: The thing I wonder about, especially since I'm at the age where I could be gone tomorrow or whatever… Something I'll never find out is if there will be analog synthesizers that look something like this in 100 years.

RH: I won't know, unless Ray Kurzweil is right and I'm jumping over the fence, which I doubt.

TO: You have to buy his pills first.

RH: I know. And eat them everyday, like 30 of them or something. [*laughs*] We won't go there. But anyway, I'm confident that they will still be there.

TO: And then that leaves the question: Will there still be some old Oberheims floating around?

RH: And will they still work? I'm so worried about my old machines because I know enough about them to understand thermal stress. It's not good to turn them on and off because they heat up, they cool down. It's bad. However, if you don't use them at all, things get worse too. The other thing is cosmic radiation, which kills the chips sooner or later anyway. Capacitors dry out.

TO: I would argue there's no reason why the technology, the stuff in these newer modules, won't be working in 50 or 100 years for the most part.

RH: But what do we do with the early digital stuff?

TO: It's due to chemicals more than the environment. I've heard about chips going bad. When I first started hearing about it I thought, "Oh, these chips will last forever." That's not true. I only know about my own stuff and there's plenty of 2 voice, 4 voice and 8 voice Oberheims that need to be changed. But you can replace them with modern versions. A lot of equipment will be running for a long time. That leads, of course, to the question of, "What should I try and improve as an analog designer?" I'm taking an approach of making stuff as much like the old one as I can. But using new technology. I'd love to be around for a hundred years to see if some of my '70s stuff is still working.

Essays

A man who knows what he likes and sees no reason to compromise.

In the mid-'80s, after producer Adrian Sherwood had an almost accidental chart hit with Gary Clail's single "Human Nature," the head of a very successful major label invited him in for a meeting. He gave Sherwood a list of their artists, and asked him to choose which ones he would like to remix. Sherwood read slowly down the list, which included some classic '80s pop acts and big-name artists who were selling records in impressive numbers. "I don't really like any of them," he confessed. The label head roared with laughter, and they went to the pub instead.

This story, really, tells you all you need to know about Adrian Sherwood, producer, remixer and founder of the long-running independent label On-U Sound. He is a man who knows what he likes and sees no reason to compromise, who has always made music for love, not money – and most encounters with him inevitably end up either in the pub, the studio or with Sherwood in the kitchen cooking up a big vegetarian meal for all comers.

Sherwood's story is a classic tale of a man following his passion. Turned on to reggae by the older sister of a school friend in High Wycombe, by the age of 14 he was DJing at afternoon sessions in the local reggae/soul club and making contacts in the specialist London shops on his fortnightly record-buying

When punk embraced reggae as a natural partner, Sherwood was right in the middle of it all.

trips. At 17 he was the junior partner in a record distribution business, servicing reggae specialist stores around the country with new music.

At first they just drove around with records released by small London labels, but they were soon importing product straight from Jamaica and then set up their own label, Carib Gems, to license tracks for UK release. Gradually, Sherwood began to forge links with innovative Jamaican artists like the dub producer Prince Far I, commissioning and sometimes collaborating on new albums for Carib Gems and then for his own label Hitrun.

When punk embraced reggae as a natural partner, Sherwood was right in the middle of it all. He toured with the Clash and the Slits, was asked to join John Lydon's post-Pistols project PiL, and in 1980 set up On-U Sound to explore the new links between post-punk experimentalism, his beloved dub reggae and the newly emerging hip hop scene. A chance meeting in New York led to a

long-standing partnership with drummer Keith LeBlanc, guitarist Skip McDonald and bassist Doug Wimbish – the rhythm section on many of the early Sugar Hill rap records. Former Slits singer Ari Up and Mark Stewart of the mercurial Bristol band the Pop Group became regular collaborators.

Around these key players, a whole series of genre-bending bands began to form, record and tour: New Age Steppers, African Head Charge, Tackhead, Little Axe. Meanwhile Sherwood continued to release reggae, with albums by big Jamaican names such as Lee 'Scratch' Perry, Bim Sherman and Junior Delgado. On-U became synonymous with a certain quality, its diverse releases unified by the clever packaging – the label's mid-'80s series of 10-inch singles with beautifully photographed B&W covers are now prized by collectors, changing hands for serious sums.

For further proof that this is a man who lives and breathes music, all you need to do is step into his living room. A couple of years back, Sherwood moved from London to the lovely town of Ramsgate, on the Kent coast, but his house is very much the same: walls plastered with posters for his records and gigs, CDs and records lining every wall and a mixing desk dominating what would have been the lounge.

ADRIAN SHERWOOD

Author: Sheryl Garratt

Collaboration has always been what he does best, so it's no surprise to find that musicians are constantly coming down to visit, or even moving down to be near him: Doug Wimbish and the Ghetto Priest have already bought homes nearby. But it is typical of Sherwood that he's also getting involved in the local music scene, forging new links and opening a rough-and-ready arts and recording space on the seafront, Shantytown.

Sherwood's story is a classic tale of a man following his passion.

Download culture has affected On-U as much as any other label, but as ever, Sherwood has been resourceful, expanding his live shows into his main income stream, and starting a new collaboration with dubstep producer Pinch. "We used to do gigs to promote the records – now it's the other way round. The records are promoting us doing live shows. So we've created a show where we're basically building a studio onstage, and making the music live. So Pinch has got a load of outputs that are coming up on an analogue mixing desk and a noise pad. I've got a pad with loads of samples, and I'm using two delays, three reverbs, phasers and a noise machine. And we're going to all

Most encounters with him inevitably end up either in the pub, the studio or with Sherwood in the kitchen cooking up a big vegetarian meal for all comers.

the big festivals, doing a show that's like dubstep meets On-U. It's not so easy to make records and sell them any more, so I'm operating on the old premise of the Jamaican sound systems. If I cut good enough rhythms, I can play them out and no one else can play them back at me."

Sheryl Garratt has edited *The Face* and *The Observer* in the UK. She is now a freelance journalist, working mainly for the *Sunday Telegraph*.

To hear Ben UFO on Rinse FM is to hear an artist truly in his element.

Sometime nearly ten years ago, at a student radio station in Leeds, someone received an application for an FM show from Ben Thomson, later known as Ben UFO, and turned it down. You have to wonder if that program director has ever heard Thomson on the air since then.

If there's a single thing that sets Thomson apart, it's his conscious desire to move forward.

Anyone who locks into Hessle Audio's show on Rinse FM when Thomson's at the helm gets pirate radio at its finest: a vivid panorama of bold new music, anchored by house, techno and bass, but easily veering through jazz, ambient, reggae and beyond. Unknown classics flow into unreleased tracks by Thomson's brilliant cast of peers – one show in 2013 began with a hectic free jazz piece, and later premiered never-before-played songs by Four Tet, Kowton and Julio Bashmore. All of it's threaded together by Thomson's neat yet unfussy mixing, and by his own humble commentary: "love the drops on this one," or, "a big personal favorite of mine at the moment, the sounds of Pépé Bradock, somehow managing to mix something very summery with something very noisy."

Pearson Sound, who runs Hessle Audio with Thomson and Pangaea, often co-hosts the show. He does a fantastic job as well. But to hear Ben UFO on Rinse FM is to hear an artist truly in his element.

If there's a single thing that sets Thomson apart from most DJs, it's his conscious desire to move forward. The art of DJing is often the art of going with the flow, doing what feels natural, playing whatever record seems right at that moment. Ben UFO is by no means above that, but he and his Hessle cohorts also feel a self-imposed pressure to challenge themselves and their audience, and to avoid treading water as much as possible. "We don't really go over the same territory," Thomson has said, adding that each Hessle Audio show "will be a markedly different selection and a different feel, and if a track is played again it will be in a slightly different context."

Thomson seems especially prone to hearing music for what it really is.

Keeping up this forward-momentum often means breaking down (or simply ignoring) boundaries, especially in terms of musical style. Pearson Sound, Pangaea and Hessle

Audio's other contributors (Objekt, Elgato, Bandshell, et al.) do this all the time in their records, either by blending elements of house and techno with hallmarks of the UK's hardcore continuum (setting a jungle-inspired rhythm at a house-y 124 BPM, say), or by lunging off-piste altogether and making something truly avant-garde (see Pearson Sound's 2013 EP, *REM*).

Thomson, who at this point is devoted entirely to DJing and running the label, does this through his sets and through Hessle Audio's A&R. He's said that his goal is to "bring loads of different stuff together under the same broad aesthetic and have it be seen as part of the same thing." This explains DJ sets which group records together in a way that's totally unconventional yet perfectly natural. It's also clear in Hessle Audio's catalog, whose stylistic individuality is evidenced by the awkward, hyphen-laden terms with which it's described ("post-dubstep" being both the most useful and the most cringe-worthy). Thomson seems especially prone to hearing music for what it really is, and ignoring the divisions that have been superimposed on it.

As it happens, electronic music is going through a phase when this is especially needed. For decades, new styles of club music arrived one after another, and although each

BEN UFO

Author: Will Lynch

was inspired by its predecessor, many of them were truly original. Today, such novel styles are a rarity – we are in an age of revival and reinvention. Originality is defined by the ability to re-synthesize what's come before in a way that's clever and compelling. This is exactly what Ben UFO does better than just about anyone else.

His DJ sets group records together in a way that's totally unconventional yet perfectly natural.

If that's a fairly abstract explanation for Thomson's success, there's a more concrete one as well: he's a pro who takes what he does very seriously. "I'm naturally fairly introverted," he says. "I don't participate in a lot of the wilder things people typically associate with DJing. I don't go to after-parties that often and I'm normally completely sober when I DJ." It's impossible to imagine Thomson blowing off a gig, or even half-assing one. On Rinse FM, he dutifully "big ups" anyone who tweets at him, be they industry figures or fans. He dismisses notions of his own importance as "something people keep saying" or "something people have come up with." Many DJs see success as a personal

victory. Thomson, who downplays his own success despite having hit the #21 spot in *Resident Advisor*'s Top DJs of 2012, sees it as "a responsibility."

This makes him a slightly odd fit in the big leagues of the DJ world, at least in terms of personality. Baby-faced, soft-spoken and occasionally wearing granddad spectacles, he's not someone you'd expect to see at superclubs like Ibiza's Space, though by now he's played there plenty of times. He's also found himself on plenty of enormous festival stages – a far cry from the intimate spots he loves, like London's Plastic People or Hamburg's Golden Pudel. It's not always easy.

"I find myself in situations where I'm completely petrified quite a lot," he says. "There's always a really nerve-wracking ten or 15 minutes before I go on stage and play to a lot of people. But I think it's good to put yourself in situations where you feel terrified, or where you're not naturally comfortable. You come through the other side and feel the adrenaline rush – it's amazing."

Will Lynch is the associate editor of *Resident Advisor.*

Horsepower have always been credited for a sound that became the origin of dubstep, but their ethos is also a crucial part of the story.

When dubstep blew up in the mid-'00s, Horsepower Productions finally began to make sense. A few years previous, their music seemingly existed outside of everything – a pared down version of 2-step which had no contemporary peer. Nowadays, they're regarded as a foundational figure in one of the biggest electronic music genres in the world.

"What We Do" expressed an identity – this is us, this is our style.

You won't find them headlining festival stages, however. The production collective has remained a cult concern, at least partly deliberately. Horsepower have always been credited for a sound that became the origin of dubstep, but their ethos – the way they cultivated a sense of belonging to an underground that could never be wholly consumerized – is also a crucial part of the story.

Horsepower were originally Benny Ill, Nasis and Lev Jnr, though from 2002 Benny Ill largely produced alone under the moniker. (He was joined in 2009 by Jay King and, on the 2010 album *Quest for the Sonic Bounty*, the four reunited.) Their legacy, however, was built on the first three 12-inch releases they put out on Tempa, the seminal label run by Neil Jolliffe

and Sarah Lockhart, AKA Soulja, who also started the club night FWD>> where many game-changing dubs were first tested.

It's somehow no accident that the collective's first release came out the same year as Oxide & Neutrino's "Bound 4 Da Reload" went to #1 in the UK chart. As the likes of Luck & Neat, Sweet Female Attitude, Artful Dodger and MJ Cole dominated the UK pop charts, Horsepower went in an opposite direction. It sounds a bit like a mission statement. The subtleties of the production and the structure of "When You Hold Me" would have placed it beyond most A&R's agendas, yet its samples, crackling atmospherics and wobbling bass made for a track that stood apart – a sound that would only later became a blueprint for innumerable dubstep tracks.

Horsepower, quite simply, went deeper. "When You Hold Me" set out the template, employing samples of gunshots taken from a film. Ill, when he DJs, has said that he sometimes likes to include rainforest sounds playing throughout his sets. This is done in service of creating a vibe – a tactic Burial would later utilize to great effect in his own productions.

On the flipside of "When You Hold Me," "Let's Dance" similarly set out a clear agenda. The early '00s saw the arrival of another style

of minimal 2-step – the stark sublow and eski beats of Jon E Cash, Wiley, Platinum 24 and Terror Danjah that were designed to be MC-ed over. "Let's Dance"'s wordless, driving 2-step could be read as an obvious message. Although there was always fluidity between grime and dubstep – Skepta rhyming over Skream's "Midnight Request Line" at FWD>> being a particularly memorable example –grime was about getting lost with the MCs, whereas dubstep was about getting lost in the production. Horsepower drew the line.

From now on the sounds would be darker, what was "girly" would be gone.

Despite 2-step's move toward the charts with tracks like Genius Cru's "Boom Selection," DJ Pied Piper's "Do You Really Like It" and Daniel Bedingfield, Horsepower continued to pursue their own trajectory with their next two Tempa releases: "Gorgon Sound" dug deep into dub soundscapes while "Triple 7" was garage evolving in pirate frequencies. A notable twist on Tempa 003 was how the driving bassline on "Vigilante" became the voice of the tune – it literally feels like it's trying to say something. The title of "What We Do"

BENNY ILL

Author: Melissa Bradshaw

expressed an identity – this is us, this is our style – and in remix form had the sort of outer space experimentalism that placed it in a King Tubby/Lee Perry/Adrian Sherwood/Mad Professor tradition.

In 2001 Horsepower also put out a release on seminal jungle imprint No U Turn's sub-label Turn U On. On the flip, "Givin' Up On Love" was the crew's most arresting mo ment to that point. Its sweetly sad female vocal, and stunning, minor-keyed production was like a goodbye to a garage love affair. Again there seemed to be a message, this time melancholic: From now on the sounds would be darker, what was "girly" would be gone.

pursue Horsepower's reference of UK garage culture to hip hop and dub styles, and the musical possibilities contained therein.

It's not hard to hear the impact of Horsepower's sound today. Countless producers used the template as a jumping-off point for their own experiments and imitations. Burial's evocations of a garage underground come directly from Horsepower's inspiration. Indeed, it's impossible to picture the dubstep scene that would come to be built without Horsepower's foundational take on garage, and their secretive, coded messages.

Grime was about getting lost with the MCs, whereas dubstep was about getting lost in the production.

There were no love songs (at least in the standard sense) on Horsepower's first two albums. While grime seemed to evolve more on its own terms, at least until Dizzee Rascal's *Boy In Da Corner*, Benny Ill continued to

Melissa Bradshaw is a writer based in London. She is interested in sound system culture past and present, and has a PhD in literature and psychoanalysis.

Funk, as heard in Purdie's playing, is accent and swing; pocket, propulsion and abundant personality.

There are funky drummers and then there's the man renowned as *the* funky drummer, Bernhard "Pretty" Purdie. A ubiquitous session player and sometime bandleader who's supplied the rhythmic backbone on literally thousands of recordings, Purdie's presence on classics like Aretha Franklin's "Rock Steady" assured him a hallowed place in the annals of breakbeat history. But the funk that's defined this stickman's work for over five decades has never been simply based on open bars of digitally pillage-able beats. Funk, as heard in Purdie's playing, is accent and swing; pocket, propulsion and abundant personality. Describing the admittedly not-so-smooth nature of his press rolls, he affectionately refers to them as "biscuits." It doesn't get much funkier than that.

The signature creation of this consummate timekeeper is a rhythm as tricky as it is irresistible; a convergence of bass, hi-hat and snare syncopation once described by *The New York Times* as "a groove that seems to spin in concentric circles as it lopes forward... and if you can listen without shaking your hips, you should probably see a doctor." This is the Purdie Shuffle. And though, naturally, no one quite plays it like its originator, it's been replicated (or at least approximated, or at the very least accidentally approximated) on records as diverse as Led

Zeppelin's "Fool in the Rain," Death Cab For Cutie's "Grapevine Fires" and Juelz Santana's "Dipset (Santana's Town)."

Appropriately, the Shuffle has down home roots. Purdie's native Elkton, Maryland, to be specific, where as a youngster the fledgling drummer developed his rhythmic invention while attempting to capture the energy and *whoosh* of the trains that passed near his family's home. A prodigy behind the kit, by age 8 he'd joined a local big band. By 12 he'd formed his first group as leader. And by the time he graduated high school and enrolled at Morgan State University in Baltimore, he was playing in multiple bands and holding down nightclub gigs at a pace less suited for a student than a full-time professional musician.

In 1961, he packed his bags for New York City, determined to become just that. As legend has it, Purdie – never short on confidence – eventually attracted the attention of record producers by hanging out around recording studios wearing a sign identifying himself as "The Hitmaker." If his knack for self-promotion got his foot in the door, his drumming kept him in the building. A stream of steady session work commenced, Purdie cutting demos and certified hits for the likes of Mickey & Sylvia, Les Cooper, Doris Troy and others. The sessions came so fast, furious and far ranging,

Purdie maintains that he even re-cut various early Beatles drum parts (though one Richard Starkey notably claims otherwise).

What's indisputable is the quality of Purdie's best-known work. On James Brown's "It's a Man's, Man's, Man's World," his lithe hi-hat triplets and rimshots push the momentum of one of the most dramatic songs in recorded history. On B.B. King's classic blues "The Thrill Is Gone," his backbeat is the portrait of strength through restraint. For Gil Scott-Heron's "The Revolution Will Not Be Televised," his cavalcade of ghost notes, rolls and open hi-hat *pssssts* (another signature lick) are the musical reflection of a growling agitation and unrest.

His lithe hi-hat triplets and rimshots push the momentum of one of the most dramatic songs in recorded history.

As Aretha Franklin's musical director on albums like *Young, Gifted and Black*, Purdie's inventive pulse is as readily identifiable on ballads like "Day Dreaming" as iconic funk bombs like "Rock Steady." Roberta Flack and

BERNARD PURDIE

Author: Jeff "Chairman" Mao

Donny Hathaway's "Where Is the Love" is unimaginable without the drummer's bubbly bossa-like accompaniment – the essential third voice in a conversation between two soulful giants. And on Steely Dan's "Home at Last," the quintessential Purdie Shuffle gets a proper showcase within a typically meticulous Fagen-Becker number.

Purdie cult favorites have also proven their lasting power. The punishing opening break from "Soul Drums," the title track to his debut LP, won wider adoration when it was sampled by Beck for *Odelay*'s opener, "Devil's Haircut." Boom-bap before boom-bap, songs like "Coffee Cold," from his sessions with *Hair* composer Galt MacDermot, were similarly revived years later by tracksmiths like Dan the Automator, Prince Paul and DJ Premier. And the sides he cut as both a leader and sideman (with Johnny "Hammond" Smith, Charles Kynard and Ivan "Boogaloo Joe" Jones) for Prestige were the grooves from which London's acid jazz scene of the early '90s culled continual inspiration.

Even a lost obscurity like *Lialeh*, his privately pressed soundtrack to a no-budget porn film, became a hotly pursued piece of Purdie groove-ology on the '90s "beat-diggin'" circuit before being officially reissued in 2003. Purdie was so prolific in the '70s – session drumming

for James Brown, Miles Davis, Cat Stevens, Hall & Oates and countless others – he's in hindsight credited almost by default for beats that have long existed in a mysterious vacuum like Melvin Bliss' "Synthetic Substitution," one of the most sampled breaks in history.

What the best of these recordings exemplify – and what Purdie's oeuvre in its entirety fundamentally represents – is a dedication to service. "The two and the four," is what he once famously told Amhir "Questlove" Thompson was the key to keeping food on the table. Though perhaps a suitable enough mantra for a more pedestrian hired gun, Purdie's actual approach to his trade was far more sophisticated. Whether it meant showing flash or laying in the cut, he understood how a piece of music could best benefit from him as a supporting player. Drumming may have long been Bernard Purdie's job. But through the exuberance of his playing, he never let us forget it's also his passion.

Jeff "Chairman" Mao is the co-author of *ego trip's Book of Rap Lists* and *ego trip's Big Book of Racism*. He resides in Harlem with his wife and kids, their cats and his record collection.

Raster-Noton has effectively existed as a homestead on the frontier of digital art.

By 1999, the Berlin Wall was dust for a decade, and a new threshold was in view. Though the next millennium would not begin, technically, until 2001, the year 2000 hovered just ahead in the popular imagination with a mix of portent and promise. This anticipation in mind, the German record label Noton invited an international assortment of musicians to contribute to a monthly series of recordings titled *20' to 2000*.

Each participant was directed to record what they felt might play on a home stereo for the 20 minutes just before bells would bring in 2000. A dozen in all, these contributors included a veritable who's who of experimental electronic titans: Thomas Brinkmann, Scanner (AKA Robin Rimbaud), Mika Vainio (of the duo Pansonic) and Wolfgang Voigt. Their music, a mix of emotionally remote glitch and ambient, signaled a considered ambivalence about the future. The releases were as stark in their packaging as they were sonically: Composed of standard-size CDs, the outer two inches of which were fully transparent, encased in nearly mark-less clamshells, each connected to the next with small magnets, resulting in something like the vertebrae of a squat cyborg snake.

Among the participants were Carsten Nicolai, who had since the mid-'90s run Noton as his own concern, and Olaf Bender, who had around the same time founded – alongside Frank Bretschneider – the label Raster-music. The imprints shared an interest in viscerally ascetic, ecstatically minimal tracks. Music that whittled the rhythmic intent of techno down to myriad displays of patterning.

How many techno musicians have work in the collection of the Museum of Modern Art?

The series not only announced the beginning of a new chronological mindset, but coincided with a merger: Noton and Rastermusic would become Raster-Noton. Since the 1999 union, visual design and sonic experimentation have been its hallmarks. The label has released a sequence of recordings that, while originating from a variety of musicians, can be heard to collectively explore a shared territory. Raster-Noton has effectively existed as a homestead on the frontier of digital art, waiting for the rest of the planet to catch up.

Today, of course, data visualization is pervasive, but its accepted norms can be tracked back to the early efforts of Bender, Nicolai

and the cohort they assembled at Raster-Noton, most notably Ryoji Ikeda, who has made a name for himself by filling art spaces with immersive barcode projections. The expressly global label has served as a safe haven to Russian-born CoH, Swedish tape-music tinkerer Carl Michael von Hausswolff, British broken techno duo snd (Mark Fell and Mat Steel) and to a crew of Americans, among them sound artist Richard Chartier, microsound explorer Kim Cascone and William Basinski, best known for his work with decaying tape loops.

The label has also been home to the unceasing productivity of Bender and Nicolai themselves. Nicolai's solo releases, usually under the name Alva Noto, can often sound less like individual records than like the latest in a series of missives from a rarefied landscape. He is also a prolific collaborator, having recorded with artists as diverse as Ryoji Ikeda, with whom he shares a love of immersive data environs, and Ryuichi Sakamoto, whose melodic proclivities offer a useful counterpoint. Those efforts have increasingly made him as prominent in art galleries as he is in clubs. (How many techno musicians have work in the collection of the Museum of Modern Art?) His books, such as *Grid Index* and *Moiré Index*, look exactly like his music

CARSTEN NICOLAI & OLAF BENDER

Author: Marc Weidenbaum

sounds: geometric structures whose complexity is rooted in slight shifts rather than sweeping gestures.

Like Nicolai, Bender is as much a graphic innovator as musician. It is a distinction that he willfully blurs, as in the title to his 2008 album, *Death of a Typographer*. The music found within has the cadence and intent of techno, but registers as barely a sequence of blips – the blueprint for techno in the form of a click track. Bender generally records under the moniker Byetone, and is given to koan-grade pronouncements about his dedication to luxurious aridity. He once told an interviewer that he prefers the phrase "how less can I do" to "how much can I do."

It was music that whittled the rhythmic intent of techno down to myriad displays of patterning.

In 2013, Bender and Noto opened for global synth pop act Depeche Mode. Bender and Noto's project for this stadium-proportioned enterprise was Diamond Version, a trio with the Japanese musician Atsuhiro Ito, a virtuoso of the fluorescent light bulb,

which he wields like an especially theatrical Jedi knight. This association with Depeche Mode was not implausible, despite the seeming gap between their audiences. In the year prior to the tour, Diamond Version began to release a series of hard-hitting, club-teasing EPs on the Mute Records label, a longtime residence for Depeche. Around the same time, Noto contributed a remix to a single by VCMG, the two-man supergroup comprised of Depeche Mode's original songwriter Vince Clarke, and the man who inherited those duties when Clarke left the band, Martin Gore.

The beats of Diamond Version are more louche than much of what Bender or Noto have previously produced – the effect is less white-wall gallery, more opulent urban lounge – but the dance party tonalities only serve to disguise a trenchant minimalism that is of a piece with their collective catalogs. Diamond Version should be heard not as deviating from their more abstract Raster-Noton activities, but as another layer in the social graph that is Bender and Noto's combined artistic vision. For we know what happens when new layers are added to corresponding yet inherently distinct data sets: familiar patterns are disrupted, and a new moiré emerges.

Marc Weidenbaum founded Disquiet.com in 1996. He's written for *Nature* and lectures on the role of sound in the media landscape.

Cosey Fanni Tutti put her own beauty to the test in ways that challenge and interrogate the meaning of the term.

Christine Carol Newby begat Cosmosis begat Cosey Fanni Tutti. This Trinitarian catechism offers three names for three moments in the ongoing, unfinished story of a visionary British artist whose itinerant trajectory from Hull to London to Norfolk to the universe and back defines the kind of wild upward arc that someone with a fancy degree, citing Gilles Deleuze, might call "a line of flight." It's a suitable phrase for a rare bird indeed.

Cosmosis dates from the period of COUM Transmissions, a communal experiment by a set of like-minded wayfarers keen on calling the bluff of '60s countercultural slogans and imperatives by actively practicing freedom up to its distasteful and scary consequences. As names go, "Cosmosis" usefully conveys the insolently absolute ambitions of a young, radical avant-garde partisan birthing a new world on the fly out of ready-to-hand scraps, making do with what is right before her, and pushing it as hard as possible.

There is nothing more ready-to-hand than your own body, and, accordingly, in her performance work with COUM, this became a startlingly flexible, powerful and accurate instrument with which to pry into other people's desires and fears, their prurience and their innocence often blurring in

the process. Being "beautiful" helps, but Cosmosis/Cosey put her own beauty to the test in ways that challenge and interrogate the meaning of the term. As a working photographic model/actress in London, Cosey was accustomed to allowing her image to be transformed and disseminated by an industry that trades upon fantasies of female exposure, vulnerability and nudity.

In the COUM Transmissions gallery exhibition "PROSTITUTION," Cosey recontextualized the pornographic magazines in which her image had been disseminated by juxtaposing them with the material detritus of her own bodily processes, turning what could have been a standard sexist framework for the distribution of objectified flesh into something violently alive, risky and – yes – empowering. The reactionary tabloid headlines this show triggered convey the extent to which Cosey's actions challenged the public's willingness to confer full self-sovereignty onto the bodies which that same mainstream media was all too happy to serve up in Page Six-style spreads.

Then came a crossfade from the art world to music, albeit music of a sort designed to deform the category itself. In a fittingly noisome act of birth, the art collective COUM begat the band Throbbing Gristle

and, in the process, Cosmosis became Cosey, the creator of images / sounds / textures / ruptures / events equally essential to the band and transformative of her own identity as an artist. Blowing militant heat and alien cool on the cornet, delivering surgical strikes on a heavily processed guitar, Cosey gave Throbbing Gristle not one but two of its most distinctive instrumental components, defining the sound of the band in both its "ambient murk" and "mutant pop" modes.

What is striking about Cosey's sonic contribution to Throbbing Gristle is its variety and range.

Some of TG's finest hours are crowned with her assured vocal delivery, but she's equally compelling as a slyly intuitive improviser. The seagull honk of processed cornet and the agitated scrabbling of Cosey's guitar are equal partners with Chris Carter's sequenced architecture, Sleazy's archive of eerily intimate tapes and Genesis P-Orridge's charismatic purr. Within this organic ecology of sounds and personalities, what is striking about Cosey's sonic contribution to Throbbing Gristle is its

COSEY FANNI TUTTI

Author: Drew Daniel

variety and range, an emotional spectrum ranging from the soothing pastoral lull of "Hometime" to the imperial dancefloor majesty of "Hot on the Heels of Love" to the scalding noise workouts documented in their live incarnation (a heritage recently and brilliantly revivified by the Carter Tutti Void album *Transverse*).

This capacity for change and growth is at once central to Throbbing Gristle's poetics and particularly acute in the longer arc of Cosey's own subsequent career. In her life-long musical and personal partnership with Chris Carter as Chris & Cosey and, later, as Carter Tutti, the twin poles of Cosey's split personality as icy chanteuse and fiery inst-rumentalist were centrifugally heightened in opposition to each other.

Floating above the intricate latticework of Carter's spiraling synths and precision-tooled drum programming, Cosey's voice and sounds have offered a consistently human point of contact, a constant reminder of embodiment – yet at their furthest sonic extremes they reach past human frames of reference towards vistas of cosmic/extra-terrestrial scope, jarring fragmentation and blurry abstraction, losing their links to the standard expectations of what a horn, a guitar or a voice ought to sound like.

The legacy of her work is too extensive to define within a small space, but even a provisional attempt would have to identify a core paradox: the way that radical indepen-dence and radical fidelity interpenetrate. By allowing herself to transform and change from Christine of Hull to Cosmosis of London to Cosey of Norfolk and, beyond that, the Great Sonic Unknown, Cosey became, in the process, ever truer to herself, and her own mission.

By synthesizing her work with and against that of her partner(s), Cosey's immersion in the meshwork of collaboration only further drew out what makes her voice, her sounds and her body of work singularly inspiring and persistent: self-exposure as a militant mode of honesty, one which passes through noise, ugliness and abjection and emerges out the other side into an expanded field of reference. In a time when the monoculture of the internet and the mass dissemination of digital tools threatens to further homog-enize a glutted marketplace of increasingly transient and trivial signifiers, the raw directness, stubborn force, and sheer beauty of Christine / Cosmosis / Cosey Fanni Tutti's body of work holds fast.

Drew Daniel is the author of *Twenty Jazz Funk Greats* and *The Melancholy Assemblage: Affect and Epistemology in the English Renaissance*. He is one-half of the band Matmos.

One part Paradise Garage, one part Los Angeles hippie freakazoid and two (or more) parts punky-funk British attitude.

Riding on an airport transfer bus recently, I overheard a DJ telling his manager his plan for the current year. There was the extra studio time, which would in turn bring him more gigs, as well as propelling him up into the *Resident Advisor* Top DJ list. It was important, he said, that he built up a team around him, as though he was describing a cyclist in the Tour de France or a heavyweight boxer. This is the life – and professionalism – of the modern DJ. Charts plotted, courses taken, plans actioned.

For Harvey, there are no chart placings, there is only music.

At the other end of the spectrum lies Harvey Bassett, AKA DJ Harvey. It's doubtful that Harvey has ever spent time on a tour bus plotting an entry into the *RA* list (if he even knows what it is), much less methodically constructing a "team," though with Heidi Lawden as close associate for over 20 years there's scant need for one.

Harvey is cut from a different kind of cloth to today's aspirant deck spinners. He's gone from teen punk drumming sensation through to elder statesman of the global party scene, all the while maintaining a certain world-weary diffidence about the absurdity of it all. Although he's some way from emulating the success of the billboard-touted DJ, he still has the pulling power to lure a hardy band of converts to rave to his unique brand of dance music: one part Paradise Garage, one part Los Angeles hippie freakazoid and two (or more) parts punky-funk British attitude. For Harvey, there are no chart placings, there is only music.

Harvey Bassett was born in the early 1960s in London, but was raised in Cambridge, about 50 miles north of London, in an era when the fallout from the zippy '60s, Pink Floyd's fenland home, was still felt. While still in school Harvey, inspired by punk rock, joined a local band, Ersatz, on drums, and received the anointment of John Peel who played the group's records on his Radio 1 show. But it was the shock and awe of hip hop's arrival that propelled him towards a future in dance music. In the mid-'80s, Harvey and a pal busked it over to New York City, clueless and keen, in search of those Young Soul Rebels: hip hop's founding fathers.

They walked around Washington Square Park showing people photos of their heroes and asking where they lived (for anyone not familiar with New York in the '80s, this is way more demented than it might sound now). They even briefly lived with the Rock Steady Crew. Crucially, however, they voraciously devoured the then-thriving NYC underground: The Saint, Area, Nell's, The Roxy and so on.

Harvey is cut from a different kind of cloth to today's aspirant deck spinners.

When Harvey returned to the UK, he found himself one of the earliest adopters of house and techno. "I'd play 'Strings of Life' at the Mud Club and clear the floor," recalls S-Express's Mark Moore. "Three weeks later you could see pockets of people come on to the floor when I played it and go crazy to it and they turned out to be people like DJ Harvey."

By this time, Harvey's exploits as a DJ revolved around an ad hoc sound system, TONKA Hi-Fi, that also included Rev, Marky and Choci, among others. As well as throwing parties in Cambridge and London, they held a residency at the Zap (often followed by impromptu shindigs on the beach). But it was at Moist, a club run jointly with Heidi, where he established his reputation as a risk-taker, as likely to play an old acid rock record as a current Mr. Fingers 12-inch.

DJ HARVEY

Author: Bill Brewster

The Ministry Of Sound, then new, anointed him resident alongside the likes of Justin Berkmann, and he would frequently do the graveyard shift on both Fridays and Saturdays, playing into the morning on the best sound system ever seen in the UK to that point ("like steering the Titanic," Harvey once memorably described it). During his MOS stint, Harvey paired up with record dealer/DJ Gerry Rooney for the short-lived but influential Black Cock, the daddy of the modern edit label.

His final salvo in the UK came via the persuasive Sav Remzi, whose Blue Note club helped kickstart London's East End renaissance. New Hard Left was part of a raft of influential nights at the tiny club in Hoxton Square and proved something of a swansong for Harvey who relocated to Los Angeles shortly after 9/11. This brief sojourn turned into a life-changing move. Harvey now lives full-time in Venice Beach. The United States is also where he's found his studio voice, producing remixes and, more significantly, albums from both the Map Of Africa and Locussolus collaborative projects.

For a time, Harvey was marooned in the States, waiting for a Green Card that would allow him to resume travelling once more. Not that he minded that much. He was off in Hawaii, the owner of a club and enjoying the island paradise. During this moment, however, a quiet mania grew on numerous internet forums (my own, *DJ History*, added its own ludicrous noise to the hubbub). His return show in London last year, sold 1,000 tickets in a few hours, while his now infamous Sarcastic mix from 2001 caused a worldwide trainspotter meltdown, as eager disciples tried to separate the Hudson Fords from the John Fordes.

His now infamous Sarcastic mix from 2001 caused a worldwide trainspotter meltdown.

But what makes Harvey such a compelling DJ is not his collection of records. It's the ease with which he controls a party, whether he's spinning Double Exposure or the latest German import. In fact, strip away the hype, the bombast, the internet overheating and the fanboy worship, and what you have is quite simple: One of the world's best party DJs.

Bill Brewster is the co-founder of DJHistory. com, and the co-author of numerous books about DJ culture, including *Last Night a DJ Saved My Life and How to DJ (Properly)*.

Badu has always presented herself, flaws and all, on record.

When people recount meeting Erykah Badu, a lot of them describe her as being other-worldly. A little bewitching. Slightly "not human," if you will. It seems no one can escape the inexplicable magnetic grip of the Texan-born performing artist, mother, doula and uncategorizable other born Erica Abi Wright. As Roots bandleader and drummer Questlove once wrote, "Raphael Saadiq and I had an affectionate joke about her: never look her in the eye for more than five seconds, because her brain will be your brain."

"Never look her in the eye for more than five seconds, because her brain will be your brain." – Questlove

Neo-soul was lapping at the toes of an audience already warmed by D'Angelo's *Brown Sugar* when Badu delivered her 1997 debut album, *Baduizm*. The 14-track album was covered in a thin film of grit, as the self-professed "Analog Girl" preferred to keep her music underdressed than unnecessarily adorned. Her vocals were lithe and channeled jazz mistresses of times past, buoyed by elements of hip hop production. Through

Baduizm, Badu conveyed a cool strength while relaying the realities of life and love.

While "neo-soul" is a term that Badu has said doesn't sit entirely well with her, she deserves credit for cracking it open. Badu took a modern approach to a stately genre, upgrading its moving parts so it could be understood by a new generation. Bagging four Grammy nominations and two wins, *Baduizm* represented the jazz- and soul-in-flected sound of a woman awake and present – a formidable equal in intellect and musicality amongst men.

Through *Baduizm*, Badu conveyed a cool strength while relaying the realities of life and love.

Badu's debut album introduced a woman who possessed allure and commanded respect. Both aspects were reflected in her position as the sole feminine force within the powerhouse collective dubbed the Soulquarians that included the likes of Questlove, J Dilla, James Poyser, Q-Tip, Common, Bilal, Mos Def and Talib Kweli. As Questlove has recounted, the aforementioned names were falling over themselves

at the opportunity to bunker down with Badu during her *Baduizm* studio sessions, drawn into her seductive orbit. As she coolly asserts on the Soulquarian-rich *Mama's Gun*, "I'm the envy of the women and I rule the men."

Perhaps envy isn't the right term. Badu has always presented herself, flaws and all, on record. Working hard and receiving little pay (the steadfast lament of "The Grind") and admissions of vulnerability and being lost in love (the three-part opus "Out My Mind, Just in Time") make her eminently relatable. Only someone with an unwavering sense of self could so readily reveal all these sides of her life. It's hard to get to that enviable Zen place – which, knowing Erykah, we imagine as a haze of nag champa, healing crystals and an endless supply of tempeh – which is in part why we look up to her. Incorporating mention of two baby daddies (make that three now) into a song titled "Me" is a true boss bitch move, made by a woman who's intimidated by very little.

This strength is conveyed most clearly during Badu's live performances – an important dimension of her artistic persona. During the 1997 recording of her album *Live*, she tested out "Call Tyrone," an acidic ode to a deadbeat boyfriend (rumored to be inspired by Andre 3000, father of her child Seven),

ERYKAH BADU

Author: Marisa Aveling

which turned into a classic moment in Badu history. The footage of her looking like an African queen while laying it down displays Badu's power as an entertainer, but even without the visuals, the shriek of female fans responding with a guttural "PREACH" is evidence enough.

Over the years this fearlessness – or her willingness to address fear and work through it – has led to some forceful statements. A particularly infamous example came in 2010 with the clip for her shimmering track "Window Seat." Through the course of the video, a determined yet weary-eyed Badu walks with purpose through Dealey Plaza, an area in downtown Dallas made notorious nearly 50 years earlier as the site of John F. Kennedy's assassination. As Badu presses forward, she peels off her clothing, item by item, until she stands naked in front of passersby, only to be shot by an unseen killer. Blue blood spills from her head, pooling to form the word "groupthink." The video ends with Badu reciting a monologue that closes with the statement, "A single person within a circumstance can move one to change. To love ourself. To evolve."

Marisa Aveling is the managing editor of *FRANK151* and a contributing editor to *Wax Poetics*. She is currently based in Brooklyn, New York.

Perpetually self-effacing, Gareth Jones deflects the spotlight at all times.

The importance of Gareth Jones is twofold. First, there are his own achievements – his discography as a producer and mixer over more than 30 years and his part in the growth of the mighty Mute Records machine – which are considerable by any standards. But beyond that, he is emblematic, a perfect archetype of the quiet but vital figures who all too often get written out of music history, the industry ninjas moving in the shadows and shaping history. To understand his place in the scheme of things is to dig beneath the hype and better grasp how sounds and cultural ideas are spread and shared among artists and condensed into forms that reach the wider world.

Jones himself would almost certainly balk at the idea of shaping history, though. Perpetually self-effacing, often uncomfortable and always deadpan in interviews, he deflects the spotlight at all times, unfailingly complimentary about the talent and personality of those he has worked with (even those, like the notorious Diamanda Galas who, by Jones's own admission, have reduced him to tears in the studio).

He may have worked on some of the most influential electronic records of all time, from John Foxx's *Metamatic* on, he may have resided in Berlin and worked in the legendary Hansa studio just as the madness of the post-punk Neue Deutsche Welle movement was interfacing with the global mainstream, but to hear him speak you'd never get the sense he felt he was doing anything important. Beyond the occasional wry mention of certain musicians' eccentricities, this is someone talking about their job. Paradoxically, though, it's precisely this refusal of his own influence, and this concentration on detail over grand gesture, that makes him so influential.

In his quiet way he has constantly fed into the creative process of whoever he has worked with.

For those of us raised on the old-school music press version of rock 'n' roll history, it's easy to fall for the myth of the flamboyant genius, of grand culture clashes and violent flashes of inspiration that alter everything in an instant. These things are real, and are, of course, part of what we love about music culture. But anyone who's ever been involved with a band, a scene, a crew or a company knows that this is not all that creativity is built of: a band entirely full of wild, exploratory firebrands would fall apart in a second, any group or subculture needs people with their feet on the ground or at least willing to put in work that isn't obviously anecdote- or publicity-worthy.

Alan McGee and Tony Wilson, inspirational though they might have been to young musicians, would never have been able to form and maintain Creation and Factory without Dick Green and Alan Erasmus by their sides. It's questionable whether the first flashes of inspiration that gave birth to the dubstep scene could have made stars of Skream, Benga and co. without the limelight-shy Sarah Lockhart working away on FWD>>. And in the studio, even the most radical sonic explorers and frenzied live acts need someone who can translate their vision and energy into something that still makes sense when it's separated from its source and committed to tape.

None of which is to say that the work of someone like Jones is only about supporting and facilitating the work of the big names he works with. Though he may do his absolute best to appear almost invisible, stripping away traces of his own ego wherever possible in person and in his contributions to records, that doesn't mean his role is as a neutral conduit of information. When it comes to

GARETH JONES

Author: Joe Muggs

trying to square the sounds in people's heads with those which come out of speakers, there's no such thing as transparency – that's the great myth of "fidelity" that leads to so much confusion in understanding music production.

This concentration on detail over grand gesture is the thing that makes him so influential.

So while it might be nigh on impossible to find a "Gareth Jones sound" that links John Foxx to Nick Cave, Diamanda Galas to Erasure or Einstürzende Neubauten to Emmy the Great, you can be absolutely certain that his influence is strong on the way their releases sound. Whether as a direct influence on technique (as with his application of the sampler technology that he'd discovered with Depeche Mode to the industrial sound sources of Neubauten) or a transmitter of sonic ideas (someone who could understand the sonic and technical links between the wildly different voices of Galas and Erasure's Andy Bell), in his quiet way he has constantly fed into the creative process of whoever he worked with. And his Zen-like dedication to turning studios into a "safe space" where ideas can be played with, used or discarded with ease is never a neutral quality either: though on the surface it simply eases the creative process, in reality it is a huge and direct contribution to that process.

In fact, only the people who were there can ever truly understand the alchemy of great studio work – it hinges on so many microscopic moments, decisions and flukes, that no amount of anecdote or technical documentation will ever explain how certain things came to be or who was responsible for them. Indeed the same applies to the wider life of music as it disseminates through industries and cultures. And it's this that makes it so very hard to assess the place of people like Gareth Jones, whose still waters run deep, and whose greatest contributions may have been to the most microscopic but crucial decisions that few even remember let alone note as epochal. But when we are telling and writing musical history, we should always remember the importance of those people, however little they may big themselves up.

Joe Muggs is a writer, ranter, A&R, DJ with the Slugrave crew, occasional beatmaker, spoken word performer and general aging raver.

Liebezeit decided it was more important to think in cycles than in bars, contrary to the dictates of the Western avant-garde.

Among the many posthumous bequests of the German experimental music scene best known as Krautrock was its impact on rhythm. Neu!'s Klaus Dinger conceived the motorik Dingerbeat, identified by Brian Eno as one of the most important of the '70s. By the time of 1977's *Trans-Europe Express*, Kraftwerk had reduced their sound to a fast-shifting, mechanical clatter with surprisingly funky properties which would form the underpinning for both synth pop and hip hop. Around the same time in Munich, Giorgio Moroder was conceiving the sequencer patterns that drove Donna Summer's "I Feel Love" and would set the template for disco.

However, the most discreet and far-reaching reconfiguration of the rock beat came from Can's Jaki Liebezeit. Now in his early '70s, Liebezeit is still active, puttering back and forth to a studio in Cologne. His work space is filled, utensil-like, with an array of multi-ethnic percussion instruments, as well as a customized drum kit on which he still performs and records with artists like Burnt Friedman or the four man collective Cyclopean. He operates quietly, with a minimum of fuss – it is possible to imagine that he has never taken a drum solo in his life. Yet it is his very restraint which makes him among the most significant figures in 20th century rock, one who has opened up its landscape to terrain still being explored.

Jaki Liebezeit was born in 1937, in a small village near Dresden. He was of the generation affected by the trauma of World War II and the Nazification of Germany, but it is a subject on which he generally keeps his thoughts to himself. It is clear, however, that along with fellow Can members Irmin Schmidt and Holger Czukay he felt a connection between the aftermath and ruin of the War and the need to innovate, to reconstruct music as a means of restoring to Germany its artistic soul and sense of self-worth.

It is possible to imagine that he has never taken a drum solo in his life.

Liebezeit disliked rock 'n' roll as a teenager – he found its rhythms trite and, in any case, there were plenty of would-be rock drummers. Nonetheless, Liebezeit grew up in an American-occupied zone, so he took his first jobs as a fledgling sticksman playing at concerts for US soldiers, and, consequently, was exposed to the overbearing influence of American tastes on West German culture.

Next, Liebezeit turned to jazz, meeting bandleader Manfred Schoof in Cologne, and for a while enjoyed playing in the style of Art Blakey. Then, during a lengthy spell with a group in Barcelona, he began to tune into North African radio stations and experienced alternative approaches to rhythm. In 1961, long in advance of mainstream fascination with world music, he bought an LP of Indian music and from there began to study mazier, less thudding options for percussion.

When he returned to Germany, he found the jazz scene taken over by the inventions of Ornette Coleman. However, for Liebezeit, "free" jazz was anything but, instead representing an end point in the development of the genre. Liebezeit decided it was more important to think in cycles than in bars, contrary to the dictates of the Western avant-garde. Minimalism, discipline, fluidity, repetition, a "monotony" of sorts – these would become his watchwords as he sat down for the first jamming sessions at Schloss Nörvenich with his fellow Can members, all of them in their own way seeking to cast off the restraints of their own academic, classical backgrounds as well as the banal, preset dominance of Anglo-American rock. It was time to begin again.

Can were well-named – cylindrical, enablers of content. Rather than pointlessly embark on ostentatious, virtuoso solos, they provided a setting in which sound ideas, an overall,

JAKI LIEBEZEIT

Author: David Stubbs

organic energy, could flow freely. Liebezeit's unconventional approach was crucial. He didn't merely hold down the backseat, in the old rock parlance. He was an equal contributor in the collective, in which, according to Krautrock ideals, there were "No Führers!", his percussion floating in the mix alongside guitar, keyboards, bass, vocals.

For all his ultra-disciplinarianism, Liebezeit's was a discipline without dogma.

Liebezeit worked in tandem with bassist Holger Czukay, who was hardly a Stanley Clarke of the fretboard. Even so, in his minimalist zeal, Liebezeit urged Czukay to play even less, once threatening him with an axe for failing to do so. But for all his ultra-disciplinarianism, Liebezeit's was a discipline without dogma. His playing was truly "free" in that it unmoored Can. His refusal to observe the predictable, tethered, earthbound, restrictive regularity of rock 'n' roll accounts for the levitation the group achieved – that dervish-like sense of "take-off" on "Father Cannot Yell" on *Monster Movie*, or midway through *Tago Mago*'s "Paperhouse," as his kit seems to transmogrify into a set of rotor blades. Liebezeit's playing on the title track of *Future Days*, his refusal to put his foot through the pedal but simply maintain a cyclical pattern, contributes to its sheer weightlessness. His willingness to abandon the role of conventional sticksman also benefits *Tago Mago*'s "Aumgn," whose controlled bedlam is pebbledashed with flurries of intelligent, percussive decision-making. His insistence on a machine-like, metronomic approach, meanwhile, is key to *Future Days*' "Moonshake." Cut in 1973, it's a prototype for a machine music still several years away.

The fresh highways, ambient airspace and post-rock options 21st century music has at its disposal has much to thank Liebezeit for. He is worth dozens of higher-profile, glorified rock drumming legends, but his self-sacrifice means he is rather less fêted. In Cologne he commutes quietly to work, unmolested by the populace. It's tempting to say that they should build a statue for him. However, Liebezeit is all about sublimating the ego in rock – converting all that selfish energy into the larger, collective effort, being sensitive and alert to the overall need. It's not just a great philosophy for playing, but also for living.

David Stubbs is the author of *Fear Of Music: Why People Get Rothko But Don't Get Stockhausen*. His new book, *Future Days*, a study of Krautrock, is to be published by Faber & Faber in 2014.

A sound that could only be born in a city like Lisbon.

In one of Buraka Som Sistema's most visceral music videos, the action shifts between people in their homes dancing in webcam-like clips and a thumping, sweaty club where those same clips are projected in front of pumping fists and bobbing heads. Connecting the two scenes are the furiously throbbing beats and flat, impenetrably cool bilingual vocals of the Lisbon-based outfit's "We Stay Up All Night," a single off their 2011 album, *Komba*. The result is an impeccable audiovisual metaphor for a group that perpetually struts the line between local and global, home and away.

Growing up in the suburbs of Lisbon, producer João Barbosa (AKA Lil' John, Branko and J-Wow) and DJ Riot (born Rui Pité) first played together in a grungy rock band called Blanket. When that group folded, Lil' John and Riot went on to found a series of electronic music projects, including the jungle/drum & bass outfit Cooltrain Crew.

Around this time, they also started collaborating with Kalaf Ângelo, a poet, musician and MC, who had came to Lisbon from Benguela, Angola. He performed spoken word steeped in his immigrant experiences, and became one of the only African contributors to the Portuguese press when he began writing a weekly column for the *Público*

newspaper. Ângelo's addition moved the trio to experiment with yet another style: kuduro.

The knock-kneed, stumble-step syncopation of kuduro was exhilaratingly new.

Created in Angola by DJs and musicians in the late '80s, kuduro chops up bits of Caribbean soca and zouk, Angolan semba (a relative of Brazilian samba) and traditional African percussion rhythms into a frenetic dance music. It's a sound that can be heard pumping out of car windows and reclaimed sound systems in the ghettoes of Angola's capital city of Luanda – and a sound that swirled through the immigrant communities of suburban Lisbon when Riot and Barbosa were growing up there in the '90s. Kuduro wasn't exactly hip in Lisbon in the early '00s, though – and it was barely known at all outside Angola and some parts of Portugal.

Buraka Som Sistema is largely responsible for changing that. Barbosa, Ângelo and Pité started a club night where they chopped and screwed kuduro samples with other electronic genres. They called the event Buraka Som Sistema. (Buraka was the

neighborhood where the event was held, and "Som Sistema" means sound system in Portuguese.) When the police shut the club down, the group decided to keep working as a performing outfit. They added Angolan producer Conductor (Andro Carvalho, previously of hip hop crew Conjunto Ngonguenha), who had been a regular at the club nights. Later, the lineup was completed by Blaya, a Brazilian artist who started out as a dancer with the group and evolved into one of its singer/MCs.

Buraka Som Sistema has always taken their role as unofficial ambassadors for the genre seriously.

The group founded its own label, Enchufada Records, in 2004; released their debut EP, *From Buraka to the World*, in 2006; and dropped their first full-length, *Black Diamond*, in 2008. But the buzz began almost immediately, with critics and fans trading tracks and posting videos as fast as the group could create them. Some of the hype came from early, high-profile collaborations and support from famous fans like Diplo and M.I.A. But most of the excitement was a result of the sheer freshness of the group's sound. The knock-

JOÃO BARBOSA & KALAF ÂNGELO

Author: Rachel Devitt

kneed, stumble-step syncopation of kuduro was exhilaratingly new: The word kuduro is a play on Angolan slang for "hard-ass," and the ferocious energy of the music kicks and punches its way out of the speaker.

Buraka Som Sistema has always taken their role as unofficial ambassadors for the genre seriously. They've traveled to – and recorded in – Angola frequently, working hard to give credit for samples and seek out collaborators like Angola's DJ Znobia and Angoloan-Portuguese MC Pongolove. And their videos regularly feature Angolan street scenes, bursting with color, gritty with the hardships of life in the ghettoes, and overflowing with regular folks engaged in vibrant, hip-shaking, leg-twisting kuduro dance.

But there's much more to Buraka Som Sistema than just a Western-facing redesign of a specific type of African music. Their live show is among the most energetic in a scene full of laptop-shackled DJs, while the group's albums pop and sizzle with tastes of grime, drum & bass, dubstep, South African kwaito and Brazilian baile funk. Collaborators have included funk carioca artist Deize Tigrona, Cape Verdean singer Sara Tavares, grime MC Afrikan Boy and electro-tropical outfit Bomba Estéreo. And their albums offer up far more than beats: *Black Diamond* addresses

issues ranging from the diamond trade to militarism in Africa. *Komba*, meanwhile, was named for an Angolan ritual that celebrates a person's life seven days after their death.

A group that perpetually struts the line between local and global, home and away.

In other words, Buraka Som Sistema's sound is one that could only be born in a city like Lisbon, a post-colonial, multicultural urban mecca that Enchufada describes as "the city where the African, South-American and European continents meet to eat, drink and dance the night away." But it's also a sound that speaks powerfully to the globalized society we live in, one where – as DJ Riot once put it – America and the Western world can no longer think of themselves as its center.

Rachel Devitt is World Music editor for *Rhapsody* and *Google Play*. She is also a freelance writer and an ethnomusicology PhD.

Just Blaze took a classic hip hop formula and moved it convincingly into the 21st century.

The first shot across the bow was Jay-Z's "Girls, Girls, Girls." Justin Smith had placed a few beats with rappers before, but a single with the president of Roc-A-Fella Records was high-profile exposure on a different scale. Despite an inauspicious release date less than a month after 9/11, the song was a Top 10 hit and heralded a new, modern iteration of the classic hip hop sound. This rugged, sample-based approach would be spearheaded by Kanye West and the young Smith, AKA Just Blaze. Blaze lacked Kanye's flair for flamboyant self-promotion, but his music spoke volumes – and his impact on hip hop has been just as immense.

At the turn of the century, New York rap was having an identity crisis. The biggest hits were coming out of the South and many producers and rappers in the Rotten Apple were trying, usually unsuccessfully, to jump on the Southbound bandwagon. Tellingly, Jay-Z's singles in the two years prior to "Girls" had been largely produced by noted sample eschewers Swizz Beats and The Neptunes.

Just Blaze grew up across the Hudson from Manhattan and was proudly New York in his sound, unafraid to use soul samples and drum breaks hard enough to make you forget that Atlanta and Memphis existed. His tech-savvy intellect and encyclopedic knowledge of the golden-era hip hop of his youth combined to produce cutting-edge music that clearly fell in the lineage of New York City but was anything but retro.

As a Computer Science student in the late '90s at Rutgers University and an inveterate tech-head who wrote his first computer program at nine years old, it was only natural that the music-obsessed young man started interning at a studio. It was there, at the Cutting Room in Manhattan, that Just began making the connections that would eventually lead to the house of Roc-A-Fella.

What had seemed painfully stale and behind the times became cutting edge in his hands.

After what he's described in an interview with hardknock.tv as a "year-long hazing period" at the Roc-A-Fella home studio baseline engineering second-tier projects and having his beats rejected by the higher ups (a period in which he never even met Jay-Z), Justin finally got his chance to step up to the next level. The label showcase album *La Familia* was his coming-out of sorts, and although none of the songs he produced were picked for singles (the Neptunes would eclipse the rest of the album – and most of the pop world – with "I Just Want to Love U (Give It 2 Me)") these productions would mark the beginning of a new sound.

Blaze is a notorious record collector. This shouldn't be a surprise considering his productions, but the extremes that he's taken it to are noteworthy. In those first years of major-label income, "I was probably spending two or three thousand dollars a week on records," he estimated in a 2011 interview with *Complex*. This digger's mentality is at the core of hip hop, going back to the days of Bambaataa and Kool Herc. It's as old school as you can get, and gives his work a grounding that uniquely offsets the modern sheen. Simply put, by the early '00s Just had found a way to take the classic hip hop formula of sampled soul layered with tough drum breaks and move it convincingly into the 21st century.

What had seemed painfully stale and behind the times became cutting-edge in his hands. Jay-Z's *The Blueprint* (including "Girls") and its follow-up leaned heavily on this sound, both in the many beats from Blaze and in those from Kanye West, who was also working similar territory. "The big horns, the hard drums and the vocal chops," as Just put it in *Complex*, had been thoroughly mastered,

JUST BLAZE

Author: Andrew "Monk-One" Mason

and he was duly rewarded by being named Roc-A-Fella's main in-house producer.

Music that clearly fell in the lineage of New York City but was anything but retro.

If "Girls" put Just Blaze on the map, Cam'ron's "Oh Boy" in 2002 redrew the topography. The call-and-response vocal sample – sliced precisely from an old Rose Royce ballad – was a trick that he (and Kanye) would thoroughly exploit. It was far from the only trick Blaze had in hand, though. His obsession with recording techniques and curiosity about the latest gear meant he always made the most of the recording studio. Before the widespread availability of vinyl emulators like Serato, for example, he was using CD decks to drastically change the pitch of vocal scratches while keeping them in tempo. Quirks of technology were cleverly incorporated into the music: for Memphis Bleek's "We Get Low" he used the usually-muted SMPTE signal that synchronizes tape as an audible element of the beat.

As Blaze passes the decade mark of making hits, he has hardly stood still. The man who once told the *Wall Street Journal* that "DJing and producing go hand in hand" has returned to those fundamentals, spinning sets that showcase his grasp of club dynamics, even as his musical vision has expanded beyond them.

While keeping firmly grounded in cutting-edge hip hop via his work with Kendrick Lamar and XV, the arena-rock feel Just explored with songs like Fabolous's Supertramp-sampling "Breathe" has given way to a growing enthusiasm with the new genre selling out arenas: EDM. Witness his collaboration with Baauer that resulted in the hybrid dubstep/trap hit "Higher" and his recent house music experiments. "I grew up on house just as much as I grew up on hip hop," he told hard-knock.tv last year, and it shows. If this is the future of the classic New York sound, it's in good hands.

Andrew Mason is a founder of – and contributing editor to – *Wax Poetics*. He also heads a record label, Names You Can Trust.

Kerri Chandler has spent his career enriching the simple things.

Kerri Chandler's life has been filled with music from day one: piano lessons, gospel influences, a DJ dad with a basement full of vinyl. Born in the late '60s, he grew to be a purveyor, mastermind and ambassador of the so-called Jersey Sound, a style championed by artists like Blaze and Jomanda, labels like Movin' Records and, last but not least, a fabled club named Zanzibar and its DJ heavyweight Tony Humphries.

Rooted in gospel traditions, but also influenced by the bourgeoning Chicago house tracks of the time, house music from Jersey offered a soulful alternative and a safe harbor for kids like Chandler looking for a way into the music industry. Starting to DJ at the tender age of 13, Chandler's biggest inspiration was his dad's record room. Located in his grandmother's house and later celebrated in the title to the first compilation on his Madhouse imprint – *A Basement, A Red Light & A Feelin'* – young Kerri spent hours going through thousands of classic disco jams.

Chandler learned the ropes as a producer, however, by making rap instrumentals. It wasn't until a friend pushed him to do "house stuff" that he switched gears. A debut house EP on his short-lived Express Records label in 1989 featured "Get It Off," a tribute to his recently deceased girlfriend. It contained a "rip" that he later said was the sound of "someone taking her away from me and changing my whole groove." The track eventually became one of his most popular and influential works, the "rip" sound appearing in countless other tunes.

Rooted in gospel and soul music traditions, house music from Jersey offered a safe harbor for kids like Chandler.

In a genre that is often reduced to an unsophisticated four-to-the-floor kick drum approach, Chandler has spent his career enriching the simple things. His basslines are instantly recognizable, tweaked to perfection. Emotional synths make frequent appearances, imbuing tracks with pathos and uplift in equal measure. Highlights include "She's Crazy," a song recorded as his grandfather swigged Jack Daniels and sang an old favorite. "Inspiration" was done in a single hour with vocalist Arnold Jarvis, and remains a deep house evergreen. (No mean feat, given that house music is rarely lauded for its brilliant songwriting.) Another one of Chandler's jewels goes by the unassuming name of "Track 1." Part of an EP for the seminal NYC club institution Shelter, it perfectly encapsulated the vibe and style of the club at a time when "deep" was house's reigning prefix.

Regardless, Chandler isn't content with simply DJing and producing. He's a Renaissance Man. The story goes that he could build a turntable with a screwdriver, a light bulb and a box of matches. But this MacGyver-styled myth isn't that far off. Chandler studied electrical engineering, and he proudly geeks out on the latest technology, whether it be self-built synthesizers, customized rotary mixers or a laser system that allows him to virtually grab records and play them. Pioneer consults with him when they want to build their latest gear. But he also supports niche designers too: You're just as likely to see him mixing records on the DJ Deep-designed portable rotary DJR-400 mixer.

His basslines are instantly recognizable, tweaked to perfection.

But the thing that keeps Kerri Chandler relevant is his constant hunger for the new and the current (while, at the same time, never forgetting his past). So many of his peers tip too far one way or the other, chasing a quick

KERRI CHANDLER

Author: Gerd Janson

buck or reliving past glories. Seeing him play for a well-versed crowd with an affinity for history and nostalgia at the British institution that is the Southport Weekender is as entertaining and refreshing as watching him playing to a mass of hedonistic sunbathers at Monday's Circoloco madness at DC-10 in Ibiza. He has successfully found a way to neither break his back nor bend his knee.

The story goes that he could build a turntable with a screwdriver, a light bulb and a box of matches.

And that is probably the most striking thing about Kerri Chandler's career. Nothing ever feels forced, calculated, or rehearsed with his countless productions and remixes, his DJ persona or even the way he's guided his record labels through the years. Like the best of New York's and New Jersey's iconic house and disco figures – Masters at Work, François Kevorkian or the godfather Patrick Adams – Chandler doesn't follow a business plan. It's the spur of the moment and a voracious appetite for opportunities, the same inspiration that hit a kid knee-deep in his father's record collection.

Gerd Janson is a DJ, label owner and (sometime) music journalist based just outside of Frankfurt. He's been a Red Bull Music Academy team member for more years than he can remember.

A man who has continually lived in the future.

Lee 'Scratch' Perry changed the way we think about sound. During the last 50-something years, his constant quest to push the boundaries of accepted practice in record production has yielded significant and lasting musical innovation. He's also a complex, contradictory being whose dramatic public displays and baffling pronouncements have made him one of the music world's most enigmatic figures, a sonic shaman who follows a unique artistic and personal trajectory.

Although his Black Ark studio was only operational for a handful of years during the late '70s, the supreme (and extreme) examples of sonic brilliance he conjured there are continually referenced by a range of practitioners in other realms, influencing the ambient excursions of Brian Eno and dub techno incursions of Pole, as well as the trippy house commandeered by the Orb, and the entire expanding universe of dubstep. He even helped bring out the bolder side of rap super-stars such as Jay-Z and the Beastie Boys, who drew directly from Perry's visionary productions, as heard on the former's "Lucifer" (which samples the Perry-produced "Chase the Devil"), and the latter's *Check Your Head* album (with its TV samples and Jamaican music snippets clearly inspired by Perry's 1975 *Revolution Dub* set).

Perhaps most significantly, Perry's work with Bob Marley remains unparalleled, the teacher-student relationship belying an unbreakable bond that lasted until the singer's untimely death. Perry's time with the Wailers represents a pinnacle of their respective careers, as heard in the immortal *Soul Rebels* and *Soul Revolution* albums, and later collaborations such as "Jah Live," "Punky Reggae Party" and "Who Colt the Game." Perry was also among the first to utilize dub mixing techniques, and his Black Ark masterworks helped transform dub into an art form, as heard on the landmark *Blackboard Jungle Dub* album, as well as later works like *Super Ape*.

Lee 'Scratch' Perry sought to challenge the limits of reggae.

Perry's impoverished childhood was spent on the edge of a sugar cane estate in Kendal, Hanover, a particularly impoverished and neglected part of Jamaica. Refusing to be beaten down by the brutality of the sugar industry, he became a renowned card sharp and domino player, and excelled as a dance champion. Then, in the early '60s, while bulldozing roads during a construction project, divine voices directed him to Kingston to pursue music. Finding a place in the stable of

Coxsone Dodd, Perry precipitated nearly every shift in Jamaican music. He helped ska to solidify at Dodd's Studio One, where he worked closely with the Maytals, the Wailers and Jackie Mittoo. Moving away from Dodd in 1966, he was briefly an in-house producer for WIRL (West Indies Records Limited), where he helped usher in the rocksteady style, and then adopted the Upsetter persona while working for Joe Gibbs with "I Am the Upsetter," a track aimed squarely at Dodd's head.

In late 1968, he ushered in the reggae craze with "People Funny Boy," this time aimed at Gibbs, which used a mutated rhythm inspired by the beat of Pocomania, one of Jamaica's African-derived forms of Christian worship, offset by the bawls of a crying baby, taken from a sound effects record. The following year he and his Upsetters toured Britain promoting the instrumental hit "Return of Django," and once he paired the Wailers with the Upsetters, he prepared the group for the international stardom they would achieve upon signing with Island Records.

Following further innovations in the dub and deejay styles, after establishing his Black Ark studio, a tiny space with rudimentary four-track equipment, Perry scored a contract of his own with Island, yielding excellent albums by Max Romeo, the Heptones, Junior Murvin,

LEE 'SCRATCH' PERRY

Author: David Katz

George Faith and Jah Lion, as well as the dub masterpiece, *Super Ape*. Leading British punk group the Clash asked Perry for assistance with their "Complete Control" single in 1977, and Paul and Linda McCartney made use of Perry's services around the same time, evidence of his growing international renown. However, as Perry sought to challenge the limits of reggae through the drastic application of phaser, echo, delay and other non-standard recording techniques, Island began rejecting creations such as *Return of the Super Ape*, *Roast Fish Collie Weed and Cornbread* and the Congos' wonderful *Heart of the Congos*, one of Perry's most outstanding productions with a harmony group.

While bulldozing roads during a construction project, divine voices directed him to Kingston to pursue music.

The Black Ark became a focal point for radical Rastafari consciousness and political insurrection, and as various pressures came to bear, a drastic personal metamorphosis saw the emergence of a troubling Perry persona named Pipecock Jackxon, who closed the doors of the Ark and covered the walls with impenetrable graffiti. By the time the studio perished in a mysterious fire, Perry became a nomadic soul, focused on serving the Almighty through sound and sculpture, cladding himself in mosaic costume garb. His post-Ark work is characterized by multi-tracked stream-of-consciousness proclamations, leading Linton Kwesi Johnson to refer to him as the "Salvador Dali of reggae," and drawing comparisons with fellow Afrofuturist space cadets Sun Ra and George Clinton.

Work for Island in the Bahamas and recordings made in Amsterdam and New York in the early '80s were decidedly patchy, but Perry has since made a mind-boggling array of albums of varying quality, the most important of which were crafted with Adrian Sherwood and Mad Professor, longstanding colleagues whose work was largely influenced by Perry's earlier innovations. *Time Boom*, from 1987, was a real return to form, and 2008's *The Mighty Upsetter* and its *Dubsetter* companion, the most recent works with Sherwood, were quality sets proving that the Upsetter still has something relevant to relate.

His relocation to a remote Swiss mountainside village may seen improbable, but the life he has created there with wife Mireille, has worked wonders on his psyche. Now free from the booze, spliff and meat consumption that contributed to earlier negative frames of mind, the 77 year-old Perry continues to perform and record all over the world. Although he may no longer operate as a producer in the conventional sense, his recorded output continues to challenge, reflecting the outlook of a man who has continually lived in the future, intriguing the legion of fans attracted to his undeniable genius.

David Katz is the author of *People Funny Boy: The Genius of Lee 'Scratch' Perry*.

The Sheffield scene dispensed with guitars, and chords, altogether.

"We're just a footnote in most histories," Martyn Ware says in the 2001 documentary film, *Made In Sheffield*. "But the Sheffield scene in its entirety had a huge impact." His commendable modesty disguises the truth. No one alive did more to forge the Steel City sound than Martyn Ware, founder of The Human League and Heaven 17, chart-topping producer, electronic evangelist, thinker, theorist and synth pop pioneer.

Ware has confirmed that the metronomic hammering of Sheffield's steel industry was a factor in shaping his approach to sound. But something less tangible, yet arguably more formative, was also in the air: a certain attitude to life, an awkwardness, a bloody-minded stubbornness. This manifested itself politically (the red flag flew over the town hall for a while and, circa the Miners' Strike of 1984-85, the surrounding county became nicknamed the People's Republic of South Yorkshire).

More importantly, it also manifested itself artistically. When punk rock was on the rise in the south, Sheffield reacted by going even further. *Sideburns*, a punk fanzine, famously printed three guitar chords with the caption "This is a chord. This is another. This is a third. Now form a band." The Sheffield scene dispensed with guitars, and chords, altogether.

Ware received his first musical education from glam rock. David Bowie and Roxy Music were important, but so were less arty, more poptastic figures like Marc Bolan, Gary Glitter and the Sweet. His interest in Motown and disco was a counterpoint to the more challenging end of his taste spectrum like Kraut-rock, Debussy, Steve Reich and a love of electronics initiated by the groundbreaking Moog soundtrack for Stanley Kubrick's *A Clockwork Orange*.

Cutting a flamboyant dash around town in his green fur jacket and stack-heeled boots, Ware became an integral figure at a council-funded theatre/performance space called Meatwhistle, the hub of an intensely creative circle of musicians who would form ad-hoc bands with endlessly-shifting line-ups. One such band, the Dead Daughters, became Ware's most significant dalliance. The line-up of Ware, Ian Craig Marsh and singer Adi Newton (later of Clock DVA), solidified, after a name change, as the Future. The band's manifesto was "No standard instrumentation." Everything besides vocals was to be synthetically generated. When synths, previously available only to millionaire prog rockers, came down sufficiently in price, Ware bought a monophonic – no chords! – Mini Korg 700S on hire purchase, while Marsh fashioned a Roland System 100 into a makeshift drum machine.

When Newton's anti-melodic singing style chafed with Marsh and Ware's pop-friendly direction, they parted company. Ware head-hunted school friend and sci-fi obsessive Phil Oakey, walking into his flat with *Trans-Europe Express* in one hand and Donna Summer's "I Feel Love" in the other, declaring "We can do this." The Human League was born. Debut single "Being Boiled," which mixed radical veganism with misremembered Eastern theology over a bracingly stern electro bassline, eventually went on to sell half-a-million copies. In the meantime, the League recorded two albums for Virgin – *Reproduction and Travelogue* – whose sparseness was leavened by a dark wit and underlying pop instinct.

The band's manifesto was "No standard instrumentation."

The schism opened when, legend has it, Ware failed to turn up for a photo shoot. Whatever the immediate cause, Oakey admits, "There's always going to be tension in a group with me and Martyn in it. Because we're both pompous and arrogant." Oakey and Wright kept the name, leaving Ware "incandescent with anger." He and Marsh recruited another Meatwhistle alumnus,

MARTYN WARE

Author: Simon Price

Glenn Gregory, to form Heaven 17, whose debut album *Penthouse & Pavement*, with a sleeve depicting the members as slick corporate executives, was a satire of the acquisitive aspirations of Thatcher's Britain. Instead of the grubby gig circuit, Heaven 17 performed their "synthetic music with soul" to backing tapes in discotheques.

Marsh and Ware then launched the British Electric Foundation, an umbrella organization with a mock-corporate structure and a faceless, anti-star policy. Their first release was the instrumental, cassette-only *Music for Stowaways*, but the first B.E.F. album proper, 1982's *Music of Quality and Distinction Volume 1*, paired an array of defiantly uncool vocalists (Bernie Nolan, Gary Glitter) with covers of immortal pop classics.

Heaven 17's second album, *The Luxury Gap*, broke them into the big time, largely due to the titanic "Temptation," a global smash which narrowly missed out on the UK #1 spot. It also featured some of the earliest uses of the Roland TB-303 bass synthesizer (later an integral element of acid house), and the Linn LM-1 drum computer.

Ware's growing studio know-how made him a sought-after producer. He helped relaunch the career of Tina Turner, a former B.E.F.

collaborator, when he produced her comeback hit "Let's Stay Together," giving him a credit on the best-selling album of her career (the multiple-platinum *Private Dancer*). He also produced Terence Trent D'Arby's debut *Introducing the Hardline*, and Erasure's chart-topping *I Say I Say I Say*. Further B.E.F. volumes followed in 1991 and 2013, while Heaven 17 continue to function as a working entity, producing new material as well as performing the classics. Martyn has also recorded with fellow synth pop legend Vince Clarke as The Clarke & Ware Experiment.

In recent years, Ware has been exploring the possibilities of 3D sound. In 2011, building on work he began at the National Centre for Popular Music in Sheffield, he conducted an experiment on behalf of the Noise Abatement Society on a busy street in Brighton, using a six-point sound field to create ethereal textures with the aim of distracting people from the sound of traffic. The results, analyzed by a psychobiologist Harry Witchel, suggested that it acted as a calming influence. Proof, perhaps, of something Martyn Ware has known all along: the sounds around us really do alter the things we do, and the people we are.

Simon Price worked for nine years at *Melody Maker*, and 12 at *The Independent On Sunday*. His book, *Everything (A Book About Manic Street Preachers)*, was published by Virgin in 1999.

One of the most idiosyncratic voices in contemporary electronic music.

"I'm floating free I'm floating free I'm floating free I'm floating free / Between the stars between the stars between the stars between the stars." Repeated in a bodiless drift against a synthesizer that seemed to flicker against the black void of space, these words announced the arrival of one of the most idiosyncratic voices in contemporary electronic music. As one-half of Closer Musik, Matias Aguayo – alongside Dirk Leyers – helped to cement Kompakt's place in the techno firmament. On his own, Aguayo has gone on to create one of the most fertile hybrids of European and South American dance music currently operating.

Aguayo is a singular ethnic fusionist, a musical Shaman of the wee morning hours.

The dance music world spins fast and fleeting; Closer Musik peaked early and petered out quickly. After the duo split, Aguayo would release another of Kompakt's central missives with the cavernous techno pop of *Are You Really Lost?* in 2005. The album was a lightless room of sorts, an empty-space approach to vocal-led techno and house music that had a strange almost mystical physicality. Sometimes formed solely around samples of grunts, stitched into off-base rhythms against synthesized gurgles and tumbling drum machines, these sparse, spacious creations somehow seemed both completely at home with the Superpitchers and DJ Kozes peopling Kompakt's roster but also wholly fractured and foreign. There's no party summons in *Are You Really Lost?*; it's a strange brand of navel gazing, a gray and off-black colored companion piece to late nights alone.

Still, we might not be telling his story at all if Aguayo hadn't massaged those first efforts at electronic exotica into not only a woolier, weirder expansion of both his own music and perhaps most importantly, as the germinating concept for his famed Bum-BumBox parties and Cómeme label. Several years after relocating to Buenos Aires in 2003 Aguayo and a crew of friends began what was essentially an audio flash mob experiment around South America. Straining against what he began to see as a restrictive Argentinean club culture, Aguayo sought a space that could reshape itself in a moment to *that moment*; he needed a roaming club scene whose energy was shaped not only by the selectors behind the boombox but also by the whims and energies of those in attendance. A space cleared of ceilings or walls, formed by the constant shakings of things, of flesh. Beginning in Buenos Aires, the BBB crew hit various spots in the city with just a boombox and an mp3 player and performed short DJ sets, eventually expanding to larger mobile sound system setups. Aguayo and company would announce locations via social media outlets or simply by word-of-mouth, and the BumBumBox events eventually came to embody sudden sparks of creativity in micro-community settings, stressing inclusivity as a kind of post-modern folk art spilling across the neighborhoods of Buenos Aires and – eventually – throughout South America.

Emerging as a sonic nod to these urban pavement galas was Aguayo's own label, Cómeme. Minted in 2009, the brand has become the hub of electronically-oriented takes on various strains of ethnic music. South American and African rhythms were the source driving the label's debut split between Aguayo and inner-circle compatriot, Rebolledo. Elsewhere, it might seem reductive to pare the label's libidinous sprawl down to "fun," but it's the word that seems closest to bridging the gap on just how much body-flail terrain they've covered over the years. Cómeme has housed pulsating, static-punched trance (Barnt's "Geffen"), strobey Autobahn anthems (Philipp Gorbachev's

MATIAS AGUAYO

Author: Derek Miller

fantastic "Gas Lady") and roughened jackin' house (albums by both Rebolledo and Daniel Maloso), all pulled together via the curatorial vision of Aguayo.

The playfulness upon which his label's staked its name has also snaked its way through Aguayo's own work. Guided by the cheeky, loose-limbed spirit of one of 2008's omnipresent summer anthems – "Minimal," a wink-and-nod play on the very techno scene from which he emerged – Aguayo's two albums since Cómeme's start increasingly embrace its tongue-in-cheek brand of Southern Hemisphere electronica. 2009's *Ay Ay Ay* saw Aguayo transforming himself into a kind of glossolalian beatboxer, littering his floor-bent beats with vocal incantations, all undercut by a kind of blissful narcotic sway; 2013's *The Visitor* upped the ante, increasingly using guest voices to people the shadows of his evermore complicated, almost alinear rhythmic odysseys.

And this is just the abbreviated list of his accomplishments over the last decade plus. Whether it's his own growth as a producer into a singular ethnic fusionist, a musical Shaman of the wee morning hours, his forays into the art of the instant carnival or his oversight of one of electronic music's most compellingly colorful outlets, there's enough to argue for his singular status within the dance music realm.

Derek Miller has written about music for *Stylus Magazine, Pitchfork, eMusic, Village Voice* and *Resident Advisor*.

Metro Area have always existed in elegant opposition to the crassness of the masses.

If house is a skeletal version of disco, as Kelefa Sanneh once wrote in *The New York Times*, Metro Area's music is a colorful musculoskeletal chart – vibrant, open, exploratory. It has the grandeur of disco, the adventurousness of boogie, the sparseness of house, the insistence of techno. It is at once meta and primal, commentary whose most resounding message comes via how well it functions on the dancefloor.

These songs are ideals laid out and pounded into your skull.

Morgan Geist and Darshan Jesrani are disco nerds. Today, that may sound like no big deal – New York is now seemingly filled with straight, white guys who are just as obsessed with the gay, black/Latino music of yesteryear – but back when Geist and Jesrani launched their joint venture, disco just wasn't cool. The pair met after striking up a friendship via an online mailing list – their tastes growing up in the '80s were eclectic (Geist had a stronger New Wave background, while Jesrani preferred R&B) but they intersected with disco, house and techno. They had to find each other. There weren't the scenes in various parts of the world – the Netherlands, Norway – that visi-

bly produce new disco now. Earlier this year, James Murphy – another straight, white, New York disco guy-hag – discussed his disco dabbling during the early days of DFA as part of the Red Bull Music Academy. "It sounded like a terrible idea," he said. It wasn't.

"We consider ourselves to be making dubs of old tracks that never really existed," Geist told *The New York Times* in 2002. Indeed, much of their production work resides between song and track – vocals are sparse in the rare instance that they appear at all (the group has only one full-on vocal track to its name, 2007's "Read My Mind"), but hooks abound, melodies veer into surprising breakdowns, new ideas burst out of old ones. The amount of space the guys leave in their mixes gives their songs an invisible club-like frame, and parts dance out to dazzle you – the synth splats of "Dance Reaction," the deflating bounce of the bassline of "Miura," the drum filtered to go "whoo" in "Caught Up," the analog instruments that pepper their digi-funk: strings, flutes, horns, piano. Both Geist and Jesrani were influenced by the electronic elements of '70s prog rock – each part of their music is a sound effect and the effect is thrilling.

Metro Area's music has gleamed to the beat of its own drums as other spins on disco

have come in and out of fashion: the unimaginative disco house that they heard bastardizing '70s and '80s sounds in the late '90s, the ironic celebration of Italo trashiness that was electroclash, the disco re-edits and Johnny-come-lately pseudo connoisseurs of today. For their craftsmanship alone, Metro Area have always existed in elegant opposition to the crassness of the masses. And if that individuality is too implicit, just ask. Either member will tell you exactly what they think of current dance music. "We were motivated both by inspiration and frustration," is how Jesrani recently explained their first 12-inch to *MTV Hive*.

It is at once meta and primal, commentary whose most resounding message comes via how well it functions on the dancefloor.

However much snobbery drives Geist and Jesrani, their music never sounds stuffy thanks to an almost slapstick sense of sonic experimentation and the uniformly propulsive effect of their tracks. These songs are ideals laid out and pounded into your skull. And

METRO AREA

Author: Rich Juzwiak

though their music functions as criticism of others, they're just as hard on themselves. While discussing "Miura" to *Turntable Lab*, Geist recalled, "We mixed it on a huge vintage mixer and I think we both regret that to this day because it sounds really knocky and shitty to us." That song was voted #1 on *Resident Advisor*'s poll of the Top 100 tracks of the '00s. It is, without question, their mostbeloved track – and it sounds shitty to them.

Back when Geist and Jesrani launched their joint venture, disco just wasn't cool.

Seemingly never satisfied, the men of Metro Area have spoken about single tracks taking sometimes up to a year to complete. Though they have been active for almost 15 years, they have only 25 released tracks (and an intro) to their name. The sophomore album they once spoke of apparently has been scrapped. The hollow virtues that the besieged music industry holds dear – rapidity, familiarity, vulgarity – are all overtly rejected by Geist and Jesrani. The triumph of Metro Area is the triumph of taste.

When Metro Area released their one and only album in 2002 – a compilation of 12-inch cuts and some new tracks – their hipness level temporarily elevated to uneasy heights. Jesrani recalled to *New York* magazine that during a Paris gig around this time, Geist told him, "The people who are yelling loudest will hate us in six months."

If their public profile shrank in the years after 2002, it was just as well. Industry respect for the duo has never abated, and their music comes packed with its own applause, anyway. (Listen closely to their meticulous productions and you'll hear live handclaps often woven into their sound.) Geist and Jesrani launched Metro Area to be the change they wished to see in the world. What they became was a simultaneous tribute to – and essential part of – dance music history.

Rich Juzwiak is a Brooklyn-based journalist. He currently works as a staff writer for *Gawker*.

Modeselektor was born in a period of transition.

"Mutability is our tragedy, but it is also our hope. The worst of times, like the best, are always passing away" wrote the Roman philosopher Boethius in the 6th century. Almost 15 centuries later those words wound up in the mouth of Christopher Eccleston playing a savvy Manchester beggar in the Factory Records mythologizing *24 Hour Party People*. Indulge the irreverence a moment longer: while Boethius was contemplating the nature of history, he could've easily been remarking on the back catalogue of Berlin techno duo Modeselektor. Besides the fact they sampled Eccleston's stirring speech on their track "The Rapanthem," these two East Berliners know more about mutability than most.

For starters, Modeselektor was born in a period of transition; Gernot Bronsert and Sebastian Szary met on a Berlin dancefloor in the early '90s. Or rather, a makeshift dancefloor at one of the crop of illegal acid house parties that sprang up in the newly re-united capital like desert flowers after the fall of the Berlin Wall. But while togetherness was the spirit of the times, dance music was still under purism's spell. So it was like the proverbial bull – or monkey, maybe – in a china shop that Modeselektor swung onto the scene, ripping up the rulebook to build on the energy that brought them together.

Making their own music to play out was a natural progression from a few years spent DJing raves, as was collaborating with a local visual crew to create monstrous live shows that took them all over Europe. By 2001 they'd caught the ear of Ellen Allien who signed them to her label BPitch Control and their path was set. After several 12-inches came their mission statement: 2005 debut album *Hello Mom!*, a perfect exercise in the kind of genre-disregarding experimentation that has come to define the modern dance music landscape.

Even at their most pounding, Modeselektor remain sonically experimental.

From the compressed, glitchy dancehall of "Silikon" to the Turkish folk music inspired groove of "Hasir," *Hello Mom!* skipped and slipped playfully between, over and under the lines. So it was that a brash party number like "Kill Bill Vol. 4" could cozy up to the celestial "Ziq Zaq" without so much as batting an eyelid. Techno was the nucleus around which the album orbited, but Modeselektor was more intent on making connections than carving out a niche. Time and time again the duo proved the elasticity of techno's form,

its inherent desire to imagine new futures and landscapes. "In Loving Memory" is perhaps their debut's finest demonstration: it opens as pure ambience before introducing static and dust, setting off microscopic elements on a collision path. The resulting friction builds into a lolloping groove that in turn melts into ecclesiastical ecstasy.

Modeselektor are not afraid of exclamation marks, literal or musical. It was, of course, their energetic live sets that first got them noticed. Yet it is the roundness of their emotional world that set them apart. Silliness is as valued as spirituality, a contemplative moment as important as an escapist release, a party-hard aesthetic on equal terms with impeccable sound design. Never is one sacrificed for the other. Even at their most pounding, Modeselektor remain sonically experimental; ever curious.

With albums number two and three – the exhibitionist *Happy Birthday* and the more introspective *Monkeytown* – the impact the duo's free-spirited approach has had on the wider music community became clear: Thom Yorke, French rappers TTC, American rappers Antipop Consortium, UK indie rockers Maximo Park and Australian experimentalists PVT joined reggae vocalist Paul St. Hilaire on Modeselektor's ever-increasing

MODESELEKTOR

Author: Ruth Saxelby

collaborator list. The results reached further than ever before, taking their sound to new territory – and territories. Cloud shifting ambience made room for bubbling dubstep, and power-tool techno rumbled next to dubbed-out orchestral grooves.

Time and time again the duo has proved the elasticity of techno's form.

Much of their work could be called prescient: Modeselektor did ballsy stadium dance music way before America caught on and called it EDM. Moderat, their melodramatic side project with Apparat, predated the current wave of producers switching their game up to that of a live band. Perhaps most tellingly, their work with Thom Yorke set the pace for the densely textured, skittering landscapes the Radiohead frontman went on to create with Atoms For Peace.

Not that Bronsert and Szary are hanging about for slaps on the back. They're already onto the next thing: a new album with Apparat was released this year, which reconfirmed their often overlooked talent for heartfelt electronic pop, and more collaborations with Sound Pellegrino Thermal Team are imminent. For Modeselektor are all about inclusion – be it musically, collaboratively or emotionally. It's how they began and why they continue. To be inclusive is to accept change and to embrace evolution; to challenge the status quo and resist fixity – for themselves or their beloved Berlin. They embody their city's changeability, its summer breeze and severe winter. It's that inherent mutability that gives them life.

Ruth Saxelby is the associate editor of DummyMag.com and also contributes to *Pitchfork*, *The Guardian* and *Dazed & Confused* amongst others.

Moritz Von Oswald has continuously redefined the genres he's been involved in.

Few individuals in electronic music have proved themselves to be more innovative, individual and timeless than Moritz von Oswald. Over the course of two-and-a-half decades, he's continuously redefined the genres he's been involved in, melding aspects of techno, house, dub reggae and the avant-garde with peerless elegance, spread across a range of revered projects.

Von Oswald's musical career started behind the drums in Neue Deutsche Welle group Palais Schaumburg, playing and later collaborating with fellow studio obsessive Thomas Fehlmann. After the group disbanded in 1984, he went on to dabble in related side projects as a session player, producer and engineer, before discovering house music and appearing on a handful of energetic but disposable dance releases in 1989. By early 1991, though, his attention shifted towards the rapidly developing sounds of US techno, and he followed his new musical partner Mark Ernestus to Detroit to seek out the creators of the revolution engulfing Europe's dancefloors.

Musical pilgrimages feature regularly in the von Oswald story, and it seems the influence of these journeys have had a profound impact on his subsequent output. In Detroit, while Ernestus was chasing the latest releases from the city's hottest techno labels of the day, von Oswald was apparently focused on picking up rare or obsolete music equipment. The pair quickly forged relationships with Detroit's techno luminaries, who were as impressed by the Germans' ability to circumvent early '90s technical shortcomings (like a lack of MIDI synchronization) as von Oswald and Ernestus were with the futuristic music of figures like Juan Atkins, Blake Baxter, Eddie Fowlkes and Jeff Mills.

Over the next couple of years, the Detroit-Berlin exchange became a functioning creative partnership, with native talents from both cities crossing the Atlantic to work in each other's studios, play gigs and make music collaboratively in various permutations. As von Oswald's confidence as an engineer for techno's innovators blossomed, he set the foundations for his reputation as one of Germany's studio master craftsmen, a position he later cemented with his work at the highly respected vinyl mastering plant, Dubplates & Mastering.

By 1993, von Oswald and Ernestus were ready to make their own major contribution to the techno canon. The first release on their Basic Channel label, "Enforcement," was a fierce, stripped-back techno affair in the mold of Jeff Mills' contemporaneous Waveform Transmission series. Arriving in a plain white sleeve with a bare minimum of label or artist information, it set the stage for its follow-up, "Phylps Track," recorded this time under the artist name Basic Channel and recognized as the primary template for their signature (and much copied) dub techno sound.

Built out of cavernous reverbs, gradually modulating single chord loops, and thundering shards of studio effects, the Basic Channel series transplanted the hypnotic echoes of classic Jamaican dub onto a powerhouse techno frame, to spectacular effect. Over the next two years and nine Basic Channel releases, von Oswald and Ernestus continued to deliver their distinctive vision of techno, creating a unique body of music that was innovative and influential in equal measure. The series was an underground sensation, bolstered in no small part by their refusal to do interviews or release any information about themselves. This anonymous stance aptly mirrored the gray-scale mysteries of the music within, and of course, sent the techno world into a flurry of speculation and rumor over its creators' shrouded identities.

As if in anticipation of the burgeoning legion of Basic Channel imitators (many of whom still exist today), 1994 saw von Oswald and Ernestus perform something of an about

MORITZ VON OSWALD

Author: Lee Smith

turn with the launch of their Main Street label. Working under the Round moniker, they surprised conservative techno purists with "I'm Your Brother," an unashamed US-style vocal house track that at the time seemed worlds apart from the bleak minimalism of Basic Channel. It was followed by the classic "New Day," an end-of-the-night vocal house masterpiece, and the pair's Maurizio project, a more languid, spaced-out take on the Basic Channel style that sounded sublime on dancefloors and headphones alike. But their flirtation with deep house was fairly short-lived, and Main Street's next release saw the duo delve even further into the dub vortex.

Musical pilgrimages feature regularly in the von Oswald story.

As before, von Oswald and Ernestus decided that the only way to truly understand the music they wanted to make was to visit its birthplace and meet its protagonists. Accordingly, they embarked on a pilgrimage to Jamaica, where they formed a long-standing relationship with vocalist Tikiman, AKA Paul St. Hilaire. The third Main Street release was not so much dub techno as it was pure electronic dub, with St. Hilaire's silken vocals carrying a sparse yet resonant backing track set at reggae's classic supine tempo. Another label and recording moniker, Rhythm & Sound, was started to showcase this new direction, and von Oswald's own techno and house output was effectively put on hiatus for a further ten years, though he continued to steward other acts of a similar ilk via his involvement with a series of sub-labels including Chain Reaction and Imbalance. Concurrently, von Oswald and Ernestus again created a kind of European collaborative hub for their chosen genre, utilizing Ernestus' Hardwax record store in Berlin as a base for a new galaxy of dub-orientated reissues, traditionally-styled reggae labels and a steady flow of their own original works.

By 2007, von Oswald had started extending his reach beyond the tight-knit world of Hardwax and its associated activities, and was working regularly as a remixer, producer and engineer for a range of artists. When he and Ernestus announced the end of their partnership that year, he formed the Moritz von Oswald Trio with Sasu Ripatti and Max Loderbauer, going on to release three acclaimed albums that explored the possibilities of electronic live jams with a subtle avant-garde edge. He also began slowly relenting on his anti-press stance, reasoning that his work was no longer just about himself, and that he owed his colleagues the chance to bring their music to a wider audience via increased engagement with the media.

Emerging as humble, wise and warm in interviews, he nonetheless remains elusive when it comes to the nuts and bolts of his studio magic, preferring to discuss the contexts and concepts behind his music in more general terms. Most recently, he's reignited his collaboration with Detroit's techno forefather Juan Atkins, and the pair's resulting *Borderlands* album pulls off von Oswald's by-now inevitable feat of sounding unprecedented and ageless. It's just the latest articulation of von Oswald's manifest talents; as an engineer, a collaborative lynchpin and, most importantly, a musician of singular and seemingly unending skill.

Lee Smith is a freelance music writer and reformed club promoter from Brighton, UK.

Mulatu Astatke powerfully synergized American pop, soul and funk with traditional Ethiopian music.

With its rolling grooves, orchestral arrangements, funky horn sections and remarkable singers, Ethiopian pop music's so-called golden age of 1969 to 1974 bears scant resemblance to any other African style of the time. It possessed a harmonic and depth absent from most other African music, and Mulatu Astatke, more than any other Ethiopian composer or arranger, was responsible for that magic.

Born in 1943, Mulatu Astatke left the Ethiopian capital, Addis Ababa, in 1959 to study at Lindisfarne College in Wales, where he acquired his passion for music. Three years later he enrolled at London's Trinity College of Music, where it flourished. He played congas and jammed early versions of Ethio-jazz at Ronnie Scott's venue, in addition to soaking up other Afro-Caribbean styles. That's apparently where he began thinking about how the Western 12-note scale might be combined with the five-note pentatonic scales and 6/8 grooves used by northern Ethiopia's azmari griots. "If we can expand the melody we can also improve the harmony," Astatke said in a 2007 interview. "That is what I call a cultural revolution."

Astatke's syncretic tendencies ignited at Boston's Berklee School of Music, where he transferred to in 1963. After studying vibra-phone and percussion at Berklee, he moved to New York, where he befriended Tito Puente and began soaking up the Cuban, Dominican and Puerto Rican rhythms that were permeating the city. However, it was all African music to Mulatu, who added an Ethiopian tinge to the local flavors of tracks such as "The Panther," "Soul Power" and "Playboy Cha Cha" on his debut album, *Afro-Latin Soul*.

There was as much James Brown as Duke Ellington in hits like "Gubèlyé" and "Yègellé Tezeta."

Astatke later admitted that he wished he had titled that 1966 full-length *Ethio Jazz*, which would have emphasized the "African contribution" to the sound. But to those in the know, *Afro-Latin Soul* was a revelation, establishing Astatke's methodology in blending the 3/2 Latin clave with the azmari's traditional *chik-chicka* rhythm, usually in 6/8.

Astatke returned to Ethiopia in 1969 just as its musical "golden age" was getting underway. American pop, soul and funk synergized with traditional music powerfully during this fertile period, which lasted until Emperor Haile Selassie was deposed by a military coup in 1974. He performed with and wrote for Tewodros Tadesse, Kuku Sebsebe, Betsat Seyoum, Sèyfou Yohannès, Menelik Wossenachew, the azmari traditionalist known as Teje and singer-composer Girma Bèyènè. Astatke integrated the traditional kebero drum and krar lute into his jazz ensemble, but there was as much James Brown as Ellington in Astatke hits like "Gubèlyé" and "Yègellé Tezeta."

In 1972, Astatke returned to New York to record *Mulatu of Ethiopia*. His hardest-swinging album features a lovely instrumental version of "Kulunmanqueleshi," a traditional song that became an Ethiopian hit when sung by Tilahun Gessesse. However, his first Ethiopian recordings – the singles collected on *Ethiopian Modern Instrumental Hits* and his 1974 album *Yekatit Ethio-Jazz*, which were themselves anthologized on volume four of Francis Falceto's indispensable Éthiopiques series on Buda Musique – are stunning examples of Ethio-jazz fusion at its apex. Astatke's Fender Rhodes piano rubs up against wah-wah guitars and Feqadu Amde-Mesqel's tenor sax.

In 1973, Duke Ellington came to Addis Ababa during a tour of Africa he undertook in a jazz-ambassadorial capacity. Astatke showed

MULATU ASTATKE

Author: Richard Gehr

him around town and arranged an Ethio-jazz version of his own favorite composition. "Dewel," based on Orthodox Church music, is perhaps the most beautifully trancelike of Astatke's works. Astatke performed on piano with Ellington's orchestra, foreshadowing the time after the military takeover when Astatke's most ambitious and progressive music would be made in collaboration with Americans and Europeans.

Ethiopian pop music's so-called golden age of 1969 to 1974 bears scant resemblance to any other African style of the time.

In some sense, *Inspiration Information Volume 3*, Astatke's 2009 collaboration with eclectic British combo the Heliocentrics draws from the same spring that fed his relatively obscure but no less remarkable appearance on *Tchew Belew*, a record by the great accordion player Hailu Mergia and the Walias in 1977. Following the success of the Heliocentrics project, Astatke formed a new band, Steps Ahead, to release his first album of new material since the '80s in 2010.

Three years later, he released the most ambitious album of his life. Modeled on similar sonic panoramas by Ellington and Miles Davis, with *Sketches of Ethiopia*, Astatke has said, "I am talking about all of Ethiopia, from North to South, from East to West. And even about the diaspora communities! Ethio-jazz is now played all over the world. And its successors are as interesting, if not more so, outside Ethiopia." From Ethiopia to the West and then back again, his oscillating and ever-expanding musical vision is once again moving into the land of the 12 in order to replenish the realm of the five.

Richard Gehr currently writes for *Village Voice*, *eMusic*, *SPIN* and *Relix*. His book about *The New Yorker* magazine cartoonists will be published by New Harvest in 2014.

Mykki Blanco is just out here trying to be a pop star.

While queer theorists, hip hop scholars and art rap disciples are busy trying to claim Mykki Blanco as their respective patron saint, Mykki Blanco is just out here trying to be a pop star. Equipped with a skill set that combines an ear for beats and a knack for hooks, a stunning visual sensibility with a fierce attitude and a natural gift for performance, she has all the tools in place for a successful crossover from underground to mainstream. Whether the world is ready for a cross-dressing rap artist to scale the charts is another question entirely.

The ascent of Mykki Blanco – born Michael Quattlebaum Jr. – among tastemakers and culture commentators was surely helped along by the shock value inherent in the video for "Join My Militia (Nas Gave Me a Perm)." Half gangly Rumpelstiltskin, half menacing mermaid, Blanco donned an all-black outfit of weave and lingerie, aggressively delivering her cryptic rhymes. Along with the haunted house-hop laid down by Arca, her demeanor struck a chord with the low-BPM club avant-garde and provided toothsome Tumblr fodder.

If "Join My Militia" was an abrasive hit into left field, "Haze.Boogie.Life" saw Blanco swinging for the fences, baseball bat in hand. The song itself was a fully-formed dancefloor-obliterator, aimed at clubs and SUVs. Sinden and Matrixxman provided an instrumental that zapped and palpitated, bringing in a bulky low-end for the hook. Blanco dished out catchphrases left and right, drilling her martial glam braggadocio firmly into listener's heads. The way she arranged her mantra-like syllables around the beat constituted a clinic in delivery.

Blanco deserves to be treated as an artist and not as a museum piece.

The video for "Haze.Boogie.Life" perfectly exemplified Blanco's performance of gender fluidity. Constantly switching outfits, perms, makeup and accessories, she covered a dizzying range of personas on a scale from diva to thug. Blanco's intonation varied, slightly but noticeably, throughout the track. In combination with each scene, her tone of voice seemed to change, fitting to whichever persona was given the spotlight. It was a simple audio-visual trick, but it cleverly reminded that voice – like gender – is a mere shade rather than an absolute and inherent trait.

As art rap in its truest sense – performance art written through rap – Mykki Blanco pro-vided the radical template for what Kanye West would go on to deliver to a much larger audience 14 months later with *Yeezus*. But if Kanye's appropriation of underground bass music's dark side provided a language for him to vent against the 1% (i.e. himself), while still securing the #1 spot on *Billboard*'s album charts, Blanco's reception is burdened with an entirely different subtext.

Kanye's persona fits neatly into hip hop's long-established masculinity codex (more so than early in his career – which is again a different discussion). Mykki Blanco stands apart. In fact this very separation played a major role in why she has been able to garner so much positive attention on a pre-mainstream level.

Constantly switching outfits, perms, makeup and accessories, she covered a dizzying range of personas on a scale from diva to thug.

That reception is a testament to the changing climate within the world of hip hop, where just a few years prior, an openly gay rapper would have quickly drowned in

MYKKI BLANKO

Author: Anthony Obst

the abyss of message board hate slurs. Frank Ocean's coming out has been widely discussed and, for the most part, embraced. Rappers like Zebra Katz and Le1f have built fan bases within a community that's long been plagued by homophobia. "Queer" is no longer barred from the discourse of "rap."

Denominating a sub-genre on the basis of sexual orientation is problematic, though. It's a harsh reminder of the continued reign of heteronormativity that Mykki Blanco is often viewed as an exotic "other," discussed largely within academic contexts, pushed into a margin – even if it's a wider margin than ever before. Just as Michael Quattlebaum has been fleeing from backwards notions of masculinity and gender, his escape from academia has been just as forceful. Symbolically ("I'm not going to be some sort of gay political dress-up doll") and physically (he's dropped out of college multiple times.)

Mykki Blanco's media reception hints at the way she's being filtered: At the time of this writing, Blanco has not been featured in *The Source*. *XXL* first covered her a year after *The New York Times* ran a piece. At that point, *Village Voice* already granted her a cover story. Among the first publications to write about Blanco? The Italian edition of *Vogue*. Her narrative is not written through the usual

course of aspiring rap stars – partly because some outlets still view her as a subject that doesn't relate to their audience.

Mykki Blanco provided the radical template for what Kanye West would go on to deliver with *Yeezus*.

Though one might argue that Blanco's entry point into the music industry initially came more through her art grind than a rap grind – after all, her rap persona was birthed in the context of a video project – she has proven herself to be one of the most exciting hip hop artists to emerge over the last couple of years. Her musical talents can stand on their own, and as their creator, Mykki Blanco deserves to be treated as an artist and not as a museum piece. *Betty Rubble: The Initiation*, her 2013 EP, could easily sit next to the likes of Kanye, Pusha T, Trinidad James or Lil Wayne. Her hard-hitting trunk-rattlers, fierce delivery and devastating one-liners deserve a larger audience.

Anthony Obst writes about rap and beat music for Red Bull Music Academy, *Live For The Funk* and *Juice*. His byline has also appeared in *Spex* and *okayplayer*.

Nik Void may play the guitar, but she is the epitome of a modern artist.

On February 20, 2007, the artist Jo Mitchell, who has carved out a niche recreating infamous gigs, turned her attention to the world's most notorious industrial music event. The Concerto For Voice And Machinery II was a re-staging of a gig by the German group Einstürzende Neubauten, Fad Gadget and Genesis P-Orridge at London's Institute of Contemporary Arts on January 3, 1984. At the original show, the band used chain saws, pneumatic drills and cement mixers on stage (there was also a piano, but only as raw material for the performers to destroy).

Her brutally unconventional playing style mocks the preening self-regard of appalling musical plate spinners.

In the 20 minutes the show lasted before the power was turned off by worried ICA officials, the band drilled though the stage, with the aim of burrowing through the basement of the venue down into the tunnels under The Mall which connect Buckingham Palace to the Houses of Parliament. As Neubauten member Alexander Hacke said retrospectively, their Dadaist/Situationist action had "failed." It is worth mentioning this because Mitchell's act of retromania was also a failure in artistic terms. It took a valid and insurrectionary act and repackaged it as a toothless "rock gig" – an exercise in headline-grabbing "shock and awe"-style entertainment that was actually closer to *Stomp!* than to the original event.

Nik Void, a London-based musician and artist about whom little biographical material is known, exists in a continuum with Neubauten as a member of industrial/noise/dance unit Factory Floor. Likewise, she also resides in the same spectrum of "performers" as Frank Tovey, AKA Fad Gadget, as both blur the boundaries between music and art. And she has concrete links to Genesis P-Orridge, as she has worked with the Throbbing Gristle singer's former bandmates, Chris Carter and Cosey Fanni Tutti. (The trio, as Carter Tutti Void, released a live album called *Transverse* in 2012 on Mute, a thrilling blend of live electronics, throbbing primal rhythms, guitar noise and baleful vocal utterances.)

If Neubauten and company were burrowing out of the ICA, then Void – notionally at least – is violently digging her way into the gallery. Popular music has always been regarded as the slightly inferior cousin to contemporary art, but there are very good reasons why Factory Floor were offered a residency at the ICA and has worked with the artist Haroon Mirza and the composer Peter Gordon. Void may play the guitar, but she is the epitome of a modern artist.

Let's start with her name. To presume that Void is some kind of sub-Richard Hell or Johnny Rotten nomenclature of punk nihilism is to miss the point entirely. She, as a personality, does not exist. She has removed herself entirely from the picture, an idea picked up from the entirely more progressive (pre-superstar DJ) culture of house and techno. In private Void says that if she has the attention of a large audience, she doesn't want to waste their time with the self-indulgency of solipsistic lyrics or the soap opera drip feed of biographical detail. She wants people to become entirely absorbed by the art or music itself.

She has become an absence. There is just noise.

This is something that is common among dance music pioneers ranging from Underground Resistance to Burial, and it is only the hackneyed rock press who see the idea of a faceless electronic music producer as a tan-

NIK VOID

Author: John Doran

talizing mystery that needs to be cracked at all costs. (The same applies to the name Factory Floor. Those who presume it is merely a gauche reference to the Mancunian post-punk label are mistaken – although there is some convergent evolutionary history at the root of both names. The band are concerned with stepping away from the ego-fuelled cult of individuality promoted by rock music and presenting themselves as an absence; a faceless machine of process. They are simply a factory that produces noise.)

Her name and her methods of production are in complete harmony. The way that women in music are objectified and objectify themselves is an extremely complex subject. In terms of pop music alone, the ways in which Britney Spears, Madonna, Lady Gaga, M.I.A. and Shakira are all objectified (and to what extent they are in control of this process themselves) vary wildly. Void has objectified herself completely but not in terms of sexuality or gender. She has rendered these factors irrelevant to herself by reducing what she is purely to sound.

Her early Factory Floor tracks "Lying" and "Wooden Box" – hardly exercises in baroque songwriting themselves – have given way to a form of singing so pared back that it almost demands new terminology. She sings through vocal effects, which obscure what she is saying. To muddy the water even further, a lot of what emanates from her is purely guttural noise and nonsense words. She samples these recordings and then splices them up into a mosaic of exhortations and sound fragments, dropping them back into the mix like a house music producer would with the disembodied voice of an R&B diva, except with even less sense or context. There is literally nothing of the essence or biography of her in her own records. She has become an absence. There is just noise.

Her name and her methods of production are in complete harmony.

While her role as the guitarist in Factory Floor is becoming more minimal as the band journey away from their maximal noise roots, she is also in the process of developing her own sound as a solo performer which involves a huge wall of guitar noise using bowing and other non-standard rhythm and feedback techniques. The continuing development of a unique and overwhelming Nik Void sound means she sidesteps the usual misogyny that female rock musicians often face from those desperate to prove that women musicians (somehow) lack chops.

But, more importantly, her brutally unconventional playing style mocks the preening self-regard of appalling musical plate spinners. The ventriloquists concerned with prissy technical ability as a pure form of entertainment. As much as these artists now appear antiquated and completely out of step, perversely, Void's improvised brutalism and instinctual primitivism have marked her out as a thoroughly modern artist.

John Doran is the editor of TheQuietus.com. He regularly contributes to *BBC Radio 6 Music*, *Metal Hammer* and *VICE*.

Nile Rodgers turned pleasure into a principle.

I don't know to what degree two generations' collective love for Nile Rodgers inspired the enormous response to his, Daft Punk and Pharrell's "Get Lucky." Certainly the sight of Rodgers – gaunt and bewigged thanks to the cancer that almost killed him, gamely contributing his signature *chik-a-chik-chik* rhythm playing – gave flesh to survivordom as concept. Cancer or not, it was good to hear Rodgers on a hit again. As one-half of the creative force behind Chic, one of the '70s greatest bands, he turned pleasure into a principle, helming a guitar-bass-drums combination as lissome as any in rock.

Years of apprenticeship for Luther Vandross and Ashford & Simpson toughened the groove of bassist Bernard Edwards and drummer Tony Thompson, but the feather-light and shrewd use of the space between the strings and vocals of his employers, coupled with a visual ethos copped from Roxy Music, inspired Rodgers to create disco whose depiction of a cocktail-hour elegance trembled with anxiety. Like the ballerina in *The Red Shoes* who can't stop turning and turning in a widening gyre, Rodgers and Edwards' characters flash rictus grins. The studied blankness of Norma Jean Wright's vocal on 1977's "Everybody Dance" complements the diamond-drill concentration of Edwards' bass, an

approach that peaked on 1979's "My Feet Keep Dancing": as the singers turn the title into a mantra, strings saw away, going higher and higher, one note at a time, a ruthless danse macabre.

These types of stompers constitute the bulk of Rodgers' legacy. As you're reading this sentence a radio station somewhere in the world is playing "Le Freak" – and why not? Written after Studio 54's unyielding door policy banished Rodgers and Edwards on New Year's Eve 1978, "Le Freak" stacked chants and serious guitar riffage like a Funkadelic track given a glam-rock gloss. The Edwards showcase "Good Times" is even thicker and funkier – perfect sample-fodder.

Rodgers created disco whose depiction of a cocktail-hour elegance trembled with anxiety.

But Chic also recorded tracks whose decelerated tempos blurred differences between sophistication and despair, often punctuated with Rodgers' acerbic solos. The manic strings of "My Feet Keep Dancing" turn woozy on "Will You Cry," on which Rodgers' guitar doubles those strings

with eye-opening precision. "Tavern on the Green" is a two-minute Wisteria about a tourist trap. "When You Love Someone" marries both approaches: meditative at first, euphoric later. Rodgers' ten-note hook drips like Chinese water torture until a tempo and chord change in the last minute, during which Edwards and Thompson join him and singer Luci Martin.

Production work kept Rodgers solvent after Chic's fortunes dwindled. It began with two highs: the Chic-in-all-but-name Sister Sledge album *We Are Family* and Diana Ross' *diana*. However, two commercial disappointments (in the States at least) foreshadowed Rodgers' mid-'80s identikit approaches. A spooked Carly Simon tiptoes into the stuttering electronic bricolage of "Why" from the *Soup for One* soundtrack, while on *KooKoo* Debbie Harry and Rodgers-Edwards couldn't create a compelling frisson.

David Bowie's *Let's Dance* reanimated Rodgers' career. Bowie fans who mourn the phase that this album heralded may point to Rodgers' original intentions and despair: Rodgers thought he was going to make an art rock record, the best chance for him to prove, according to an interview with *Rolling Stone*, that black artists have other interests besides "dancing, making love and

NILE RODGERS

Author: Alfred Soto

stuff like that." But Bowie hired Rodgers to transform folk demos into tub-thumpers suitable for arenas in Australia, Vancouver and Los Angeles. What "the '80s" signify as music and ambition began with the cannon-like boom of the drums on "Modern Love," gated beyond recognition.

The strings saw away, going higher and higher, one note at a time, a ruthless danse macabre.

It worked: Bowie and Rodgers got their hits. For *Like a Virgin*, Rodgers returned to the *diana* template: Madonna as Diana Ross backing Chic, with a Synclavier tagging along. The arrangements push the limits of her insouciance, but Rodgers' guitar is at its lithest on "Angel," for which he reprises the pizzicato trick, and both Synclavier and Madonna take off on the wordless portion of "Over and Over"'s bridge.

As Rodgers has admitted several times in the last decade, the '80s were hard. He accepted too many production assignments that required him to inject funk where none existed or to reanimate commercial corpses. The credits get drearier until a last-gasp assignment turned into a triumph. Sliding into the late Ricky Wilson's slot, Keith Strickland did a nimble bit of Rodgers mimicry on the B-52's *Cosmic Thing*. "Love Shack" and "Roam" depend on the watercolor hues and rhythm slinging that Rodgers took to the top of the charts a decade earlier. Indeed, imagine "take it hip to hip / rockin' through the wilderness" coming out of the lips of Alfa Anderson and Norma Jean Wright.

The prestige jobs faded in the '90s. Bernard Edwards dying of pneumonia in a Japanese hotel room ended the hope of another Chic album, but in recent years as the influence and affection for the band has grown Rodgers has taken his own version on the road. The publication of a chatty memoir coincided with a cancer diagnosis that he has apparently beaten. Before the good news, though, there was a Daft Punk album to make. Whether he contributed to the titles of the songs on which he played we don't know, but it's impossible not to listen to "Give Life Back to Music" and "Lose Yourself to Dance" without connecting those slogans to the grooves he lays down. Their greatest living creator knows: grooves end with beginnings.

Alfred Soto is an instructor and media adviser at Florida International University. His work has appeared in *the Miami Herald*, *Village Voice* and *SPIN* and he blogs at *Humanizing the Vacuum*.

Patrick Adams proved soulful dance music knows no expiration date.

When Patrick Adams once observed that the finest disco recordings were on par with anything Beethoven, Bach or Tchaikovsky wrote, such was the beauty of their arrangements, he might very easily have been describing his own work. The Harlem-born-and-bred producer/arranger/composer's credits festoon an array of classics from the disco-boogie era, from the manic Moog moves of Cloud One's "Atmosphere Strutt," to his studio collective Phreek's dedication to nightlife revelry, "Weekend," and salacious hyper active workouts like Musique's "In the Bush."

Adams keyed on the fragility of a lyric while maintaining a pulse geared for the dancefloor.

If any single figure's catalog transcended the genre – keying on the emotional warmth or fragility of a lyric or melody while maintaining a pulse geared for the dancefloor – it was Adams. With a few simple creative chord changes, a rendition of a Motown standard like Inner Life's cover of "Ain't No Mountain High Enough" – co-produced with frequent collaborator Greg Carmichael – could be reinvented as a slab of symphonic disco

euphoria. In the B-sections and breakdowns of an instrumental jam like Cloud One's "Disco Juice," Adams creates a wistful tension between the sustained synth and vibraphone's notes and the rumbling congas and kicks below.

His string and rhythm arrangements on Donna McGhee's cult classics "Make It Last Forever" and "It Ain't No Big Thing" manage the trick of adding lushness while enhancing the song's intimacy. And on Adams' own personal favorite, Inner Life's "I'm Caught Up (In One Night Love Affairs)," he hitches his Holland-Dozier-Holland-inspired songwriting to click track snaps and a typically impassioned Jocelyn Brown vocal, evoking longing and contemplation amidst our heroine's liberated love carousel.

None of this was by coincidence. Growing up in the shadow of Harlem's Apollo Theater, as a teenager Patrick Adams befriended the stage manager at the world famous venue, eventually regularly sitting in on sound checks and passing out music charts to the orchestra. A few years of playing in bands, absorbing the tutelage of veteran producers like Gene Redd at recording dates, and tinkering with his own two-track reel-to-reel at home honed his sensibilities and technical chops.

His first big break arrived when he guided Black Ivory, a trio of fellow uptowners that included a young, falsetto-ed Leroy Burgess, to a deal with Perception/Today Records. At just 20 years of age, Patrick produced the group's classic sweet soul number, "Don't Turn Around," and was hired as the label's A&R director. Listening back now, Black Ivory's debut LP exemplifies all the signature traits of the Patrick Adams sound – an ear for affecting melodic changes (the striking ballads "I'll Find a Way" and "Find the One Who Loves You") and arrangement smarts (an aching version of Michael Jackson's "Got to Be There" that unexpectedly, jubilantly breaks into Isaac Hayes' "Shaft" on its outro).

He'd continue to employ them to great effect upon leaving Perception/Today in the mid-'70s, helming a series of terrific 45s (Pete Warner's "I Just Want to Spend My Life with You," Mayberry Movement's "I Think I'm in Love," Daybreak's "Everything Man," Four Below Zero's "E.S.P.") that made little noise upon release but have been heavily championed by rare soul aficionados in the years since. A group out of Tupelo, Mississippi whose hometown provided the partial inspiration for its name ("Tupelo" begetting "Four Below"), Four Below Zero's 1976 single in particular set the template for Adams' sublime and sophisticated brand of emotive dance

PATRICK ADAMS

Author: Jeff "Chairman" Mao

music – rhythmically irresistible with the most relentlessly upfront hi-hat this side of Lee Perry's Black Ark, but with intricate strings and a soulful as hell group vocal. That track would initially appear on P&P Records, a Harlem world indie run by a promoter named Peter Brown and his wife Patricia. P&P provided such a forum for Patrick Adams' work that its name is still commonly, if mistakenly, assumed to stand not for "Peter & Patricia," but "Peter & Patrick."

With a few simple creative chord changes, a rendition of a Motown standard could be reinvented as a slab of symphonic disco euphoria.

With P&P and its associated labels, Patrick Adams and Peter Brown emphasized the kind of funky DIY experimentation the majors – for whom Patrick had begun making inroads with as a producer and arranger for hire – couldn't be bothered with. This meant releasing Patrick's one-man-band jamming as Cloud One, or funky break-beat laden oddities like the Golden Flamingo Orchestra's paean to NYC's Guardian Angel

foot patrols, "*The Guardian* Angel Is Watching Over Me." Mysterious singers (Marta Acuna? Margo Williams?) came and went through P&P's revolving recording door – their names and voices preserved on records, their stories blank Discogs entries still awaiting updates.

But Patrick's sound continued to flourish. In a shrewdly calculated move, he embraced anonymity as well – spinning off collaborative group projects for other labels with his "P.A. System" writers/singers/musicians like Stan Lucas, Leroy Burgess and Kenneth Morris under aliases like Phreek, Rainbow Brown, Sine, Inner Life and Musique. This, so radio jocks like Frankie Crocker could rock them all without appearing to play favorites. Dovetailing with his major label productions for the likes of Herbie Mann, Eddie Kendricks, Candi Staton and others, Adams was deemed "The Uncrowned King of Disco" by industry trade magazine, *Record World*.

For most producers or musicians such notoriety could have boomeranged as a career death knell when the inevitable disco backlash set in at the close of the '70s. But Adams adapted his aesthetic, sculpting essential Paradise Garage-era spins like Shades of Love's "Keep In Touch (Body to Body)" and Skipworth & Turner's "Thinking About Your

Love" – proving soulful dance music knows no expiration date. A hook-y Linn drum-fueled smash like Wish's 1984 hit "Touch Me," featuring longtime vocal muse Fonda Rae, affirmed this yet again when UK songstress Cathy Dennis' cover version went global in the early '90s.

As hip hop became a creative force, he even diversified his skill set by turning to engineering, working out of seminal golden era recording hotbed Power Play Studios and lending his seasoned studio touch to classics by Salt-N-Pepa, Dana Dane and, most notably, Eric B. & Rakim on the duo's seminal *Paid in Full* and *Follow the Leader* LPs. In other words, Patrick Adams not only endured but thrived across eras, much like the beloved recordings that bear his name and sonic stamp. May they long remain in rotation where the happy people go.

Jeff "Chairman" Mao is the co-author of *ego trip's Book of Rap Lists* and *ego trip's Big Book of Racism*. He resides in Harlem with his wife and kids, their cats and his record collection.

Paul Riser arguably exerted as distinct an influence on the Motown sound as anyone.

The 2002 documentary *Standing in the Shadows of Motown* is the kind of thing that can comprehensively put the skids under the defining idea of pop as the product of a solitary, driven individual pulling all the strings in the single-minded pursuit of their vision. Examine the history of Motown in any detail, in fact, and it begins to look less like a grand plan and more like a remarkable succession of happy accidents; a fortuitous confluence of talent, industriousness and old-fashioned star power that just happened to flow through the Detroit greater metropolitan area for a decade or so, resulting in some of the greatest pop music ever made.

Suddenly, here he was amongst a gang of gun-toting hoodlums who called themselves the Funk Brothers.

As Paul Justman's extraordinary film poignantly illustrates, most of the musicians who actually played the music that built Motown toiled in anonymity. It wasn't until the release of *What's Going On* in 1971 that the label finally began crediting some of those players on album covers. Amongst the handful of people whose name might have caught the eye before then was Paul Riser, Motown's principal arranger and orchestrator, who arguably exerted as distinct an influence on the Motown sound as Smokey Robinson, Holland-Dozier-Holland or James Jamerson.

Detroit-born Riser graduated from Cass Technical High School in the city's mid-town district, where he'd studied classical and jazz trombone. Cass Tech's list of notable alumni reads like a who's who of post-war black music: Donald Byrd, Curtis Fuller, Diana Ross, Ron Carter, Greg Phillinganes and Dorothy Ashby are just some of its former students. Less familiar might be the name of Dale Warren. Before joining Stax Records where, amongst other things, he masterminded legendary funk band 24-Carat Black, Warren did a tour of duty as lead viola for Motown's in-house string section.

"I knew Dale Warren from Cass," Riser recalled in an interview last year with *Soul Source*. "One day, he called and told me there was a paid position playing trombone at Motown, and that I should come down." Riser was somewhat skeptical. "I knew nothing about Motown. I hated R&B and most other forms of pop music, with the exception of some of the Atlantic stuff that I'd heard my brother and sister play, people like Ruth Brown and Ray Charles, but I reluctantly agreed."

Riser's inaugural gig at Motown HQ on 2648 West Grand Boulevard was an eye-opener. The studious 23-year-old's strict religious background had, by his own admission, left him short on street smarts. Suddenly, here he was in the raucous atmosphere of Studio A, the converted basement garage nicknamed "the Snakepit," amongst a gang of gun-toting hoodlums who called themselves the Funk Brothers. "It was something of a shock for me to see the way the other musicians behaved," he said in that same interview. "They would drink, get high, fight sometimes and just generally behave badly. I just wasn't used to music being performed this way."

Beneath the rowdiness, however, Riser quickly identified a tightly-knit group of dedicated musicians, as disciplined in their own way as he in his, and worked hard to fit in. "Boy, was I shocked to see how much effort it took to make music!" he remembered, when lecturing at the Red Bull Music Academy in 2011. "It takes so much stamina to sit there and hear take 15, take 20, take 30. Not that I respected the music itself so much, but I respected what it took to get the music, the end product."

PAUL RISER

Author: Paul McGee

This somewhat scornful opinion was far from atypical amongst Riser's classically-trained peers elsewhere in the world of R&B. Over at Chess in Chicago, Charles Stepney didn't mince words regarding what he described as "musically stupid" recording artists. Meanwhile, Philly soul pioneer Thom Bell was set for a career as a concert pianist, or even a conductor, before having his head turned by Little Anthony & the Imperials. Did these men find themselves gravitating to R&B out of frustration at the lack of opportunities for black composers in the classical idiom? Perhaps. But Riser, finding life as a Funk Brother a little too labor-intensive, saw Motown as the ideal setting in which to flex his orchestrator's muscles and develop his creativity at the same time.

"I loved doing orchestrations, particularly with strings," Riser once told journalist Rob Moss. "String players are usually better disciplined than horn players and certainly more than rhythm guys – and that suited me. The producers didn't put any pressure on me. They would give me something to work on and just say, 'Go do your thing, 'which I appreciated because it gave me a lot more confidence." One of his main duties was to add what he called "sweetening" to a song. For example, the Temptations' "My Girl" was a pretty, but rather sparse ballad before Riser went to work on it. "Smokey [Robinson] had given it to [the Temptations] without strings, but they thought it was 'square' and they didn't want to do it. In fact, they hated it! I put the strings on and everything changed."

The secondary hooks, counter-melodies and sparkling flourishes all owe something to Riser's input.

Riser's orchestral break leading into the final key change of "My Girl" has become as crucial to the song as the main melody or the lyrics, and is characteristic of his work across the Motown catalogue; the secondary hooks, counter-melodies and sparkling flourishes heard in everything from "Dancing in the Street" to "Papa Was a Rolling Stone," the desolation of "What Becomes of the Broken-Hearted" (co-written by Riser during a Spinners session), the brooding menace of "I Heard It Through the Grapevine" and the sweeping drama of "Ain't No Mountain High Enough" all owe something of their impact and enduring power to Riser's input, the latter song being one of his personal high-water marks.

Shortly after Motown finally left Detroit for Los Angeles, Riser moved on, continuing to do outstanding work with a broad range of artists from Aretha Franklin, Luther Vandross and Phil Collins, to modern-day keepers of the flame like R. Kelly, whose "Step in the Name of Love" was arranged by Riser, and Raphael Saadiq, who called upon Riser to add a touch of authenticity to the painstakingly crafted Motown pastiches on his *The Way I Feel* album. He's a long time out of the shadows.

Paul McGee was born in Liverpool before the Beatles broke up. He lives and works in Berlin, Germany, and has written about music, films, TV and popular culture for *Q*, *MOJO*, *The Arts Desk* and *The Word*.

It's nearly impossible to imagine electronic music without Robert Henke.

Artistic influence is usually about one's work or technique rubbing off on someone else. And Robert Henke, the driving force behind Monolake, has certainly been influential in that way, with a discography of adventurous techno that's informed a generation of electronic musicians. In his capacity as an artist and academic, Henke has made computer music his life's work. But it's an arguably minor offshoot of that pursuit that made Henke one of the most uniquely influential figures in music of the last decade – a producer that changed the way production works generally, for people whose music might bear nothing of the dub ripples and digital clicks that have defined Monolake through the years. You can probably picture electronic music without Monolake, but it's nearly impossible to imagine electronic music without Robert Henke.

Monolake began in 1995 as the duo of Henke and Gerhard Behles, a fellow computer music academic, and their wispily dubby early sides helped forge the sound signature of Basic Channel's foundational Chain Reaction imprint. The tracks, together with field recordings Henke made in China, found their way onto *Hongkong*, Monolake's full-length debut. Behles left the group after *Interstate*, their second album, and aside from a brief period in 2004 when Torsten

Pröfrock, AKA T++, made Monolake a duo once more, it's otherwise been Henke's project alone. Since going solo, Henke has maintained Monolake's original headiness while also exhibiting palpable artistic restlessness: he cultivated evocative ambience on records like 2009's *Silence* but remorselessly stripped it bare on chilly 2012 follow-up *Ghosts*.

Henke remains one of Ableton Live's most adventurous users and boosters.

When Behles left Monolake in 1999, he did so to focus on another side of their partnership, a company he and Henke helped found called Ableton. Their product, Live, was basically a digital audio workstation, but it didn't look or act much like comparable software. At that point, DAWs were lending the ease and flexibility of hard disk storage to a comparatively ancient recording paradigm, one that had been around since multitrack tape machines first found their way into recording studios. On a program like Cubase or Pro Tools, you could record takes ad nauseum and edit without a razor blade, but making music on a computer

was still more or less a linear process made up of a few discrete stages: composing, tracking, mixing and, if it came to it, reinterpretation for live performance.

Live's conceit was that your computer doesn't have to act like a recording studio if you don't want it to. It got there by loosening the hold of time, formerly one of the most critical constraints on the recording process. Behles and Henke were deeply influenced by granular synthesis – where samples are divvied up into milliseconds-long slivers of sound called grains, which can then be recombined into new sounds – and it found its way into the features that set Live apart.

His is a sound that's immersive in a way that pummeling club music aspires to but rarely reaches.

Granular methods provided the technological framework for "warping," a beat-mapping and time-stretching process that let all of the musical material in a Live session sync up effortlessly. It was also the metaphor behind the "clip view," a screen that concep-

ROBERT HENKE

Author: Jordan Rothlein

tualized a recording session not as a series of sounds playing down a timeline but as a matrix of musical fragments – "clips" – that could be played in any order and rearranged with simple drags and drops. With linearity no longer a necessity, those discrete stages of recording were suddenly a lot blurrier: you could compose and recompose from tracking through mixing – or completely do away with the finished product altogether, choosing instead to perform the track live with near-infinite variability.

Since Live first became commercially available in 2001, this paradigm shift has left an indelible mark on all sorts of music. Electronic music grew longer, loopier, denser and freer as Live let producers build music from whatever constituent parts they wanted, and the results could stretch out in whatever direction they pleased. You can hear it as much in the minimal techno of Richie Hawtin's M_nus label as in the lysergic churn of Flying Lotus, and it's all over Monolake as well: beats and glitches give way to unrecognizable sounds as compositions take on delectably strange shapes.

Live has long been deeply intuitive and remarkably easy to use compared to other DAWs, which has made producers out of plenty who may have otherwise found pro-duction needlessly complicated and creatively counterintuitive. It's not much of a stretch to say that Live has done more to demystify, democratize and decentralize electronic production than any other development save the internet in the new millennium.

Ableton Live's conceit was that your computer doesn't have to act like a recording studio if you don't want it to.

Henke has said he passed on a director position at Ableton because it might impede his work as an electronic musician, but he's remained central to the company over the years. He's sat on Live's specification team, helping to set the general agenda for the software, and he's designed a number of its on-board effects and instruments. He curtailed his official involvement in the company at the end of the '00s as he took on academic appointments at the Berlin University of Arts and at Stanford, but he remains one of Live's most adventurous users and boosters. Monolake live shows now feature Henke positioned behind a Live-equipped laptop, flinging digital shrapnel between surround channels in service of a sound that's immersive in a way that pummeling club music aspires to but rarely reaches.

Perhaps what's most impressive, though, is that it's no longer strange to see a performance based entirely around "playing" a laptop. Brian Wilson, a pioneer of studio-instrumentalism, famously stopped touring with the Beach Boys during much of their prime so that he could focus his attention on recording. These days, it's business as usual to play your studio like an instrument, fold it shut, slide it into a backpack and look for the next place you can plug it in and start recording again.

Jordan Rothlein writes about electronic musicians and their machines. He is the tech editor of *Resident Advisor*.

The world's best known and longest-serving rhythm section.

Jamaican music's mule-headed internal focus is, at once, its greatest strength and greatest weakness – it stays largely true to itself, but is pretty much unable to engage with the music business at large. Unless, of course, you're Sly Dunbar & Robbie Shakespeare, the world's best known and longest-serving rhythm section. Thanks to an enthusiasm for off-island music – Robbie is a Bob Dylan nerd; and it was an obsession with Sylvester Stewart & the Family Stone that gave the teenage Lowell Dunbar his nickname – they are the island's most consistent innovators. What lifts them above even their most persistently pioneering peers – Lee Perry, King Tubby and Prince Buster, for instance – is how they took ideas from rock and soul, reggae-ized them and sold them back into the same genres they'd taken them from.

Sly & Robbie made genuine Jamaican reggae music that found a place in the global mainstream.

By showing a metronomic understanding of groove, the ability to spice it up when called for and a love for all things musical from Philly to folk, the duo backed and/or produced a range of artists that took in Serge Gainsbourg, the Rolling Stones, Simply Red, Madonna, Joe Cocker, Gwen Guthrie, Paul McCartney, Joan Armatrading, James Brown, Sting, Sinead O'Connor, Grace Jones and, Robbie's idol himself, Bob Dylan (they're on *Infidels*; he returns the favor by blowing harmonica on their *Language Barrier* album).

Into this rock world, Sly & Robbie brought a rhythmic reliability, honed by years in Kingston's studios where cutting 20 tracks a day left little room for retakes and getting it right was what got you more work. It was with Jamaican pragmatism that Chris Blackwell put the duo at the core of the Compass Point All-Stars, the house band at the state-of-the-art recording studios he established in Nassau, Bahamas, in the late '70s. He knew they would get the job done, and that is where they worked with many of the aforementioned acts.

Exciting as this international brand-building might have been, it was back home in the reggae world where Sly & Robbie made their biggest impact, as any return was always a creative and spiritual event. Working with Jamaican superstars such as Gregory Isaacs, Frankie Paul, Culture, Dennis Brown, the Mighty Diamonds, Sugar Minott and Yellowman, they produced music that was

more about passion than efficiency or innovation. Indeed, it's a mark of how grounded the two of them remain, that rather than permanently larging it off rock star-size paychecks, as soon as they'd finish working they'd leave the luxury of Blackwell's Bahamas complex to hang out in their modest Kingston studio / office making music, often simply for their own enjoyment.

Cutting 20 tracks a day left little room for retakes. Getting it right was what got you more work.

The duo have been, between them, members of such legendary Jamaican session crews as the Aggrovators, the Upsetters, Skin, Flesh & Bone and the Revolutionaries, and regularly at the forefront of seismic rhythmic shifts. It was, however, as their independent playing 'n' production operation, Taxi Productions, where they were able to show what they were truly capable of, as two things set them apart from Kingston's rank and file studios: they weren't sound system operators they had an international rather than strictly Jamaican perspective. Sly & Robbie were determined to make genuine Jamaican reggae music that would find

SLY & ROBBIE

Author: Lloyd Bradley

a place in the global mainstream as regular pop music rather than something exotic or leftfield.

It helped that they were tech heads. They had always been quick to seize on the latest in instrument and (to a degree) studio technology on their frequent travels to the UK, the US and Japan. British reggae maestro Dennis Bovell remembers showing them rudimentary Moog synthesizers in the '70s and Sly & Robbie soaking up everything they couldn't have found in Jamaica, shipping gear home and introducing it to the domestic industry.

They wanted to make sure the technology was serving them and not the other way around.

In the next decade, Sly & Robbie were the first on the island to use, respectively, a computerized drum kit and a Steinberger headless bass. Hardly innovative in the post-disco, early '80s mainstream, their reasons for going with those particular instruments not only shines a light on why they were so successful, but also says a great deal about them as musicians. Sly explained

that they needed the computerized sound (the Steinberger bass was much crisper and more precise than a regular model) to remain relevant, but the digital notes had to be *played*, traditionally, to get the nuances, the feel and the imperfections. "Otherwise," he chuckled, "they won't be needing us any more." They wanted to make sure the technology was serving them and not the other way around.

Sly & Robbie not only advanced contemporary Jamaican music in Jamaica. They advanced it into the world's pop and rock mainstream. Among others, they took digital reggae to the Grammys with Black Uhuru's *Red*; made dancehall tuneful again with the Chaka Demus & Pliers combination tunes; produced ragga pop that was still ragga with Half Pint's "Greetings"; and got Beenie Man into the US charts.

Given that since then, reggae and reggae-related music has increasingly figured as part of the mainstream pop and rock landscape, Sly & Robbie, perhaps more than anybody else, should be hailed for providing the platform on which it could build on its own terms. And yes, that includes Bob Marley.

Lloyd Bradley, former sound system owner and pirate radio broadcaster, is the author of the best-selling *Bass Culture: When Reggae Was King* and *Sounds Like London: 100 Years of Black Music in the Capital*.

Tom Oberheim embodies networks of ideas and currents in music.

Music technology is often not so much about invention as connection. You can't take Tom Oberheim and put him next to a picture of a single circuit design, or a single machine – like Bob Moog and his ladder filter or the Minimoog. At least, you can't do it and hope to do him any justice. What Oberheim has achieved over the years is to guide the connections between technologies. And he himself embodies networks of ideas and currents in music. From Herbie Hancock and Vangelis to the beats behind Run-DMC and various '80s hits, his sound has become inseparable from recent music history.

It's fitting, then, that Oberheim is one of the founders of Berkeley's Dead Presidents' Club, a coffee shop meet-up in Berkeley, California. There, he's been a regular alongside characters like late digital pioneer Max Mathews, drum machine legend Roger Linn, researcher David Wessel of UC Berkeley and other luminaries of music creation who regularly get together for breakfast. On any given morning, Oberheim is in his element, riffing on the latest curiosities, on things with knobs and things on records alike. The "lone inventor" myth is unfortunately strong in our culture, but a lot of the best musical devices have come from this sort of klatch. Sound scientists share and compete and play off one another just like musicians.

What makes Oberheim unique is just how many parts of that world he's touched. He was involved in computer design and microcontrollers so early that he could rightfully say he focused more on analog design in the '70s because digital design had already bored him. Whereas most figures from the time would categorize themselves as mostly musician or technician, Oberheim was both, through and through. His studies took him deep into physics, engineering and music, singing with the Greg Smith Singers while he was laboring on microelectronics.

Whereas most figures would categorize themselves as mostly musician or technician, Oberheim was both.

And then there are the machines. Devices like his SEM and Two Voice Synthesizer are enjoying a resurgence in popularity, following recent reissues. Like Bob Moog, Oberheim lost control of his company and his name in the '80s, only to win it back and return to make successors to his '70s hits. And those devices hold up today. They're tactile in a way that modern musicians appreciate, covered in knobs and switches.

There's the 1974 SEM (Synthesizer Expander Module), a friendly, hard-wired box used by the likes of John Carpenter and Weather Report's Joe Zawinul. It resembles the same single-voice analog synths available today – an early vision of how the sprawling architectures of science lab-style modular synths could be reduced to something affordable and accessible. The SEM was built to complement Oberheim's own DS-2 – one of the first digital sequencers – as well as other synths of the time. The modern version, the design of which was inspired by a visit to the Red Bull Music Academy in 2008, now combines digital connectivity (MIDI) with analog (Control Voltage), including conversion between the two.

Combining two SEMs in a single keyboard in 1975, Oberheim devised what he called the Two Voice (so named because it could play two voices at once, in contrast with competing models of the time). Oberheim says on his website it's still his all-time favorite design. Again, the Two Voice today doesn't look so different from other, modern designs – and that's no coincidence. Keep going, and you have Four- and Eight-Voice varieties from the '70s.

The '80s saw the Oberheim name continue to mark gear with monster polyphony at

TOM OBERHEIM

Author: Peter Kirn

value prices. The Matrix and Xpander line combined epic numbers of oscillators with rich sound possibilities, adding FM to subtractive synthesis and providing a range of filter flavors. If you don't know this gear, you know their sound. Just listen to the music of Daniel Miller, Human League, Depeche Mode, Nine Inch Nails, Tangerine Dream, Orbital or Vince Clarke.

The devices are tactile in a way that modern musicians appreciate, covered in knobs and switches.

And before the MPC became associated with hip hop, the DMX drum machine was the box of choice at the dawn of rap. Introduced in 1980, using sampled sounds for its drums, this was the device that made the beats behind Run-DMC and countless other '80s hits. (From New Order and Madonna to Herbie Hancock and the Thompson Twins, it was ubiquitous.) Roger Linn, long before designing the MPC, unveiled his own LM-1 in the same year, but the DMX's price was right – roughly half of what the Linn device cost. Crucially, DMX still provided plenty of programming flexibility, and bested the sound

quality of competitors from Roland and the like, whose gadgets mostly churned out preset sounds and patterns.

As for MIDI, it's not clear how Oberheim has wound up getting dragged into histories of its creation. Oberheim was responsible for one of the pre-MIDI technologies that introduced the idea of interconnecting gear. The Oberheim Parallel Bus worked only with Oberheim gear – one of the problems Dave Smith set out to solve with MIDI, in collaboration with Roland and other partners. But it showed the benefits of being able to sync up different gear to combine sounds. That interest in connectivity, and the intelligent reductionism that yielded iconic designs like the SEM, were years ahead of their time.

Both the machines and the notions behind them – about polyphony, about expansion and interconnections, about physical control – form part of the ethos of what makes great electronic musical instruments now. And now, just past his 77th birthday, Tom is showing no signs of slowing. The updated SEM models keep shipping, and 2013 brings new versions of the Two Voice synth and a monster called the "Son Of 4 Voice Polyphonic Synthesizer."

Tom's signature will be on every unit that ships.

Peter Kirn is an electronic musician and journalist, and editor of CreateDigitalMusic.com.

Two Flatbush-raised rappers who follow a self-sourced syllabus of spiritual philosophy books and hip hop music.

Indigo stars cluster over Flatbush Junction. Down on the terra firma, the Brooklyn enclave bustles with the intermingling commotion of old timers and Caribbean roti spots, cackling Brooklyn College kids and the corporate logos of the renovated Triangle Junction Mall; deeper still run the red and green subway lines of the 2 and 5 trains which come to a halt here.

At this juncture reside Ak and Issa Dash, two Flatbush-raised rappers who dropped out of college to follow a self-sourced syllabus of spiritual philosophy books and hip hop music – a curriculum they've spiked with a pharmaceutical cocktail of DMT, THC and LSD. They call themselves the Underachievers.

"Gold soul theory, indigos on the rise" is their motto.

They're leading the charge for Flatbush's hip hop future, but their inner base is an altogether more ethereal realm: Ak and Issa believe they're the modern bastions of the Indigo Children movement from the '70s, a theory which claims they're blessed with supernaturally savvy intuition and an ability to tap into a third eye of perception that opens up the gates to the astral world. "Gold soul theory, indigos on the rise" is their motto.

At the moment, Ak and Issa's body of work is small: 2013's *Indigoism* mixtape was the 17-track introduction into their world. They rap from a lexicon defined by references to an elevated state of consciousness. "Got my three eyes open, pineal gland is swollen / Astral planes I'm floating, God damn it, I'm free," relays Ak on the freakish, bass-saturated "Herb Shuttles." The honeyed "Potion Number 25" has Issa claiming, "We elevate, LSD make me meditate."

Two modern bastions of the Indigo Children movement.

On opening track, "Philanthropist," he outlines their mission: "First things first let me lay it down / Young indigo nigga here to take the crown." It's an adventure of discovery that peers inside the inner soul and uses the revelations found within to propel thoughts out and up through the dome and into the cosmos. Fittingly, Issa says he's dabbled in astral traveling. Press him for details and he'll recount visions of a field of dreams soundtracked by John Mayer.

Key to the Underachievers' rise is "Gold Soul Theory," a song crafted around a woozy, liquefied beat that paved the way for the duo to be invited into Flying Lotus's Brainfeeder fold. Underachievers' lore has it this way: A girl on Twitter told them she wanted to play their music to her friend "Steve." Steve turned out to be Flying Lotus, who became smitten with "Gold Soul Theory," flew them out to Los Angeles and offered them a deal. That song now sounds like the Underachievers' anthem, as Issa explains their journey, "A rebel who went searching for treasures in his soul / Fishing for gold I found a key to unlock the door / To my mind's gate, hidden with some hieroglyphs / Told me 'bout my future and my past."

Brainfeeder may be based on the West Coast, but it's their home blocks of Flatbush that have positioned the Underachievers as part of New York's fertile new rap scene. Along with high school friends the Flatbush Zombies and Joey Bada$$'s Pro Era clique, Ak and Issa are part of the Beast Coast movement. The collective has become known for a healthy embrace of New York City's '90s rap history: They merrily rap over beats by artists from that halcyon era and are happy to accept the burden of rooting part of their music in the past to further the city's future.

Glancing back to the '90s has served Ak and Issa well: One of their breakthrough singles, "The Mahdi," was based on the same Billy

Author: Phillip Mlynar

Cobham song that the Bay Area's free-wheelin' lyricists Souls of Mischief flowed over for the enduring "'93 'Til Infinity." Ak admits he was aware of the heritage when they recorded it; Issa says he'd have titled the track in homage had he been aware of the history. The lyrical content is classically indigo – Ak and Issa dub themselves the "elevated mafia" as they shift their collective conscious to "deep space" – but the execution has an extraordinary allure as they channel substance-enhanced stream-of-consciousness content through syllable-sharp rap skills. The vibe might be lifted, but there's nothing lazy about it.

They're leading the charge for Flatbush's hip hop future, but their inner base is an altogether more ethereal realm.

As the Beast Coast movement clocks up wider acclaim, the Underachievers are emerging as the spiritual heart of the movement. While the Flatbush Zombies represent a weed-sodden approach that recalls a more animated Boot Camp Click, and Joey Bada$$ settles into a zone of verbose introspection, Ak and Issa's music stays illuminated with a spiritual hue. In conversation they credit this to Capital STEEZ, the Beast Coast founder and rapper who decided to take his own life on Christmas Eve in 2012. Rumors suggest STEEZ had increasingly flirted with hallucinogenic-powered conceits to the point where he believed his life's work was better conducted in another dimension; one of STEEZ's final Facebook posts has the rapper casting himself as an alchemist who'll come back to Earth and reveal the key to world peace. Dipping between the lines of the Underachievers' music sounds like a more grounded continuation of STEEZ's legacy.

The video that accompanies "Gold Soul Theory" shows Ak and Issa sitting on chairs in a barren squat of a room while dedicating themselves to achieving an enhanced state and delving through a stack of philosophical tomes. It looks like they're manning a Flatbush Junction base for their other-worldly transmissions. Maybe STEEZ is receiving their broadcast from some other realm. Hip hop might be borne of simple elements – a rhythmic metronome and the spoken word – but the Underachievers want their music to transcend this atmosphere. They're indigos on the rise.

Phillip Mlynar writes about rappers and cats while living in Brooklyn. His work has been honored in Da Capo's *Best Music Writing* anthologies.

Everything connected to Uwe Schmidt is complicated to some degree.

Just as his music does, we begin with a question: Who is Uwe Schmidt?

We're speaking in metonymical shorthand, of course. When we ask, "Who is Uwe Schmidt?" we're really asking about the nature of his music and the coherence (or not) of his catalog. And that's complicated. But everything connected to Schmidt is complicated to some degree. Schmidt's discography operates on similar principles as the ASCII self-portrait that currently graces his website: a fractured cipher, a constellation of code. You have to zoom out and squint your eyes for the whole picture to come into focus.

Often, but not always, a new alias accompanies the investigation of a new idea.

To begin with, there's the issue of Schmidt's many aliases. That an electronic musician might adopt multiple aliases is not particularly remarkable; the phenomenon runs deep in electronic music, for reasons both practical and musical. Back when it was still the norm for artists to sign exclusive deals with record labels, the use of multiple monikers served as a loophole, freeing artists to record wherever and whatever they pleased. Conceptually, trafficking under multiple pseudonyms allowed artists to play fast and loose with genre, de-linking musical style from individual identity. Every sound could have its own avatar.

Since he began releasing music in the late '80s, Schmidt has taken this concept to an extreme. He has released major work under a handful of aliases – Atom Heart, Atom™, Lisa Carbon, Lassigue Bendthaus, DOS Tracks, Señor Coconut – but the full list is much longer. A rough accounting tallies up some 60-odd solo aliases, including Atomu Shinzo, BASS, Brown, Bund Deutscher Programmierer, Erik Satin, Hugh & Eye, i, Los Sampler's, Roger Tubesound Ensemble and, perhaps best of all, Weird Shit.

That array has allowed him the freedom to explore an exceptionally wide range of sounds. In his early years, acid, ambient and techno hung together in an uneasy standoff, and his catalog has grown to encompass all manner of glitches, pastiches and strange fusions, like cumbia digital or his own invention, acitón (acid + reggaetón). Often, but not always, a new alias accompanies the investigation of a new idea. To explore the intersection of gospel and house music, he became Geeez 'N' Gosh. When he became interested in reductionist cover versions of pop songs, his Lassigue Bendthaus alias, previously associated with spiky electro-industrial frequencies, became shortened to LB.

Some names last only as long as it takes to write a single song. For *Atom™ Presents Acid Evolution 1988-2003*, a fake compilation ostensibly surveying 15 years of acid house, Schmidt invented 15 different identities (Phresh Phantasy, 21 Brothers, DJ Roxy, DJ Marco Favati, Paul Vanderstukken, et al.), each intended to correspond to a different year in acid's perpetual revival. In truth, however, all the music was made by Schmidt. In the same year. On the same laptop.

His best-known alias, Señor Coconut, was invented as an answer to the question, "What would it sound like if sentient robots from the future learned to play Latin American music?" The answer was 1997's *El Gran Baile*, which melded Latin samples with breakbeats and synthesizers to create imaginary genres like "samba virtual" and "rumba funk." In 1999, Schmidt flipped the question on its head: What would it sound like if a Latin American combo covered Kraftwerk? The answer this time was *El Baile Alemán*, an album that proved the malleability of Kraftwerk's repertoire and a tour de force of

UWE SCHMIDT

Author: Philip Sherburne

Schmidt's ability to wrangle an uncannily lifelike sound from his machines.

Like all of Schmidt's conceptual identities, Señor Coconut is a character. (Underscoring the disconnect, the "face" of Coconut on his record covers actually belongs to Martin Schopf, AKA Dandy Jack, a longtime collaborator.) But Coconut is the rare case where Schmidt's own biography appears in the music, albeit in remixed, coded form. Schmidt left his native Frankfurt for Santiago, Chile, in 1997, and he remains there, with a wife and family. His experiences as an expatriate have undoubtedly contributed to the kind of cross-cultural interference that drives so much of his work. Living abroad is an experience of asking questions non-stop, which suits Schmidt's anti-essentialist practice perfectly.

No matter how conceptual, Schmidt's projects are never reducible to mere abstracts.

But most of the questions that Schmidt asks have less to do with identity than with the nature of music, technology and interpretation. His catalog might be the funkiest extra-polation of Walter Benjamin's "The Work of Art in the Age of Mechanical Reproduction" ever, posing ideas like:

What is the nature of musical "content," and what happens when content is poured into a vessel of a different shape?

Is "artificial pop" (Pop Artificielle, the title of LB's 1998 covers album) the opposite of "natural pop," or is pop always already artificial?

Can a musician's signature translate across musical styles?

Don't expect much in the way of explicit answers, however. In the press release for his 2013 album HD, he drives this point home, stressing that the album is a "spiritual," "musical" and "scientific work" while noting, "In the same sense in which Liedgut wasn't about Romanticism and Winterreise had nothing to do with Schubert, HD isn't about anything I'd wish to express in a lengthy text or would like to see you being able to pinpoint or sell with a flashy headline."

No matter how conceptual, Schmidt's projects are never reducible to mere abstracts; pleasure remains first and foremost among his concerns. In his live performances, Schmidt remains an entertainer par excellence, delivering ingeniously mutating drum patterns and basslines, brain-bending visuals and even flashy headlines. ("Stop imperialist pop!") It doesn't hurt that his stone-faced shtick is part Kraftwerk and part Buster Keaton, albeit without the pratfalls; standing stock-still behind a lone hardware controller, he offers a wry critique of the way rock 'n' roll theatrics have permeated electronic music.

At the same time, by emphasizing the live, real-time nature of what he's doing on stage – numerical parameters projected on a screen mirror the sonic changes that accompany his tightly controlled hand motions – he also reminds us of the ways that, too often, electronic musicians have settled for less, allowing the software to do the work for them. Ultimately, Schmidt's work boils down to the desire to make good on electronic music's promise of "progress, innovation, craft and personality," as he told Little White Earbuds. It's a simple question: Couldn't we do better?

Philip Sherburne is a Barcelona-based free-lance contributor to SPIN, Resident Advisor and The Wire.

Contributors

Ben Grieme
Photographer

Ben Grieme is a New York-based photographer. Past clients include *The FADER, Dazed & Confused* and *Bloomberg Businessweek.*

Benji B
Moderator

Benji B is a British DJ and radio presenter. He runs a monthly club night in London called Deviation and presents a weekly show on BBC Radio 1. He's been interviewing artists on the Academy lecture couch since 2005.

Carter Van Pelt
Moderator

Carter Van Pelt has been documenting Jamaican popular music as a writer, radio broadcaster and archivist/record collector since the early '90s. He can currently be found on WKCR 89.9 FM in New York City. He is also the producer of the Coney Island Reggae on the Boardwalk sound system series each summer in Brooklyn.

Dan Wilton
Photographer

Dan Wilton is lead photographer for the Red Bull Music Academy, having been involved with the Academy since 2010. Dan's work is punctuated by his candid approach, humor and unforced style. Other clients include Adidas, Converse and XL Records.

Dave Tompkins
Moderator

Dave Tompkins has contributed to *Paris Review, Grantland, Slate* and *The Wire.* His first book, *How To Wreck A Nice Beach: The Vocoder From World War II To Hip-Hop,* is now available in paperback. He is currently writing a book about Miami.

Chris Rehberger
Creative Director DOUBLE STANDARDS
Design Agency

The founder and creative director of Double Standards and co-founder of Perlon Records says the best way to describe his design approach is "playing football in your best Sunday suit on a Tuesday." Double Standards' extensive list of clients includes the Guggenheim Museum New York, Fondazione Prada, Tate Modern London, Lacoste and artists like Olafur Eliasson and Rirkrit Tiravannija.

Emma Jean Denée
Editorial Staff

Emma Jean Denée is a New Zealander based in Cologne. Formerly a DJ and radio presenter in her home country, she has been involved in shaping spoken and written words from or about the Red Bull Music Academy since 2003, and is the "station voice" for RBMA Radio.

Emma Warren
Moderator

London journalist and broadcaster Emma Warren has been writing about music since she and her friends started *Jockey Slut* in the mid-'90s. She's written for broadsheets and fanzines, curated compilations for Soul Jazz and hosted couch sessions at the Red Bull Music Academy since the São Paulo edition in 2002.

Gerd Janson
Moderator

Gerd Janson is a DJ, label owner and (sometime) music journalist based just outside of Frankfurt. He's been a Red Bull Music Academy team member for more years than he can remember.

Geordie Wood
Photographer

Geordie Wood is a freelance photographer based in Brooklyn, New York. He is the photo editor of *The FADER* magazine. His past clients include *Architectural Digest, Bloomberg Businessweek, Esquire, Newsweek* and more.

Hanna Bächer
Moderator

Originally a live sound engineer, Hanna Bächer started working for the Red Bull Music Academy in 2006, primarily contributing to interview shows on RBMA Radio. She lives in Cologne.

Heiko Zwirner
Co-Editor

Heiko Zwirner has been part of the extended family of the Red Bull Music Academy since its inception. When Many and Torsten told him about their plan to make a book, he finally found an excuse to quit his job and help them to put it together.

Jane Stockdale
Photographer

Jane Stockdale is a documentary photographer from a small town in the north of Scotland. She has shot projects with the BBC Symphony Orchestra, Arcade Fire, *Creative Review* and Oxfam. Her first book, *I Predict a Riot*, was published by Koenig Books.

Kira Bunse
Photographer

Kira Bunse is a German photographer based in Paris. Her work can be seen in *Dazed & Confused, double, Rika, ZEIT* and more. She is currently at work on her second book.

Jeff "Chairman" Mao
Moderator

Jeff "Chairman" Mao is the co-author of *ego trip's Book of Rap Lists* and *ego trip's Big Book of Racism*, and a long time host at Red Bull Music Academy. He resides in Harlem with his wife and kids, their cats and his record collection.

Jonas Lindström
Photographer

Jonas Lindström studied at the Berlin University of the Arts and the London College of Communication. He has shot for *Interview Magazine, Dazed & Confused, Husk Magazine, Wallpaper* and more. He currently divides his time between Berlin and London.

Thanks

Katharina Poblotzki
Photographer

Born and raised in Cologne, Katharina Poblotzki is a photographer with a focus on portraiture as well as reportage and fashion. She has shot for *Dazed & Confused, Spex, Intro* and *ZEIT* amongst others. She currently shares time between Berlin and New York.

Many Ameri
Academy Co-Founder / Editor

Many Ameri is a co-founder of the Red Bull Music Academy. He spends a lot of time talking – about anything but music.

Max Cole
Editorial Staff

Often found carpooling along an Autobahn, British-born Max Cole has been writing for the Red Bull Music Academy since 2005. Previously a web editor for *Straight No Chaser* magazine, he was an RBMA participant in 2003 and has released music on labels such as WahWah 45s and Far Out.

Mosi Reeves
Moderator

Mosi Reeves is a journalist based in Oakland, California. He is the R&B and hip hop editor for *Rhapsody,* and the R&B editor for Google's *Music All Access* store. He also contributes to publications such as *SPIN* and the *East Bay Express.*

Peter Langer
Photographer

Paris-based photographer Peter Langer is a former gymnast, bike messenger, long distance runner and photo blog pioneer. Langer's work is regularly published in *ZEIT,* and he is the winner of multiple Lead Awards for his architecture and still life photography.

Piotr Orlov
Moderator

Piotr Orlov is a writer, curator and creative producer who was born in Leningrad and now lives in Brooklyn. His work has appeared in *The New York Times, SPIN, Village Voice* and the Red Bull Music Academy's newspaper, *The Daily Note,* of which he was editor-in-chief during the 2013 New York Academy.

Roberta Ridolfi
Photographer

Italian photographer Roberta Ridolfi lives and works in London. She has shot for clients such as *The New York Times,* Sony, *i-D Magazine, Elle* and Stella McCartney.

Sabina McGrew
Photographer

Sabina McGrew is a photographer based in Los Angeles. Her past clients include *The Guardian, Art, Wallpaper* and Capitol Records.

Till Janz and Hendrik Schneider
Photographers

Till Janz and Hendrik Schneider are German photographers based in London. They have worked for *ZEIT,* Bureau Mirko Borsche, Munich Opera House and more.

Todd L. Burns
Co-Editor / Moderator

Todd L. Burns is the editor of Red Bull Music Academy's web magazine. Previously, he was an editor at *Resident Advisor, eMusic* and *Stylus Magazine.* He lives in Berlin.

Torsten Schmidt
Academy Co-Founder / Editor / Moderator

Torsten Schmidt is a co-founder of the Red Bull Music Academy. He has written for both fanzines and newspapers like *ZEIT* and *Süddeutsche Zeitung* and edited *Groove* and *Spex.* The two-and-a-half days of Academy couch conversations he missed over the past 15 years will still haunt him on his deathbed.

André Herrmann, Annika Riethmüller, Ata Macias, Ben Simons, Calum Morton, Carmen Hoffmann, Christiane Oehlmann, Daniel Hövel, David Eckes, Dominick Fernow, Donelle Kosch, Elisabeth Honerla, Eva Drohner, Florian Klaass, Folu Babatola, Gordon Mac, Hansa Studio Berlin, Jacqueline Springer, Jay Donaldson, Jens Nave, Johannes Ammler, Julia Egger, Julian Sporge, Katerina Leinhart, Keith Skues, Kenny White, Lars Dorsch, Laurens von Oswald, Laurent Fintoni, Linda Brownlee, Marc Schaller, Nick Wilson, Olivia Graham, Paul Steinmann, Pauleena Chbib, Peter Trentmann, Ramon Haindl, Robert Klanten, Robin Howells, Robin Schönefeld, Sergi Noé, Tina Cucu, Trevor Jackson, Veit Grünert, Werner Amann, William Bennett, Wulf Gaebele.

Over the past 15 years, the Red Bull Music Academy has taken place in twelve different cities.

Host Cities

1998 Berlin
1999 Berlin
2000 Dublin
2001 New York
2002 London
2002 São Paulo
2003 Cape Town
2004 Rome
2005 Seattle
2006 Melbourne
2007 Toronto
2008 Barcelona
2010 London
2011 Madrid
2013 New York

The Red Bull Music Academy has hosted pioneering artists from all sorts of backgrounds on the couch to lecture.

Lecturers

A

A Guy Called Gerald
A-Trak
Aba Shanti-I
Adam Freeland
Addison Groove
Adrian Sherwood
Akim Walta
Alex Barck
Alex Dröner
Alex Rosner
Alex Smoke
Alexander Bretz
Alexander Robotnick
Alice Russell
Alva Noto
Amp Fiddler
Analogue Freestyle
Andrew Jervis
Andrew Weatherall
Anton Delecca
Appleblim
Arabian Prince
Architecture in Helsinki
Arthur Baker
Arthur Verocai
Arto Lindsay
Arturo Lanz
Artwork

Assault
Atilano Gonzalez-Perez
Atom Heart

B

Babu
Bass Dee
Bass Odyssey
Bassface Sascha
Ben Long
Benga
Beni G
Benny Sings
Bernard Purdie
Bernie Worell
Bettina Costanzo
Bez Roberts
Biz Markie
Black Milk
Blu
Bob Moog
Bob Power
Boi-1da
Bok Bok
Bootsy Collins
Brendan M Gillen
Brent Fischer
Brian Cross aka B+
Brian Eno

Bugge Wesseltoft
Bun B
Buraka Som Sistema
Busy P

C

C-Rock
Caribou
Carl Craig
Carl McIntosh
Carly Starr
Carola Stoiber
Cathy Smith
Charlie Dark
Charlie Hall
Chez Damier
Chloé
Chris Palmer
Chris Stein
Chuck D
Ciaran Cahill
Claire Maloney
Clams Casino
Clare Fischer
Claude Young
Claudio Coccoluto
Claudio Rispoli
Claudio Simonetti
Clé

Clevie
Clive Chin
Cluster
Cosey Fanni Tutti
Cosmo
Craze
Cristian Vogel
Cut Chemist

D

D Bridge
DâM-Funk
Damian Harris
Dan Dalton
Dan Stevens
Daniel Wang
Daniele Baldelli
Danny Breaks
Danny Krivit
Darshan Jesrani
Dave Haslam
Dave Ralph
Dave Smith
David Matthews
David Nerattini
David Rodigan
David Swindells
Daz-I-Kue
Deadbeat

Debbie Harry
Deep
Dego
Dennis Bovell
Dennis Coffey
Dennis White
Derf Reklaw
Derrick Carter
Derrick May
Digital
Dirk Linneweber
Dittmar Frohmann
Dixon
Domu
Don Buchla
Don Letts
Doom
Dorian Moore
Dr Bob Jones
Dr Peter Zinovieff
Dre Skull
Dudley Perkins

E

Earl Gateshead
Ed Handley
Eduardo Marote
Efdemin
Egyptian Lover

Electric Indigo
El Guincho
Elmar Krick
El-P
Emmanuel Jagari
    Chanda
Eoin Brians
Erlend Øye
Erykah Badu
Eumir Deodato
Ewan Pearson
Exile

F

Fabio
Fabio de Luca
Falty DL
Fennesz
Fion Higgins
Fletch
Flying Lotus
Fonze Mizell
Francesco Tristano
Francisco López
François K
Frank Tope
Frankie Knuckles
Front 242

G

Gabriel Roth
Gareth Jones
Gary Bartz
George Stavropoulos
Georgia Anne Muldrow
Gerald Jazzman
Gerald Mitchell
Gerd Gummersbach
Gerriet Schulz
Gilb'r
Gilberto Gil
Gilles Peterson
Giorgio Moroder
Glen Brady
Go
Godfather
Goldie
Gotan Project
Grandwizard Theodore
Greg Wilson
Gyedu Blay-Ambolley

H

Hank Shocklee
Hans Nieswandt
Harry Russell
Harvey

Heiko Schäfer
Henrik Schwarz
Herb Powers
Howie Weinberg
Hugh Masekela
Hymnal

I

I-f
I.G. Culture
Ian Dewhirst
Invisibl Skratch Piklz

J

J Da Flex
J Majik
J-Rocc
James Barton
James Gadson
James Murphy
James Pants
Jammin' Unit
Jason Bentley
Jay Ahern
Jay Electronica
Jazzie B
Jef K
Jeff Mills

Jeremy Greenspan
Jeremy Harding
Jesse Saunders
Jimmy Douglass
Joe Bataan
Joe Boyd
Joe Zavaglia
Joel Martin
John Acquaviva
John Dent
John Reynolds
John Stapleton
John Talabot
John Tejada
Jonathan Rudnick
Jono Podmore
Jordi Lloveras
Juan Atkins
Julia Holter
Julian Ringel

K

Kabuki
Kardinal Offishall
Keith Tucker
Kemistry
Ken Scott
Kerri Chandler
Kieran Hebden

Killa Kela
Kim Gordon
King Britt
Kirk Degiorgio
Klaus Goldhammer
Kode9
Konrad von
    Loehneysen
Krust
Kutcha Edwards

L

L'Orchestra di Piazza
    Vittorio
Lance Ferguson
Larry Heard
Larry Mizell
Lars Bartkuhn
Lars Vegas
Lee Hirsch
Lee 'Scratch' Perry
Legowelt
Leon Ware
Leroy Burgess

M

M.I.A.
Mad Mats

Mad Mike Banks
Mad Professor
Madlib
Magic Mike
Mala
Makoto
Malcolm Catto
Malcolm Cecil
Mannie Fresh
Marc Hype
Marco Passarani
Marcus Intalex
Mario Caldato Jr.
Mark Arm
Mark de Clive-Lowe
Mark Jones
Mark Pritchard
Mark Rae
Mark Ronson
Marky
Martin Morales
Martin Schöpf
Martyn Ware
Masters At Work
Mathew Jonson
Matias Aguayo
Matmos
Matthew Herbert
Maurice Fulton
Mauricio Bussab

Megan Jasper
Mehdi
Mel Cheren
Melvin van Peebles
Michael Kummermehr
Michael Mayer
Michael Reinboth
Michael Thorpe
Michaela Melian
Mike G.
Mike Paradinas
Mira Calix
Miss Djax
Mixmaster
Morris
MJ Cole
Mo
Modeselektor
Moodymann
Morgan Geist
Moritz von Oswald
Morton Subotnick
Move D
Mu
Mulatu Astatke

N

Neil Aline
Neil Macey

Nick Coplowe
Nick Harris
Nicolay
Nigel Godrich
Nile Rodgers
Norman Jay
Nottz
Nuts

O

Oh No
Oisin Lunny
Om'Mas Keith
Oneohtrix Point Never
Orlando Voorn
Osunlade
Owusu & Hannibal

P

Patife
Patrice
Patrick Adams
Patrick Carpenter
Patrick Forge
Patrick Pulsinger
Paul Bradshaw
Paul de Barros
Paul Humphrey

Paul Kelly
Paul Murphy
Paul Riser
Peaches
Peanut Butter Wolf
Pearson Sound
Pepe Bradock
Peshay
Pete Riley
Peter Ducuipre
Peter Grandl
Peter Hook
Phaderheadz
Phil Asher
Philip Glass
Philippe Zdar
Phonte
Plastician
Premier
Prince Paul
Prins Thomas

Q

Qua
Q-Tip

R

Radar

Radio Slave
Rakim
Randy Muller
Rashad
Ready D
Recloose
Red Alert
Richie Hawtin
Rick Essig
Ritu
Roach
Rob Bowman
Robbie
  Shakespeare
Robert Feuchtl
Robert Nesbitt
Robert Owens
Roberto Maxwell
Rod Mizell
Roger Linn
Roman Flügel
Ron Trent
Roots Manuva
Roska
Ross Allen
Ross Irwin
Rude Boy Paul
Russell Elevado
Ryuichi Sakamoto
RZA

S

Sal Principato
Santa Cecilia Orchestra
Santiago Salazar
Sarah Stennett
Sascha Lazimbat
Sascha Voigt
Saxon Sound
  International
Scuba
Sebastian Niessen
Seiji
Sergi Jordà
Seth Troxler
Shaheen
Shut Up & Dance
Silver
Sinden
Sir Mix-A-Lot
Skepta
Skream
Sly Dunbar
Snowboy
Soulja
Spencer Weekes
Spinn
Spoony
Steely
Steinski

Stephen Mallinder
Stephen O'Malley
Steve Arrington
Steve Beckett
Steve Bunion
Steve Reich
Steve Spacek
Storm
Stuart Hawkes
Strobocop
Superpitcher
Sven Miracolo
Sway

T

Tadd Mullinix
Taz Arnold
Terre Thaemlitz
Terry Farley
The Original Jazzy Jay
Theo Parrish
Tiga
Tim 'Love' Lee
Tim Westwood
Tina Funk
Todd Edwards
Todd Osborn
Todd Roberts
Todd Rundgren

Todd Simon
Tom Middleton
Tom Moulton
Tom Oberheim
Tom Zé
Tony Allen
Tony Andrews
Tony Colman
Tony Dawsey
Tony Gable
Tony Nwachukwu
Tony Visconti
Toomp
Toshio Matsuura
Toy Selectah
Trevor Horn
Trevor Jackson
Tutto Matto
Ty

U

Uschi Classen
Uther Mahmud

V

Van Dyke Parks
Vince Degiorgio
Volcov

W

Waajeed
Wally Badarou
Westbam
Winston Hazel
Wolfgang Voigt
Woody McBride

X

X-Ecutioners
XRS

Y

Young Guru

Z

Ze Gonzales
Zed Bias

?uestlove

At each Red Bull Music Academy, we invite up and coming artists from around the world to become participants.

Participants

A

Aaron Cuff
AD Bourke
Ada Kaleh
Adam Pavao
Adam Turner
Adam Wright
Adi Dick
Adrien Pallot
Ahmaad
Ahu
Aidan Kelly
Akiko Kiyama
Aklimatize
Akron
Alan McAdam
Alan O'Keefe
Alan1
Ale Hop
Alejandro Davila
Alejandro Merodio
Alex Lavery
Alex McGarvie-Munn
Alex Moran
Alex Tsiridis
Alexander Hell
Alexei Michailowksy
Aliah Sarkis
Alicia Slater

Alitrec
Aloe Blacc
Alvin van Veen
Ammo
Amenta
Amy B
An on Bast
Ana Flavia Furtado
Ana Helder
Ana Pet
And.id
Andras Fox
André Laos
Andrea Balency
Andrea Langova
Andrea Radova
Andrea A. Stuart
Andreas Kersten
Andreas Pils
Andreas Rhomberg
Andreas Schmid
Andreya Triana
Andriesh
Anenon
Angel
Angela Inglis
Angela Maison
Ango
Anja Wolf
Ann Sofie Dandenne

Anna S
Annalove
Annikabeats
Ant J Steep
Aresha
Armand Vingrames
Aroop Roy
Arthur Simon
Arveene Juthan
Asma Maroof
Astroboyz
Asya
August Rosenbaum
Augusto Merli
Axel Boman

B

B. Bravo
Baaragán
Babao
Baby G
Banyan
Baris K.
Barry Iskiwitz
Bart Vercauteren
Beatbetrieb
Behr
Benedikt Roller
Benjamin Damage

Benjamin Tobias
Berghem
Bert Preiss
Bibianna Baron
Biblo
Biotek
BKR
Black Spade
Blackcoffee
Blackman
Blondtron
Boggie Roc
Boska
Boycrush
Bozak
Braiden
Brenmar
Brian Whelan
Bridgette Gower
Broke One
Brooklyn
Bruna
Bruno Silva de Morais
Bubbz
Buggy Boy

C

Cabaal
Camplaix
Canblaster
Captain Kirk
Cardopusher
Carlos Hurtado
Carola Pisaturo
Carrot Green
Catarina Pratter
Cathy Smith
Cécile
Cedric Lassonde
Celine Brunner
Cha Cha
Chantal Passamonte
Cherry Chan
Chico Unicornio
Chook
Choto
Chris Cox
Christian Richardt
Christian Miguel Strubel
Christina Asplund
Christoph Heiss
Christoph Staber
Christopher Muniz
Christopher Sauder
Christopher Wallner
Ciaran Cahil
Cinnaman
Claire Maloney
Clara Moto

Clare Conlon
Claude Speeed
Clinic
Clip
Coco Solid
Cohen
Cohoba
Colin Gerard Hanley
Colleen Murphy
Colm Kenefick
Compuphonic
Cornelia
Cortez
Cosmin TRG
Cotton States
Craig Parker
Craig Roets
Crazy Bitch in a Cave
Criss
Cubist
Culoe de Song
Cuthead

D

D. Kim
D@t@boy 78
Da-Frogg
Dainjah
Daisuke Tanabe

Dalt Wisney
Daniel Brandt
Daniel Carew
Daniel Kensbock
Daniel Magg
Daniel McKinney
Daniel Minus
Daniel Schwingenschlögl
Daniel Seixas
Danilo Radalovich
Danny Bar
Danny Mulholland
Darko Stepic
Dave Godin
Dave Ralph
David Ryshpan
David Steele
David Zahn
Davor O
De La Montagne
Débruit
Declan Kelly
Deep Blend
Deep Sixty
Defcon
Dejan Stajic
Denius
Dermot McCabe
Derrick Dasafo

Desto
Detect
Dicofone
Didem Süzen
Dioniso Abreu
Dirg Gerner
Dirk Schade
Dirk Heinicke
Dirk Rumpff
Disco Nutter
Distal
Dizmoe
Dizz1
Doc Daneeka
Dona
Dorian Concept
Douglas Greed
Drew Wackerling
Drew Ready
Dyad
DZA

E

Eclat
Ed Neeves
El Santo
Elastic Void
Elec-tic
Eli Verveine

Eliana Iwasa
Eltron John
Emma Bedford
Emma Jean Denée
Emufucka
Enlightment
En2ak
Eurok
Evian Christ
Evirgen
Evol
Exeter

F

Fabian Bruhn
Faktor
Faro
Fatima
Feebles
Felix Fuchs
Felix Lee Roy
Fernanda de Faria Cardoso
Fion Higgins
Fiordmoss
Flava D
Flex
Flic
Florian Obkircher

Fluke
Flying Lotus
Francis
Fred Cherry
Frederic de Smet
Fredrik Nyberg
Full Crate
Funktion2
Fuse One

G

Gabriel Bercovich
Gabriel Nascimbeni
Galambo
Gasoline
Gavin Wilson
Genesis
Gerhardt Derksen
Ghosts on Tape
Giganta
Glen Davison
Gökce Özer
GoldieLocks
Good Paul
Gora Sou
Graeme Blevins
Gramophonedzie
Grantham Clayford
Grassmass

Grayson Gilmour
Gregory Schmid
Grzegorz Węsierski
Guga De Castro
Guillamino

H

Harald Björk
Harry Russell
Hasan Hujairi
Heliponto
Henk Kaal
Hiram Aldo Martinez
Mata
Hiroaki Oba
Hobey Echlin
Homeless Inc.
Hudson Mohawke
Hugo Quezada
Hysteria

I

Ian Martin
Igor Kratochvil
Ilari Larjosto
Illum Sphere
Illuminated Faces
Ilya Rasskazov

Infestus
Irwin Conor
Isaac Aesili
Ishfaq
Ivana Marcinovova

J

J. Newhouse
Jacek Opielka
Jackmaster
Jacob Korn
Jakob Schneidewind
Jakub Kriz
Jameszoo
Jamie Robertson
Jamie Woon
Jan Hertz
Jan Mathes
Jane Hassen
Jared McGrath
Jason Martin
Javybz
Jay Ahern
Jayne Conelly
Jean-Pierre Gouws
Jeff Risk
Jens Christen
Jensta
Jeroen Joly

Jesse Boykins III
JetSet by Ilkay
Jil
Jiles
Jimi Nxir
Jivraj Singh
Jneiro Jarel
Joachim Knoll
Joana de Pinho
Johan Venschueren
Johan Nico Becker
Johanna Olofson
John Paul McGonagle
Jolita Pabludo
Jolly Mare
Jonas Nachtergaele
Jonas Rocha
Jonathan Morley
Jonny Nash
Jools Hunter
Joona
Jorge Caiado
Jorge Federico Bala
Joris Van Agtmaal
Joro Lee
Joystick Jay
Juan Son
Juba Dance
Judith Theiss
Juho Kahileinen

Julian Cubillos
Julian Ringel
Julie Winters
Julien Love
Julius Sylvest
Jullian Gomes
Justine Electra

K

K-Murdock
Kaan Düzarat
Kackmusikk
Kalbata
Kalle Karvanen
Kano
Karla Calderon
Kaspar
Kat!Heath!
Katcha
Katja Dürer
Katy B
Kaur Kareda
Kava
Kay C
Kevin Beyer
Kez YM
Ki En Ra
Kid Smpl
Kidkanevil

Kidragon
Kilian Hütter
Kim Nazel
King Nosmo
Kirk Oppheim
Kixly
Klem
Kloke
Knox
Kool Clap
Koreless
Kornél Kovács
Kraftmatiks
Krampfhaft
Kristijan Iljas
Krystal Klear
Kwazar

L

Lady Fuzz
Lars Winckler
Lavina Yelb
Le Domestique
Le K
Leah
Lehman Tidwell
Leo Aldrey
Leo Gunn
Lewis Tennant

Leyo
LFU
Lhasa
Lil' Dave
Linda Leigh Levi
Lorin Jessenberger
Lorna Clarkson
Los Amparito
Louis Baker
Lourenço Magalhães
Love Cult
Lowjac
Lucca
Lucrecia Dalt
Luis Davis
Lukasz Kepinski
Lukid
Lunice

M

Maceo Wyro
Maciej Kowalski
Macro Marco
Magnolia
Maja Lympics
Maldita Fan
Mano le Tough
Mara TK
Marc Codsi

Marc Gärtner
Marc Gilgien
Marcel Hall
Marcelo Schild
Mari.Cha
Marie-Ulrike Gar
Marginal
Mark Bell
Mark Fader
Marks
Markur
Markus Lang
Markus Ortmanns
Marshmello Blackbird
Martin Riegelnegg
Martin Vejvoda
Marvin Binderhagel
Master G
Mat 64
Matous Vlcek
Mats Carlson
Matt Howatt
Mau'lin
Maud Geffray
Maureen Schipper
Maurice Tutu Sweeney
Maurício F.
Max Kalis
Max Cole
May Roosevelt

Me Menni
Meczilla
Melanie Constein
Melevat
Melmann
Mersey
Miaau
Michal Bures
Michal Bojanowicz
Michat Ostapoliicz
Michelle Amador
Midee
Migumatix
Mike Konietzko
Mike Slott
Mikki Boyd
Mim
Mina
Mirna
Miss Bliss
Miss Dee
Miss Sunshine Delight
Miss Tres
Minto George
Miz Kiara
Modul
Mombus
Monica Electronica
Monika Svensson
Monishia Schoeman

Monki Valley
Monoide
Monosylabikk
Mooken
Mora Jazz
Moretimany Mokigosi
Morris Gould
Motive
Moving Ninja
Mr Hudson
Mr. Nestor
Mr. Selfish
Mr. Statik
Muhsinah
Mujuice
Mushug
Mweslee
Myele Manzanza

N

Nace
Nadia Camerara
Nadipebi
Nailer
Name
Nando Sisowak
Nando Pro
Naphta
Natalia Grosiak

Natalia Lafourcade
Natasja Van Der Horst
Nayla Haddad
Ned Ngatae
Nehuen
Neil Clarke-Smith
Nerko Basstar
NHJ
Niamh McCartney
Nicholas Mills
Nicholas Wilson
Nick Craddock
Nick Hook
Nick Jett
Nightwave
Niita Emvula
Nina Kraviz
Nino Moschella
Nire
Noel
Nuno Dos Santos

O

O.Boogie
OB
Obi Blanche
Objekt
Octo Octa
Oddisee

Ognjan Milosevic
Olga Bohan
Oliver Neels
Oliver Rath
Om Unit
Onra
Orieta Chrem
Orquesta
Ota

P

Palmbomen
Pascal Bideau
Panzah Zandahz
Parasid
Pat McMellow
Patrice Bäumel
Patrick K. Ward
Patrik Senatore
Patrysia Hefczynska
Paul Huston
Paul O'Donoghue
Paul Spyder
Paul Wunderlich
Paunch
Pawel Pindera
Pazes
Peter Petovari
Phil Darimont

Philipp Lehmbke
Philippa McIntyre
Phillip Bajak
Phillippe Egger
Phoebe Kiddo
Pick a Piper
Pieter Kolijn
Pilooski
Piper Davis
Pippi Langstrumpf
Pleasure Cruiser
Poirier
Popnebo
Princess P
Princess Shazelle
Protman
Puki
Pursuit Grooves

Q

Quest
Quicksperm
Quizzik

R

Rachel DJ
Rafik
Raggamuffin Whiteman

Raisa K
Rajesh Gupta
Ralph Tee
Rasta Root
Regina Höllerl
Regueiro
Reini Camo
Reka
Richard Eigner
Richard tha IIlrd
Riki Gooch
Rio Hunuki-Hemopo
Rizm
Robot Koch
Roberto Auser
Roberto Coelho
Roberto Nirino
Robin Meyer-Lucht
Roman Rosic
Ronald Kohn
Ronika
Ronny Elvebakk
Ross McHenry
Ruari
Rudi Zygadlo
Rui Pereira
Rustam Ospanov

S

S.T.
Sabine Röthig
Saky Dobas
Salva
Samiyam
Sammy Bananas
San Soda
Sander Mölder
Sankt Göran
Santiago Latorre
Sara Sayed
Sarah Lahey
Sarah Stennet
Sassy J
Sauce81
Savan
Sawandi Simon
Say Bean
Scary Grant
Scout Klas
Search
Sebastian Claren
Sebastian Skalski
Sebastian Wisbar
Second Mouse
Seretan
Sergey Fresh
Sergio Gobbi

Sevdah Baby
Sezy
Shadowbox
Shamanez
Shift Z
Short-E
Shroombab
Siesta
Signor Mako
Sikh Knowledge
Silvie Johanidesova
Simba
Simonne Jones
Sinjin Hawke
Sisco Umlambu
Skymark
Slavko Jascur
Sleepless
Slemper
Slide20xl
Slow
Smax
Sofie Loizou
Some Freak
Somepoe
Sonaluna
Sonicbrat
Sonja Moonear
Soon
Soul Brown

Soundspecies
Space Dimension
  Controller
Spair
Spencer Lowe
Spiritual Blessings
Spyro
Squalloscope
Standa Soukup
Star Eyes
Stefan Albrecht
Stefanie Alisch
Steph Morris
Stephan Eifridt
Steve Murray
Still Wil
Stranjah
Subeena
Submariner
Sue Bowerman
Sui Zhen
Surface
Susanne Kirchmayr
Suzanne Kraft
Sven Ismer
Sven Ellingen
Sven Hafersaat
Swede:art
Sweetalker

T

T-Man
T. Williams
TA-KU
Taavi Tuisk
Taay Ninh
Tabu
Tanya Meunier
Taras 3000
Te`Amir Sweeney
Teapot
Teebs
Tense City
Teri Gender Bender
Thato Motsepe
The Clonious
The Hustler
The Peronists
Thibo Tazz
Thilo Wierzewski
ThinkToy
Thomalla
Thomas Schneider
Thomas Degroote
Thomas Labitzke
Thompson
Throwing Snow
Thubz
Tiago Andrade

Tim Van Den Heuvel
Timmy Stewart
Timmy Schumacher
Tokimonsta
Tomá Ivanov
Tomasz Obuchowicz
Tomo Pupavac
Topnotch
Tor
Tora Vinter
Torkel Forsberg
Trancemicsoul
Tripman
Tu-kl
Tufan Demir
Tutu Sweeney
Tutuse
Typhonic

V

V Rama
Vaclav Brozik
Valerio Delphi
Varo
Vasco Fortes
Velez
Venice
Victor Flores
Victorganic

Viktor Slavik
Vilja Larjosto
Vim
Violet
Viri Hofreitz
Vlad Caia

W

Waldemar Wokolorczyk
Warren Knowles
Wild Bill Ricketts
Wojtek Dlugosz
Wolfe Tone Loc

X

Xavier León
XXXChange
XXXY

Y

Yanoosh
Yasmina Haddad
Yoav B
Yodashe
Yogo
Yosi Horikawa

Z

Zachary Loczi
Zavo
Zephec
Zeynep Erbay Zoid
Zolcan Breaker
Zuzee

:Papercutz
00Genesis
2B
2Katz
6L6

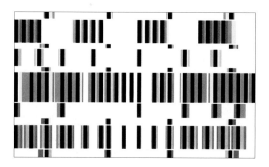

Illustration Overview

...YOU AND ME...

LINO-PRINT ON PAPER
KERRI CHANDLER X PATRICK ADAMS
66

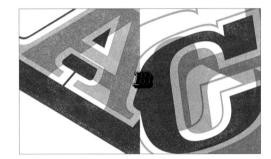

BURST OUT PERFECTION

ACETONE TRANSFER PRINT ON PAPER
GARETH JONES X METRO AREA
86

LOOKING AT THE SUBJECT IT TURNS OUT ALL WRONG

SCREEN PRINT ON PAPER
CARSTEN NICOLAI X OLAF BENDER X UWE SCHMIDT
104

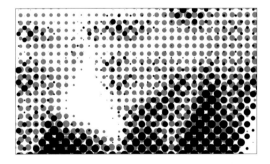

BLAZING SILENCE

C-PRINT
BENNY ILL X MORITZ VON OSWALD
124

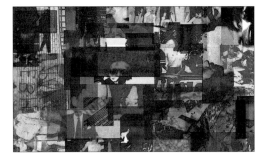
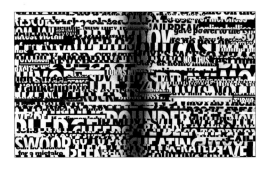

COLLECTIVE MEMORY OF A CERTAIN KIND

SPRAY PAINT ON CANVAS
MODESELEKTOR X MYKKI BLANCO
216

SOWAS KOMMT VON SOWAS

C-PRINT
ERYKAH BADU X THE UNDERACHIEVERS
236

IT COULD BE FUCKING WORSE, LOVE. IT COULD BE FUCKING SNOWING

C-PRINT
JUST BLAZE X PAUL RISER
258

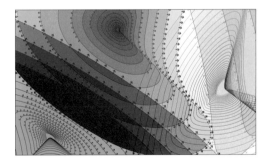

GOING ROUND IN CIRCUITS

BLUE PRINT
ROBERT HENKE X TOM OBERHEIM
280

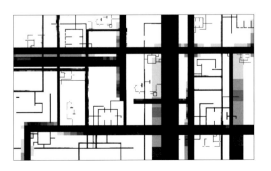

Imprint

Red Bull Music Academy

For the Record
Conversations with People Who Have Shaped the Way We Listen to Music

Editors: **Many Ameri, Torsten Schmidt**
Co-Editors: **Todd L. Burns, Heiko Zwirner**
Graphic Design: **DOUBLE STANDARDS, Berlin**

Published by **gestalten**

© Die Gestalten Verlag GmbH & Co. KG, Berlin 2013

ISBN 978-3-89955-507-3

Bibliographic information published by the Deutsche Nationalbibliothek. The Deutsche Nationalbibliothek lists this publication in the Deutsche Nationalbibliografie; detailed bibliographic data is available online at dnb.d-nb.de.

Printed by Optimal Media GmbH, Röbel
Made in Germany

This book was printed on paper certified by the FSC®.

Gestalten is a climate-neutral company. We collaborate with the non-profit carbon offset provider myclimate (www.myclimate.org) to neutralize the company's carbon footprint produced through our worldwide business activities by investing in projects that reduce CO_2 emissions (www.gestalten.com/myclimate).